A Search for Belonging

BIRMINGHAM LIBRARY SERVICES

For use in the library only

Birmingham
City Council

A Search for Belonging

Belonging

The Mexican Cinema of Luis Buñuel

Marc Ripley

WALLFLOWER PRESS
LONDON & NEW YORK

A Wallflower Press Book
Published by
Columbia University Press
Publishers since 1893
New York   Chichester, West Sussex
cup.columbia.edu

Wallflower Press® is a registered trademark of Columbia University Press

A complete CIP record is available from the Library of Congress

ISBN 978-0-231-18234-8 (cloth : alk. paper)
ISBN 978-0-231-18235-5 (pbk. : alk. paper)
ISBN 978-0-231-85109-1 (e-book)

Columbia University Press books are printed on permanent
and durable acid-free paper.
Printed in the United States of America

Cover design by Elsa Mathern

Contents

Acknowledgments

Writing this book has been a labour of love – certainly more love than labour. This may well be pointing out the obvious but Barthes was right: the author is dead. My experience has taught me that the whole process of bringing a book to life – researching, writing, refining – is never just about one person. This book would not exist were it not for the following people. Some have helped with the labour, some with the love, and others with both. To all of you: my deepest thanks.

The research for this book frequently led me to the Filmoteca Española in Madrid, and the wonderful collection of Buñuel material held in the archives there. I would like to thank Javier Herrera Navarro for being accommodating during my research trips, generous in his correspondence, and for digging out one or two unexpected treasures that influenced the direction of my research.

To Peter Evans, your comments and advice on my work have been invaluable. I greatly appreciate your input.

To Yoram Allon, Commissioning Editor at Wallflower Press, and all the editorial team at Wallflower Press, thank you for your professionalism and for ensuring that the whole process went smoothly. You have made the experience much less daunting than it seemed on day one!

I have to say a special thank you to the staff in Modern Languages at the University of Leicester, many of whom are my former teachers. Sheldon Penn, you have been invaluable in your academic and professional support. Thank you for inspiring me and for knowing how to give me the space to be inspired. Liz Jones, you are an inexhaustible source of practical advice. Thank you for showing me there is a sophistication in lucidity. Helen Rawlings, for your encouragement and support. A los hispanoparlantes en y fuera del departamento: Martín Agnone; Nuria Escudero Pérez; Sara Gómez Villa; Maria Guarnieri; Aurélie Joubert; Marion Krauthaker; Corinne Pelton; Ariane Richards; Carmen Sóñora Hernández; Anna Vives; Estefanía Yunes Vincke y Enea Zaramella: sois un equipo fantástico. Grazie, merci y gracias por alegrarme el día y por ser buenos amigos. Un besote a tod@s. Y a Clara Garavelli: muchísimas gracias por todo. Tu generosidad y apoyo no me dejan de sorprender.

Emma Staniland, I think it is best to simply say thank you for everything that you do: the motivational pep-talks, the advice when things go wrong, delicious cakes, inventive recipe tips and all of the coffees. You are a pillar of support always. In a nutshell: I cannot tell you how glad I am that I took the place of that old filing cabinet seven years ago. To my fellow northerner in the Midlands, Michelle Harrison: there are certain people – not that many – who light up a room when they are around. You are one of them.

To the students, past and present, I have been fortunate enough to teach: you have inspired and taught me more than you know. Your enthusiasm and optimism are infectious. Don't lose them!

There are other people for whose friendship and support over the years I am truly grateful: Max and Michaela Batley; Kayleigh Else; Laura Foster; Claire Galvin; Rick and Carine Hutton; Katherine Jenkins; Ryan Lever and Liz Rowlands; Alberto Martí; Becky Meredith; Alison Paskins; Karol Valderrama Burgos; Lizzie Yorke. Thank you, Yvonne Cornejo, for the impromptu film screenings and the many discussions on heterotopias. Emma Johnson, for fourteen years of plans, adventures and brilliant times. Thank you for always being there. Ian Powell, there really isn't much to say that you don't already know, so I will just say thank you for being my best friend and a consistent constant in my life.

Lastly, thank you to my parents, John and Pat Ripley, and my family for your constant belief in me and your interest in everything I do. You all make me very proud to be a part of the clan and I hope I do the same for you.

Introduction

Luis Buñuel's arrival in Mexico in 1946 after having spent eight years working in the United States would herald a new phase in the director's career. This phase was, if not always critically acclaimed, indisputably prolific until its end in 1965. But it was not necessarily a move that could have been predicted, not even by Buñuel himself. The filmmaker was unequivocal about his lack of interest in Latin America, so little that he told his friends 'that should I suddenly drop out of sight one day, I might be anywhere – except there' (2003: 197). Nonetheless, the importance of Mexico in shaping Buñuel's cinematic career cannot be underestimated. It was here that he rediscovered and honed his craft. He had not acted as the sole director of a film since his 1933 documentary *Tierra sin pan*, despite working as a producer for the Spanish Filmófono studios in 1935 and 1936, before emigrating to the United States and working at the Museum of Modern Art in New York, then spending two years as a dubbing expert for Warner Bros. in Los Angeles. Of a total of thirty-two films of which Buñuel was the sole director, twenty were filmed in Mexico.[1] The films that Buñuel shot during this time differ greatly in theme and style, and the thematics of Buñuel's Mexican cinema often eschew generic conventions and classifications in a national industry which, as Ernesto Acevedo-Muñoz has signalled, was saturated with recognisable genres such as the archetypal *comedia ranchera*, a kind of cowboy musical, and the family melodrama (2003: 5–9). Paradoxically, the iconoclast Buñuel was most productive in a national cinema whose commercial success in its so-called Golden Age, roughly from the late 1930s to the early 1950s, was based largely on strict adherence to generic conventions.[2] In fact, Carl Mora goes as far as to say that, as the Golden Age of production drew to a close, Buñuel 'gave the Mexican cinema whatever vitality it had left in the late 1950s and early 1960s' (2005: 96).

This book aims to shed new light on Buñuel's Mexican cinema by considering the spatial dynamics of the films of this period. The films that Buñuel made there have traditionally been segmented into commercial and auteurist strands. This polarity in the films' critical reception has been largely reinforced by the analytical paradigms employed in the study of these films. For the more independent movies that pepper Buñuel's Mexican period, such as *Los olvidados* (1950), *Nazarín* (1958) and *El ángel exterminador* (1962), scholars often foreground their readings in what I term the Buñuelian bedrock of Catholicism, surrealism, the bourgeoisie and Spanish identity. In turn, the lesser critical attention paid to the more commercial films has frequently focused on genre and the films' production contexts. Writing on Buñuel's Mexican output is at a juncture: studying these films through fresh and original paradigms in recent years has made a significant contribution to Buñuel scholarship and can serve as a springboard for the development of these, and other, theoretical perspectives, independently of pre-established analytical frameworks associated with the director's cinema. However, these new approaches have, on the whole, not yet succeeded in drawing together the commercial and auteurist films of the period in a convincing and sustained way. Although the period as a whole is attracting growing attention, as recently as 2016 Mario Barro Hernández emphasised that the focus of this critical attention has been largely on

> the standout works, to the detriment of the period as a whole. For this reason, it is rare to find reflections on the differences and similarities between popular films such as *Los olvidados* and other, lesser known films such as *Una mujer sin amor*. (2016: 636)[3]

The interdisciplinary approach taken in this book works to free the commercial movies from these modes of analysis; likewise, it seeks to reconsider the auteurist films independently of surrealism, Catholicism and psychoanalysis. In this way the films included – a total of nine of Buñuel's films from this period – occupy positions of critical renown and, conversely, relative critical neglect, and are simultaneously drawn together outside of the respective investigative approaches within which they have frequently been circumscribed. In concentrating on the representation of space, I actively take advantage of what Julián Daniel Gutiérrez-Albilla sees as Buñuel's position as straddling a 'liminal slipzone between Spanish, Mexican and French culture, between sexual and political discourse, between sound and image, between surrealism and commercial melodramas and between margins and centre' (2008: 8). Importantly, he emphasises that this liminal position of Buñuel's cinema requires us to think beyond disciplines when approaching his films.

In foregrounding the centrality of space in producing alternative readings of Buñuel's Mexican films, these films are displaced from their interpretive anchors by working within the domains of spatial analysis that is informed by geography and philosophy. Although a variety of spatial theorists and theories are drawn upon in my reading of the movies, I am aware that these should evidence the theory and not vice versa. As such, I provide detailed and film-focused readings of the movies themselves and how these illustrate the theoretical positions at hand. I engage extensively with past scholarship on each of the films, showing how much of this has hinted at, but never concertedly addressed, the spatial concerns that underpin the narratives of these films. At the same time, I refer to Carlos Fuentes, who describes the development of Buñuel's characters in spatial-philosophical terms, as they plunge the depths of 'the jungles of subjectivity and the oceans of society' in a quest to find 'the authentic self' (1970: 198).[4] I link his writing on Buñuel's cinema to similar philosophical elaborations of the filmmaker's work by writers and critics such as Manuel Michel, Elliot Rubinstein and Michael Wood, foregrounding Buñuel's Mexican cinema within philosophical questions of belonging and non-belonging that coalesce around Charles Chaspoul's acute assertion that 'Buñuel very often films characters in displacement, who never truly seem to succeed in inhabiting the places where they find themselves' (1997: 115).[5]

In chapter one I outline my approach and the groundwork for the research that underpins this book, beginning with a reconsideration of the thematic complexity of Buñuel's Mexican cinema. Given the paradox in writing on this period in Buñuel's corpus – namely, that certain films of this period are now attracting more attention but that this book remains one of a limited number specifically on Buñuel's Mexican cinema – I believe it is the moment to take stock of the place of the Mexican period within the whole of Buñuel's output. After reviewing the existing literature on Buñuel's Mexican films, principally in English, French and Spanish, I turn my attention towards the growing importance of space in analyses of Buñuel's cinema. I show that a spatial focus can unite the two strands of Buñuel's Mexican period by bypassing the somewhat prescriptive modes of critical analysis outlined above. Despite the novelty of this approach in Buñuel studies, I am of course not working in isolation; it is important to acknowledge the ways that a focus on space has featured in Buñuel scholarship by outlining his reluctance to represent space aesthetically and examining the trope of exile in writing on Buñuel. I then draw on a philosophical strand of writing on Buñuel that proposes that he can be considered a kind of human geographer, insofar as the characters in his films are frequently subjected to their environments and the films' narratives can be read as the struggle to resolve this tension between character and place. In addition, I detail the growing significance of the so-called spatial turn in the humanities and social sciences, and consider the relevance of this spatial turn to the study of film.

The remaining chapters are dedicated to film-focused readings of a number of movies from the period. In selecting the films for analysis, I have considered which of them share similarities or exhibit contrasts stylistically and thematically. At the forefront of my choice-making is the need to examine both the commercial and the auteurist films, side by side. Chapter two approaches the island spaces of *Robinson Crusoe* (1954) and *The Young One* (1960), Buñuel's only English-language productions. The narrative of each film presents its island setting as more than simply passive *mise-en-scène*; it is fundamental to the viewer's understanding of the films. The island spaces of both films are abortive utopias; that is, Crusoe's desert island and the game-preserve of *The Young One* are spaces of utopian intent but which fail in practice, and this has an acute effect on the physical and psychological states of their inhabitants. Connected with the idea of an abortive utopia is Michel Foucault's theory of heterotopias and this underpins my discussion of the films in this chapter. Following Foucault's brief outline of the concept, heterotopias, literally other or different spaces, have come to be considered as structured according to their own system of power or social ordering, which often contrasts with that of the society in which they are located. Thanks in part to the turn towards space in research in the arts and social sciences, heterotopias have gained currency as a field for analysis in these disciplines, and the concept has been used in writing on cinema.[6] As impossible utopias both Crusoe's island and the game-preserve of *The Young One* are shown to be unsettling spaces that subvert the romantic image of the island as an idyllic retreat through the negative mental and physical effects that dwelling there has on their inhabitants.

Chapter three delves into the similarly isolated spaces of the jungle and the desert, considering questions of exterior space and the ways in which this is shown to affect the characters placed there. The films I analyse here are *La Mort en ce jardin* (1956) and *Simón del desierto* (1965). These have not been considered at any length in Buñuel criticism as aesthetic or thematic companions; here they are taken as a pair because I propose that the spaces of their narratives – the jungle and the desert respectively – are strong examples of liminal spaces. Liminality has its roots in anthropology as a term used to define the middle period during rites of passage, whereby members of a group or tribe are separated from their society and are subjected to different laws, or indeed a suspension of laws, governing their behaviour, before completing the ritual process and achieving a reintegration into society. During this time they are, to cite anthropologist Victor Turner, in a state 'betwixt and between' (1967: 93). In this chapter I argue that the group of Francophone villagers in the former film, and Simón, the preacher living on a pillar in the middle of the desert in the latter film, are placed between spatial referents in the unfurling jungle and the seemingly limitless desert, not achieving a reintegration into any society. In doing so, I build upon the considerable body of work within the arts and the social sciences that fruitfully maps the spatial resonances of liminality. Through the analytical framework of the spatial liminal, the films' respective endings gain a new inflection which contrasts with traditional interpretations that have tended to try and neatly sew up the conclusions of these two films, ignoring the latent ambiguity of these movies by sticking closely to allegorical readings of them.

Chapter four moves towards a rather different philosophical conception of space through a focus on what has been termed the place-world. This is a concept elaborated by the philosopher Edward Casey to designate the 'inhabitation of places in a circumambient landscape' (2001a: 683). The films I use to illustrate this exploration of the place-world are two of Buñuel's most critically acclaimed of the Mexican period: *Los olvidados* and *Nazarín*. Thematically, these films are very different, with one focusing on Mexico City's forgotten street children and the other on an itinerant priest in the Mexican countryside. This is not a question of typologies of external space, however: in positioning my analysis within a geographical-philosophical perspective I avoid contrasting the films from an aesthetic viewpoint as merely the representation of the urban versus the rural. Rather, the unifying thread will centre on the body in place, in both its physical and psychological dimensions. Buñuel unflinchingly highlights diseased, decaying, dying and defunct bodies in his cinema and these two films are prime examples of this. My focus on the body in place allows for an opportunity to extend the work of scholars such as Aitor Bikandi-Mejias (2000) and Pedro Poyato (2011) on Buñuel's treatment of the body and his preference for showing the marginalised status of characters through their bodies. While Pedro and the gang of street urchins demonstrate an intimate knowledge and dextrous manipulation of both their bodies and slum surroundings, Nazarín, unlike his two female disciples, is shown to sublimate his corporeal urges, not committing himself to a grounding in any place. Again, the spatial focus of this book lays out a new interpretation of these much-commented-upon films, teasing out the latent concern with space that is shown to underscore much of the criticism written on them in order to reconsider their power as philosophical texts.

The aim of chapter five is to reposition the films I examine in the previous chapters within the unifying thread of this book: the impossibility of a home-place, or a place of belonging, within the films' narratives. This chapter is therefore a synthesis insofar as it is the point of convergence for the previous three, film-focused chapters, as well as being an analytical chapter in its own right, forging a path for further research. I do this by considering each pair of films alongside a third: *La Fièvre monte à El Pao* (1959), *Abismos de pasión* (1953) and *El ángel exterminador*, respectively. Thus, the frameworks for analysis in each preceding chapter are expanded to consider their resonances with the idea of a home-place, casting another interpretational nuance on the films analysed previously. In addressing questions of home and belonging, my discussion is inspired by phenomenological thinkers such as Gaston Bachelard, Martin Heidegger and Anthony Steinbock, upon all of whose work I draw in my reading of the films. I show that a philosophical approach to the idea of the home in a broadly phenomenological vein is well positioned to bring to light alternative readings of belonging and non-belonging, a theme at the heart of the movies analysed here. The frameworks I draw on certainly work across disciplines – stemming as they do from anthropology, geography and philosophy – and they all underscore the way in which these films, independently of their portrayal of typical Buñuelian themes, their subscription to generic paradigms or their being claimed for this or that national cinema, encourage us to think about questions of belonging and non-belonging. Claudia Brosseder has said of Buñuel that he wanted to 'let people see the realities that they usually avoid' (2000: 52).[7] The interdisciplinary spatial-philosophical approach taken in this book brings this reality to light, reading an alternative narrative through the images on screen to argue that, as Buñuel's characters show, we are not always securely in place or at home.

Notes

1 This figure does not include productions that, although filmed during Buñuel's Mexican period, were not actually filmed in Mexico. The shooting of *Cela s'appelle l'aurore* (1956) took Buñuel to Corsica, *Viridiana* (1961) was filmed in Spain, and *Le Journal d'une femme de chambre* (1964) was shot in France.

2 The chronology of the Golden Age of Mexican cinema is a matter of debate. Emilio García Riera dates this to the years of the Second World War, though admits that the term is used nostalgically, rather than with a definite sense of chronology in mind (1998: 120). Andrea Noble notes that the production output of Mexican films reached its peak of 123 pictures in the year 1950 (2005: 15).

3 [las obras sobresalientes, en detrimento del conjunto. Por ello, es raro encontrar reflexiones acerca de las diferencias o similitudes entre las películas populares como *Los olvidados* y otras menos conocidas como *Una mujer sin amor*]. All translations from sources in French, German, Italian and Spanish throughout this book are my own unless stated otherwise.

4 [las selvas subjetivas y los océanos sociales]; [el ser auténtico].

5 [Buñuel filme très souvent des personnages en déplacement qui semblent ne jamais vraiment réussir à habiter les lieux où ils se trouvent].

6 See, for instance, Elliott and Purdy (2006: 267–90) and Blum (2010: 55–66).

7 [Buñuel wollte Menschen Realitäten sehen lassen, denen sie gewöhnlich ausweichen].

Chapter 1
Re-locating Buñuel's Mexican Cinema

Where to place Buñuel's potentially problematic Mexican cinema within his overall, substantial corpus, is a more pressing question for the moment than what the movies of this period can tell us *about* place. How far can we consider Buñuel a proponent of surrealism in his artistic work? To what extent can we – *should* we – segregate the various 'Buñuels': early; middle; late; Francophone; Anglophone; Hispanic? Unlike the director's earlier French/Spanish triptych of *Un Chien andalou* (1929), *L'Âge d'or* (1930) and *Tierra sin pan*, and his later French period from *Le Journal d'une femme de chambre* (1964) and *Belle de Jour* (1967) onwards, his Mexican cinema presents a lesser degree of stylistic and formal cohesion. Whereas Elisabeth Lyon (1973) and Gwynne Edwards (2004) propose an association between Buñuel's first three movies predicated on an aesthetic basis, and Francisco Aranda lends the later films, beginning with *El ángel exterminador*, the grandiose title of the 'Great Films of Maturity' (1976: 206), the intermediate Mexican period offers a collection of commercial, genre-driven pictures peppered sporadically with more auteurist productions. The films made in Mexico constitute the majority of Buñuel's filmography as director and, as Acevedo-Muñoz suggests, the numerous, largely genre films made by Buñuel in this period prove difficult for some critics to reconcile with 'Buñuel as the European surrealist phenomenon' (2003: 11). In addition, the commercial nature of Mexican cinema during its prolific Golden Age, roughly coinciding with Buñuel's arrival in the country in the mid-1940s, meant that films such as Ismael Rodríguez's *Nosotros los pobres* (1948), starring Pedro Infante, or *Flor Silvestre* (1943), directed by Emilio Fernández and starring Dolores del Río, were constructed around generic conventions – often drawing on melodrama – and the star system in an emulation of the Hollywood model. Buñuel's own shooting schedules were largely rapid and demanding – except for *Robinson Crusoe*, filming never lasted for more than 24 days, according to the director (Buñuel 2003: 198), and the films of this period were often released in quick succession: between 1950 and 1953 he was directing two or three films per year. This has directly influenced the dismissive attitude among some critics that the bulk of Buñuel's Mexican works are little more than 'studio potboilers', or its equally flippant equivalent in Spanish, *películas alimenticias*, loosely translated as 'bread-and-butter films', the implication being these were made solely to plug a gap, financially and professionally.[1]

The culinary metaphor above is fitting, because the Mexican actor and screenwriter, Tomás Pérez Turrent, draws on his own food-related analogy to counter assertions that much of Buñuel's Mexican cinema was small fry. Asking the question of whether we can in fact speak holistically of a Mexican corpus in Buñuel's output, Pérez Turrent strongly concludes that we can answer in the affirmative. The doubt about its existence, as it were, Pérez Turrent attributes to the disparity between the Buñuel who directed *Un Chien andalou*, 'a bomb [that caused] a great impact on its first spectators', and the Buñuel who directed his first picture in Mexico, *Gran Casino* (1947), a film 'in no way exciting' (1997: 137).[2] As he documents Buñuel's critical and financial failures in a Mexican film industry driven by generic conventions and narrative codes, Pérez Turrent nevertheless finds that Buñuel found a way to work both within and against the expectations of commercial Mexican cinema, adapting to the demands placed on him while leaving his indelible stamp on the films he made there. Although Pérez Turrent adds his voice to those who separate Buñuel's Mexican corpus from his earlier and later works, he celebrates its subversive potential. The later Buñuel, he says, 'is admirable from many points of view but this is a Buñuel who has had his nails clipped'; his later cinema, in comparison, is a 'decaffeinated cinema' (1997: 142).[3] This so-called nail trimming was partly the result of Buñuel's reinsertion into an increasingly consumer-driven, Western European society where, he and André Breton lamented, to scandalise had become impossible. Continuing his defence of Buñuel's Mexican work, Pérez Turrent cites José de la Colina regarding the director's Mexican cinema in comparison to his later French cinema. De la Colina argues that the Mexican films are based on 'a density of subject matter, the carnality of the characters', which is then attenuated in Buñuel's later French period, to be replaced by an 'intellectual game and a chess set of spectres (ideas of characters more than [actual] characters)' (Pérez Turrent 1997: 141).[4] I am taking Pérez Turrent and de la Colina's categorisation of Buñuel's later French period as more abstract as a rationale for concentrating solely on the Mexican films, which they see as more realist and grounded.

Indeed, although some of the Mexican films could be seen as forerunners of the episodic narrative that structured Buñuel's mature work – the ever-changing landscapes and the series of encounters of Father Nazario in *Nazarín*, for example – my readings of these films are based on the premise that the protagonists of the Mexican films are relatable characters in largely realist – if often absurdly Buñuelian – situations. When considering the presentation of the characters' relationships to their surroundings, de la Colina's ideas of carnality and density are important. I contend that the characters of Buñuel's Mexican cinema are, as Manuel Michel puts it, placed in alienation, a position that comes to light when we consider these films as philosophical texts (1961: 27). Buñuel's greater preoccupation with form and style in his mature works could arguably be said to temper the element of carnality in his Mexican cinema, directing the critical gaze away from the protagonist and refocusing this on ludic questions of metanarrative and structural fragmentation. This conceptual shift in Buñuel's cinema emerges in conjunction with the end of the Mexican period and is evident in the films after this, beginning with *Belle de Jour* and escalating with *La Voie lactée* (1969). In fact, we do not have to look much further than the titles of the films made in Mexico to give us a clue in this respect. The importance of space and setting in grounding the narratives of the Mexican films comes across in their working, alternative and official titles such as *Island of Shame* (The Young One), *Abismos de pasión*, *Swamps of Lust* (La Fièvre monte à El Pao), *Los náufragos de la calle Providencia* (El ángel exterminador), *Evil Eden* (La Mort en ce jardin) and *Simón del desierto*. Opposite this, the titles of the later French movies are more suggestive of social satire – the understated charm of the upper-middle classes, or the idea of liberty as a phantom – exactly the genre with which Virginia Higginbotham aligns them, as she divides Buñuel's work quite simplistically into 'character studies' (*Viridiana*, *Tristana* (1970)) and 'social satire' (*Le Charme discret de la bourgeoisie* (1972), *Le Fantôme de la liberté* (1974)) (1979: 193). The density of the rounded characters and their locations in the Mexican films thus gives way to a texture of micro-narratives in Buñuel's later French works.

This book is another contribution to this growing area of Buñuel investigation. My objective is to shed new analytical light on the films of the period as a whole by excavating new critical pathways that open up the meaning of these films and recall attention equally to the more independent and the genre-driven movies. Now is the time to take stock of Buñuel's Mexican cinema, as Barro Hernández argues. My intention in this chapter is to use this opportunity to survey the roots of this compartmentalisation of the filmmaker's work from this period into two strands, looking primarily at the way this has figured in Anglophone, Hispanic and Francophone criticism, to then position my re-evaluation of these works against this limiting hierarchy. Following this survey of the critical literature on Buñuel's Mexican period, I then outline the need to turn to paradigms outside of what I term the Buñuelian bedrock of surrealism, Catholicism and psychoanalysis that have encouraged this divide, before moving on to look at the various ways in which space appears as an object of study in previous Buñuel scholarship. Finally, I position my readings of the films in this book within the broader salient trend towards spatial analysis across the arts, which is also driving innovative approaches to film.

Reconsidering the thematic complexity of the Mexican films

Writing on Buñuel has experienced something of a revival over the last two decades, especially in the period after 2000, following the centenary of his birth, and has naturally brought with it an increased focus on the films made in Mexico. Moreover, the increasing availability of even the lesser-known films of the period, for example *Abismos de pasión* and *La Fièvre monte à El Pao*, thanks to European, Mexican and US DVD distributors, has contributed to the higher level of attention paid to these films in recent Buñuel scholarship. If still precluded commensurate status with what are widely regarded as the director's most lauded productions, many of the Mexican films now feature sporadically in research on the director and his work.

The hierarchisation of the two strands of Buñuel's Mexican cinema can be traced back to the period itself. Articles on Buñuel's Mexican films in prominent cinema journals such as *Cahiers du cinéma* and *Positif* during the 1950s and 1960s tentatively scoured this nascent corpus for any traces of Buñuel's trademark style and thematic preoccupations. Peter Harcourt's evaluation of the Mexican corpus is indicative of this approach and his memory of the films of this period is 'one of seriously marred films of considerable interest' (1967: 11). The reasons why these movies are flawed, Harcourt says, are numerous: weak plot lines; stiff acting; or far-fetched narratives. For him, they can be redeemed only through the interest generated by their more overtly Buñuelian moments and traces of Buñueliana – a term that Acevedo-Muñoz uses to denote the aesthetic and thematic preoccupations such as Freudian surrealism and iconoclasm at play in Buñuel's cinema (2003: 4). Jean-André Fieschi considers that films such as *El gran calavera* (1949) and *La ilusión viaja en tranvía* (1954) served as sketches for more aesthetically accomplished films, and his praise for them is tempered; the 'creative freshness [...] frankness of regard, clarity of expression' that they possess are not enough in themselves to prevent him from ultimately categorising these as rehearsals for films such as *Él* (1953) or *Nazarín* (1966: 34).[5] The intra-corpus divisions that this approach in early writing on the period creates is driven by an attempt to 'legitimise' the study of the Mexican films by bringing them into line with the auteurist approach often employed in the discussion of Buñuel's earlier/later work, in order to 'safeguard the image of the director to the detriment of the other films, which remain overlooked' (Lillo 1994: 7).[6] Ironically, Buñuel's violent assault on the very act of spectatorship – on the single eye that stands for our collective gaze – in *Un Chien andalou*, has become a framework for viewing, interpreting and critically appraising his cinema, as his 'reputation as a surrealist encouraged a particular viewing strategy, looking for dream-like motifs that would transform over the course of the film in unexpected ways' (Keating 2010: 210), which excludes a great part of the largely realist, linear narratives of many of the filmmaker's Mexican films.

Nevertheless, the 1990s saw Buñuel's Mexican cinema revisited in earnest within new or modified paradigms in attempts to unite the two strands of this period. Gaston Lillo (1994) aims to redress the balance between the director's early and late periods, and the intermediate Mexican era. His consideration of more commercial pictures such as *El gran calavera* and *El bruto* (1953) alongside the critically lauded *Los olvidados* and *Nazarín* is an effort to bridge the gap between the commercial and the independent films. He draws on genre theory to argue that Buñuel achieves a subversion of commercial cinema in the most genre-driven of his films. His re-envisaging of certain of the director's Mexican works hinges on the socio-historical context of the films' production and viewers' reception of them and his argument is important in its focus on a variety of Mexican films. Writing a year after Lillo, Peter Evans (1995) begins to transcend the rigid commercial-auteurist dyad of Buñuel's Mexican cinema. He acknowledges the fruitful results of examining Buñuel's work through an auteurist lens, though without discounting the structures and constraints to which Buñuel was subjected. Indeed, Evans believes that 'the two Buñuels, commercial and auteurist, cannot be so simplistically polarized' (1995: 36). Evans's focus on relationships between male and female characters considered through sexual and psychoanalytical theory problematises the restrictive triad of Catholicism, surrealism and Spanish nationality, as it explodes the privileging of the masculine implicit in, for example, Edwards's framework through a consideration of female desire in films such as *Belle de Jour* opposite the manipulation of male desire that we see in *Ensayo de un crimen* (1955).

Víctor Fuentes's book in Spanish, *Buñuel en México* [Buñuel in Mexico], lays claim to be the first monograph-length study solely dedicated to the Mexican films of Buñuel (1993: 15). Fuentes recasts the work of this period in a new light, giving consideration to the generic conventions within which Buñuel often worked and the ways in which he went about subverting these, as well as suggesting new and fruitful pathways for investigation in a more philosophical vein. For instance, using Gilles Deleuze's writing on cinema, and in particular Buñuel's cinema, Fuentes highlights the fetish objects in the director's cinema that give rise to the impulse-image, a reading that I develop in chapter three of this book in relation to *Simón del desierto* (1993: 65–70; 73; 148). In addition, Fuentes draws upon the biographical details of the circumstances around Buñuel's arrival in Mexico in an attempt to consider the dynamics of exile – a theme he has subsequently developed – and the ways in which Buñuel's state as a Spaniard living and working in Mexico problematises a nationalist (specifically Mexican) reading of his films, which bear 'the hallmark of this dual nationality' (1993: 21).[7]

Catherine Dey (1999) highlights the salient trend towards a reconsideration and reappraisal of Buñuel's Mexican period, as she points out that criticism throughout the 1990s had begun to unlock a rich spring of Buñueliana through the incorporation of certain Mexican works into the Buñuel canon. Her study came as the surprisingly saccharine alternative ending to *Los olvidados* was discovered serendipitously in the film archives of the *Universidad Nacional Autónoma de México* (UNAM) [National Autonomous University of Mexico], and which I consider in chapter five of this book. Dey draws on a philosophy of ethics and begins to interrogate recurring Buñuelian themes such as the question of morality in a new light, freeing Buñuel analysis from the typical scope of surrealism. Despite the originality of her study, however, she turns almost exclusively to more auteurist films such as *El ángel exterminador* and *Viridiana* to support her argument, although *Robinson Crusoe* is also included.

Acevedo-Muñoz (2003) presents an insightful consideration of Buñuel's work within the Mexican film industry. He locates his discussion within an industrial-auteur analytical framework, focusing on the relationship between the director and the industry he was working in. Thus, films such as *Subida al cielo* (1952), *Una mujer sin amor* (1952) and *La hija del engaño* (1951) are included, framed by their production contexts, counteracting the neglect these have traditionally suffered. Unlike Dey, Acevedo-Muñoz's approach privileges what he calls 'Mexican movies' (Mexican-funded films with typical Mexican subject matter) (2003: 12–13). Although some of the most critically disparaged films find a rightful place in his study, more independent films still made within the Mexican film industry, such as *Nazarín*, and international co-productions filmed in Mexico, for example *La Mort en ce jardin* – a Franco-Mexican co-production – or *The Young One* – a Mexican-US movie – are discounted.

The centenary of Buñuel's birth in 2000 saw a series of conferences on Buñuel and their subsequent publications. The volume *Buñuel, siglo XXI* (2003) [Buñuel, 21st Century], edited by Isabel Santaolalla and others, is the result of an international conference held in 2000 and presents an ample selection of research on many of the Mexican films. Like *Buñuel, siglo XXI*, the multilingual volume in English, French and Spanish, *Buñuel: el imaginario transcultural/L'imaginaire transcultural/The Transcultural Imaginary* (Lillo 2003), is a collection of research presented at a conference at the University of Ottawa. Significantly, of these sixteen papers, seven present research exclusively on the director's Mexican cinema. The year after the release of both conference proceedings, the volume edited by Evans and Santaolalla, *Luis Buñuel: New Readings* (2004) was published. The aim of this collection was to carry out not only a re-evaluation of certain of the director's films but also a reconsideration of the man himself. This volume presents a balance between early/Mexican/late Buñuel; moreover, within the section on the Mexican Buñuel, focus is given to *Robinson Crusoe* and *The Young One*, two films which have traditionally been considered too 'international' to be absorbed into a discourse of *mexicanidad* [Mexicanness] and too commercial to be invested with the same critical value as *Nazarín* or *El ángel exterminador*.

As has been elaborated by researchers such as Fuentes, Buñuel was the site of conflation for two strands of Hispanism: the Spanish and the Mexican. The latter was the subject of a 2007 exhibition co-organised by the *Filmoteca Española* in Madrid and the *Centro Buñuel* in the filmmaker's birthplace of Calanda, Spain. As part of this exhibition, a selection of photographs taken by Buñuel during the location scouting stage for his Mexican films was included. These photographs are published in a book edited by Elena Cevera (2008), resulting from the exhibition, along with a series of short articles from Buñuel scholars and memoirs detailing the experience of location scouting and shooting with Buñuel, written by his son, Juan Luis Buñuel, and Buñuel's long-time collaborator and director of photography, Gabriel Figueroa. What is interesting about this volume is the consensus that arises between the various authors as to Buñuel's treatment and depiction of Mexico and Mexican reality through his aversion to the aesthetic frame compositions of the Mexican landscape that were a feature of Figueroa's cinematography and work with other directors of the period, such as Emilio Fernández's *María Candelaria* (1944). Their observations suggest that a consideration at length of the representation of space in these films would be a valuable and fruitful avenue to explore: while Javier Espada writes that 'these photographs also show us [...] a perception of Mexico removed from a touristic perspective and with a sensibility that often surfaces in little details' (2008: 24–5), Elena Cevera points to 'his photographs [that] refer to landscapes without people' (2008b: 15).[8] These observations clearly link with research on Buñuel's depiction of Mexico from a consideration of exile. However, as the book serves primarily as a record of the exhibition, they remain undeveloped.

Towards the end of the 2000s, more material was released which aims to reposition the Buñuel *oeuvre* within fresh theoretical frameworks. Gutiérrez-Albilla's *Queering Buñuel* (2008) as the title suggests, strives to re-read such canonical films as *Los olvidados* and *Viridiana* from a queer subject position. The strength of his work lies in his interdisciplinary approach: building his analysis on the foundations of feminist, psychoanalytical and queer theory allows him to reconceptualise Buñuel's cinema to explode the heteronormative and misogynistic discourses that he discerns in the 'textual unconscious' of the filmmaker's work (2008: 1). All five films featured in his study are from the Mexican period, and all were filmed in Mexico, with the exception of *Viridiana*. However, Gutiérrez-Albilla limits his analysis to what have regularly been hailed as the more auteurist of the Mexican films (*Él*, *El ángel exterminador*, *Ensayo de un crimen*, *Los olvidados* and *Viridiana*), a decision which again seems to suggest that some of the more commercial Mexican films do not lend themselves to extra-generic, interdisciplinary paradigms. This is echoed in Poyato's *El sistema estético de Luis Buñuel* [The Aesthetic System of Luis Buñuel] (2011). Poyato's intention is to posit a system of aesthetics, a visual and formal strand within the director's work, which serves to unify and draw together films from different periods of Buñuel's career. Like Gutiérrez-Albilla's research, this is a continuation of the trend towards an appreciation of the aesthetic possibilities of Buñuel's corpus beyond the Buñuelian predicate of surrealism and Catholicism. For instance, in his exposition of a 'morphology and genealogy of the ugly' (see 2011: 59–86),[9] Poyato coincides with work done by Bikandi-Mejias (2000) who explores the carnivalesque trope within Buñuel's cinema. However, Poyato's focus remains on the more independent films that punctuate the director's body of work. Besides the director's first three surrealist pictures, and *Tristana* and *Cet obscur objet du désir* (1977) from his later period, Poyato focuses on *Los olvidados*, *Ensayo de un crimen* and *El ángel exterminador*.

Most recently, Gutiérrez-Albilla and Rob Stone's companion volume to Buñuel (2013) gives attention to some of the most critically neglected films of the Mexican period. There are chapters focused on *Robinson Crusoe*, *Susana* (1951) and even on the international co-productions of the 1950s that Buñuel filmed in French. Their edition follows the volume on the filmmaker edited by Evans and Santaolalla in its aim of addressing all periods of Buñuel's production from revitalised, interdisciplinary perspectives. Tom Whittaker, for instance, considers the use of movement in three of the director's Mexican comedies – *El gran calavera*, *Subida al cielo* and *La ilusión viaja en tranvía* – and links the 'characters and objects [that] find themselves out of synch with the social worlds they inhabit' (2013: 226) with the struggle for modernity and the influx of migrants to the city under the presidencies of Miguel Alemán (1946–1952) and Adolfo Ruiz (1952–1958). Similarly novel is Sarah Leahy's (2013) chapter on *La Mort en ce jardin*, which focuses on the star system with relation to actors Georges Marchal, Michel Piccoli and Simone Signoret. While Signoret did not work again with Buñuel, the two former actors appeared in numerous other Buñuel films, and Leahy's focus on Marchal and Piccoli expands the writing on Buñuel and the star system, which, as she points out, has mainly considered his work with Fernando Rey and Catherine Deneuve.

The many voices I have detailed above advocate a renewed focus on Buñuel's Mexican period and are antidotes to Virginia Higginbotham's astonishing barb that the majority of the filmmaker's Mexican output is not worthy of serious attention – she claims only five of the films of this period are memorable (1979: 63) – and Paul Coates's likening of Buñuel's role in the Mexican national cinema to 'a paralysed limb of the industry' (1985: 99). It may no longer be either accurate or objective to speak of the scholarly attention given to this work as a whole in Auro Bernardi's terms as a 'malnourished minority' (1999: 8).[10] However, despite the greater balance in criticism between the two strands of Buñuel's Mexican cinema, even recent, extended studies of the director's work still reinforce their stylistic and thematic divisions, as shown in the work of Gutiérrez-Albilla and Poyato. The development of new analytical frameworks through which Buñuel's films have been studied with fruitful results has seemingly not yet been wholly successful in providing complementary readings of films from the two strands.

It has also been common to hedge any analysis of Buñuel's Mexican cinema, that is, to hasten to highlight the obvious distinctions between his earlier and later European periods to justify continuity errors or seemingly shoddy filming. The title of an article in the German newspaper *Der Spiegel* betrays such views through inter-textual reference. Headed 'The Mexican Chalkcircle', the title is a nod to Bertolt Brecht's play *The Caucasian Chalkcircle*, which depicts a peasant girl (the Mexican film industry) who finds an abandoned baby (Buñuel), eventually, and in spite of limitations, rearing the child better than its birth parents (the European film indus-tries) ever could (Anon. 1974: 112–14). Against this, the most radical voice among all proponents of the films of this era is the Mexican film scholar Gustavo García who elaborates an excoriating response to the maligning of the Mexican period, which is worth quoting at length:

> What is certain is that, in making the majority of his filmography here, including various of his masterpieces, he was not doing anyone a favour; enough of this 'messianic attitude': if Buñuel had ended up in another country on the [American] continent he would not have made anything, and let his two stretches in the USA be proof of this, one before arriving [in Mexico] and the other to make *Robinson Crusoe* and *The Young One* […] if he did not film everything he wanted to, no other ambitious Mexican director did either. (García in González Dueñas 2000: 193)[11]

Although his response is definitely spirited, García is mistaken in thinking that Buñuel returned to the USA to film *Robinson Crusoe* and *The Young One*: both were filmed in the states of Colima and Guerrero, on the Pacific coast of Mexico. Never-theless, he is very clear: Buñuel was not and should not be considered a 'saviour' of Mexican cinema. García's call to disavow this 'messianic attitude' came in 1993, at the very point when interest in Buñuel's Mexican cinema was beginning to grow, with the publication of Fuentes's and Lillo's studies, as detailed above. Now, then, is an opportune juncture to revisit Buñuel's Mexican cinema, taking some of García's spirit, to build on the salient trend towards innovative modes of analysis to unlock new readings of these films, showing how within an original approach the films can serve to complement, rather than inhibit, their respective meanings.

Beyond the Buñuelian bedrock: Buñuel and space

In order to position Buñuel's Mexican cinema within new, interdisciplinary paradigms, it is necessary to break with the Buñuelian bedrock that has underpinned
much discussion of the director's work. The traces of Buñueliana – nods towards
Freudian surrealism, religious iconoclasm, critiques of class, insider gags – that form
part of, especially, the early readings of Buñuel's Mexican films, as I have shown,
have a place in research on the filmmaker, but that place is not in this book. They are
undeniably part of Buñuel's poetics, but I am wary of reading his work principally
through these lenses. I am also hesitant to claim Buñuel's cinema for, or attribute
it to, this or that nationality: Spanish or Mexican, as Edwards goes some way to
doing. He asserts that 'the films made in Mexico bear witness in their themes to
Buñuel's essential Spanishness' (1982: 26). This assertion holds some weight, of
course: *Nazarín* is based on Spanish writer Benito Pérez Galdós's homonymous
novel, transported from Castile to Mexico; Buñuel himself admitted that *Viridiana*
was inspired by his childhood fantasy of drugging the Spanish Queen, Victoria
Eugenie, in order to sleep with her, and, humorously, that the eponymous heroine
is a sort of 'Quixote in skirts' (de la Colina and Pérez Turrent 1992: 150; 152).
Nevertheless, to suggest such an essential reading of the films is to freeze the filmic
image in one specific, monolithic meaning and to reinforce simultaneously both the
Buñuel canon and canonised frameworks for analysis within the discipline of film
studies (in Buñuel's case, psychoanalysis in particular).

Attempting to foreground Buñuel's essential 'Spanishness' in his cinema leads
us to another aspect of Buñuel studies that has gained currency: the question
of exile. Having moved to Paris from Madrid in 1925 and begun his cinematic
career there, worked in New York and Los Angeles between 1938 and 1946 as
the Spanish Civil War raged and Franco consolidated his regime, and built his
home in Mexico City, for some critics such as Fuentes (2003), Buñuel's exile
lasted a lifetime. I am aware, though, that the notion of exile in its strictest sense,
when applied to Buñuel, is problematic, given that he became a naturalised
Mexican citizen, returning periodically to Spain and even working under the
Franco regime to make *Viridiana*, a Spanish-Mexican co-production that the
Spanish censor was quick to attribute solely to Mexico following the scandal this
provoked within Catholic circles, as well as *Tristana* and to film part of *La Voie
lactée* in Santiago de Compostela. For others, Buñuel's status as exile colours the
reception of his films. Marsha Kinder, for instance, believes that 'Buñuel's career

of exile dialogizes the auteurist and national contexts, revealing that neither perspective is sufficient by itself' (1993: 291). Hamid Naficy evokes Buñuel in his writing on accented cinema – a cinema of migrants that is affected, or accented, by the filmmaker's spatial dislocation, often through exile. Naficy points to the problematic of Buñuel as an exile, as he represents 'both the epitome of exile and its most prominent exception' (2001: 55).

Chaspoul also examines the notion of exile and its (filmic) spatial resonances in Buñuel. However, his approach is different. He is hesitant to ascribe cinematic effect so readily to biographical cause and his argument is all the more interesting for it. Indeed, he asserts that, although Buñuel himself may have been an exile, he does not represent this subject in his cinema. For Chaspoul, the issue of exile punctuates his films in a more wide-ranging sense:

> If [his] physical exile comes to an end, the exile of the gaze is prolonged, for this is the true cinematographic exile. Insofar as Buñuel has never made exile a subject, but always a place which influences the *mise-en-scène* and has an effect on it, there remains an exile of the gaze despite the end of his physical exile. (1997: 113)[12]

It is important that Chaspoul considers the position of the viewer, arguing that exile as a subtext in Buñuel's cinema ends up influencing or 'contaminating' [*contaminer*] the spectator (1997: 118), leading him to conclude that Buñuel's cinema is a cinema of exile and an exiling cinema in equal measure. Although the first term may be problematic for the reasons detailed above, the second term is far more capacious, turning the spectator's gaze back on him- or herself as well as containing a patent spatial signification.

Questioning these common tropes in Buñuel analysis was not necessarily new, even before Buñuel had finished working in the Mexican film industry. Already in 1961, against questions of national cinema and the Buñuelian bedrock, Salvador Elizondo asked how else we should read Buñuel outside of these approaches: 'one invokes psychoanalysis, one invokes the Mysteries, one invokes National Incidents. Has anybody invoked the generalisation of all generalisations: man?' (1961: 2).[13] Stone and Gutiérrez-Albilla recently take up this call and advocate a rebellion against the Buñuelian canon:

> If his work has been canonized and hence subjected to fixed symbolization by the numerous studies on his cinema [...] how can one engage critically with his *oeuvre*

and yet avoid inserting his ambivalent, paradoxical and elusive films into pre-established critical models that perpetuate their subjection to symbolization? (2013: 1)

Of course, surrealism and Catholicism and transnationalism are tropes that underscore Buñuel's entire body of work. However, these motifs alone should not monopolise the study of an output as vast and as open to interpretation as his. My approach in this book follows Gutiérrez-Albilla and Stone's methodology: to break with these tried-and-tested critical paradigms in order to propose a creative, revitalised perspective on the director's Mexican work and to add one more voice to the growing call for multivocality.

One aspect of Buñuel's films that is beginning to receive more attention is that of space. Where Buñuel scholarship has highlighted the importance of setting, it has been mainly used to feed into analyses of his films that focus on the themes mentioned above. Buñuel has simply not been considered a 'spatial director' in the same way as, for instance, Michelangelo Antonioni or Wim Wenders have been.[14] He was staunchly against compositional harmony and exaggerated beauty in his films, which is all the more interesting given that seven of his Mexican films were made with cinematographer Gabriel Figueroa, renowned for his strikingly beautiful shot compositions in films such as *La Perla* (1947) and *Río Escondido* (1948), both made with director Emilio (El Indio) Fernández. Figueroa's work with Fernández is an example of lyrical nationalist films that were largely predicated on Mexican national identity as imag(in)ed through the eulogy of oppressed and marginalised social groups – often via indigenous characters. Patrick Keating (2010) draws a parallel between the Fernández-Figueroa partnership and that of Buñuel-Figueroa. He discerns numerous similarities between the two. Crucially, Figueroa's work with both directors produces 'a set of films that are designed to be interpreted in spatial terms' (2010: 202), yet while Fernández's films attracted a framework of criticism built around nationalist questions of Mexican/Indian identity, Buñuel's display a preponderance of open, ambiguous motifs. The relevance of this approach and its potential to revitalise writing on Buñuel is spelled out by Tom Conley, who explicitly acknowledges the nascent consideration of space in Buñuel's films. He writes, '[o]ver the passage of time it may be that the spatial dynamics of Buñuel's cinema may have gained force where the psychoanalytical or religious material has lost some of its luster' (2008: 45), and Conley's argument inspires my own research here.

In many ways, the spatial dynamics Conley identifies in Buñuel's cinema have always been there. Almost from the start of his cinematic career, Buñuel can be considered a director fascinated with space and the possibilities that this presents to the filmmaker. His early – and not entirely objective – documentary *Tierra sin pan* depicting the wretched lives of the inhabitants of Spain's isolated and inhospitable mountain region of Las Hurdes in Extremadura, as they struggle in vain against their environment, was a self-proclaimed filmic essay in human geography, stated explicitly as such as the opening credits roll. This is precisely the role that Elliot Rubinstein attributes to Buñuel:

> it is the 'human geography' that calls up not only Las Hurdes but all the best of Buñuel's work. In the manner of a geographer who refuses to restrict his field of study, Buñuel with passionate curiosity examines human beings in their longitudes and latitudes, their climates – their spaces. (1978: 247)

Seen in this way, Buñuel's cinema has always been foregrounded within human and spatial concerns. This is where my approach to the films I read in this book finds its place, between geographical and philosophical concerns with space. The human concern with the world that Rubinstein proposes is at the heart of Buñuel's work, is an aspect that dialogues with Carlos Fuentes's essay on Buñuel in which he surmises that tension in the director's cinema revolves around 'the decision to connect with the world or to refuse this connection' (1970: 199) Spatial metaphors abound in this essay, as Fuentes writes:

> Buñuel's characters follow a priesthood: a priesthood of the neighbourhoods, of crime, of bedrooms, of abandonment, of obsessions, of solitudes. They live out a search for their authentic self through the length and breadth of the jungles of subjectivity and the oceans of society. The identity of personal desire and of the authenticity of man in the world grants the Buñuelian priesthood a superior meaning. (1970: 198)[15]

Fuentes's imagery evokes the slums of *Los olvidados*, the jungle of *La Mort en ce jardin* and the ocean that keeps Robinson Crusoe prisoner on his island. The tension in Buñuel's cinema according to Fuentes is between freedom and isolation, as the protagonists of his films, after searching for their authentic self, discover either 'the ties of a precarious community or the sterility of a new and definitive isolation' (1970: 198–99).[16] Certainly, the trope of imprisonment is palpable in the Mexican films, often represented through confined spaces, and Fuentes lists

Nazarín's incarceration, the tomb of Catalina and Alejandro in *Abismos de pasión* and the second, irreversible confinement of the diners in *El ángel exterminador* in the church.

Similarly, Michel circumscribes Buñuel's work within the tension between confinement and freedom. Whereas Fuentes opposes isolation to freedom, however, imprisonment and liberty for Michel become alienation and de-alienation. Like Elizondo, Michel believes the beginnings of Buñuel's cinema are rooted in 'the search for man', and, as such, his output is necessarily concerned with human beings' position in the world, for 'if there is a common trait among men, it is not "an immutable human nature", but the fact of being alienated' (1961: 21; 24).[17] Michel and Fuentes's essays were originally published during and after Buñuel had finished making films in Mexico – 1961 and 1970, respectively. Alienation, as Michel has it, is arguably a more flexible term than isolation, able to convey a sense of non-belonging to both groups and places even when the person in question is not alone. It is plausible to consider the group of fugitives in *La Mort en ce jardin* as alienated in that they do not belong to their environment (the jungle) and their interpersonal relationships fail. Similarly, Nazarín's residence among the dispossessed of Mexico City and his reluctant journey with 'disciples' Ándara and Beatriz brings him into contact with others, even if he still remains alienated from them. Naturally, though, both isolation and alienation suggest a spatial dislocation between Buñuel's characters and their surroundings. This sense of non-belonging is accurately and acutely summarised by Chaspoul when he says simply that 'Buñuel very often films characters in displacement, who never truly seem to succeed in inhabiting the places where they find themselves' (1997: 115).[18] This – that the characters of the films included in this book are rarely successful in their search for a place of belonging – is the central tenet of my argument and forms the backbone of my reading of the films.

The spatial turn: geography as an exporter of ideas

It is important to point out that my focus on space and place in this book, and the way that I borrow from other disciplines such as human geography and anthropology, is part of a wider turn towards recognising the importance of space, particularly in the arts and social sciences. Barney Warf and Santa Arias make clear, '[h]uman geography over the last two decades has undergone a profound conceptual and methodological renaissance that has transformed it into one of the most dynamic, innovative and influential of the social sciences' (2009: 1). This is reflected in the move from a discipline grounded in empiricism to consider wider avenues of research and interfaces between different fields such as sociology, literary and film studies, and philosophy, meaning that researchers in these areas are increasingly turning to geographers to inform their writing. This turn towards space necessitates an interdisciplinary methodology that has been embraced by many different theorists and researchers. It also speaks to Foucault's proclamation that the 'present epoch will perhaps be above all the epoch of space' (1986: 22). To a large extent, this resurgence has been linked with postmodernism: Fredric Jameson's assertion that 'we live in spacious times' (Jameson in Thacker 2003: 1), for example, resonates with postmodern geographer Edward Soja's conception of human beings as 'intrinsically spatial beings, active participants in the social construction of our embracing spatialities' (1996: 1). The work of geographers and urbanists such as Soja, as well as Doreen Massey and David Harvey, has stimulated this spatial turn within the arts and social sciences, and their influence bleeds into various disciplines.[19] The renewed interest in space as a fruitful research area across fields is thanks to a fundamental paradigm shift, according to Foucault: whereas time, throughout the nineteenth century, was privileged over space, this is no longer the case. We now live our lives, he says, aware that 'our experience of the world is less that of a long life developing through time than that of a network that connects points and intersects with its own skein' (1986: 22).

It is possible to look back further and identify contributions to the broader trend of a reconceptualisation of the discipline of geography. Edward Relph's *Place and Placelessness*, published in 1976, is a notable forerunner of this spatial turn and a concerted effort to excavate a fuller notion of place outside of empirical geography. Relph writes of the 'almost total failure of geographers to explore the concept of place' (1976: 1). His focus is on place as we experience it emotionally, and in this his work is coetaneous with and paralleled by that of geographer Yi-Fu Tuan. Perhaps Tuan's most well-known text is his study of the affective relationship between people and their environments (1990), in which he echoes Gaston Bachelard's neologism topophilia, or the love of place, an idea that I discuss in chapter five when considering the ways that Buñuel depicts the home. Like Relph, Tuan underscores the tendency of geography towards a more strictly scientific epistemology, and positions his own work in opposition to this:

Environment [...] is not just a resource base to be used or natural forces to adapt to, but also sources of assurance and pleasure, objects of profound attachment and love. In short, another key word for me, missing in many accounts of livelihood, is *Topophilia*. (1990: xii)

Both Relph and Tuan present convincing cases for a concerted focus on the significance of space and place within the field of human geography, and Paul Rodaway considers Tuan in particular as '[v]ery much defining "humanistic geography" for a generation' (2011: 426), due to his reaction against positivist models of geographical analysis.

The resonances of this spatial turn in various disciplines are myriad. In philosophy, for instance, Edward Casey (2009), whose work inspires my readings of *Los olvidados* and *Nazarín* in chapter four, has produced insightful work in phenomenology concerning the human relationship to his or her lived surroundings, while Dylan Trigg (2012) has investigated the link between place and memory, and the role that places play in shaping our sense of self. In literary studies, Elizabeth Jones (2007) examines the interface between geography and literature, considering the importance of the home through the life writing [*autofiction*] of three twentieth-century French authors. Similarly, Andrew Thacker (2003) carefully outlines the importance of space in literary analysis. Thacker's project is the portrayal of space in modernist literature and he traces the concepts of influential spatial theorists such as Foucault, Bachelard and Heidegger before applying these concepts to his reading of the works of notable authors such as James Joyce and Virginia Woolf. Moving beyond literature alone, the volume edited by theologian Daniel Boscaljon (2013) on the representation of the home in art and narrative includes considerations of poetry, prose, film and television. The contributions are varied in their scope and demonstrate the permeations of spatially focused analyses across disciplines. The spatial turn also provides the impetus for the edited volume published by Jaimey Fisher and Barbara Mennel (2010a). Although focused specifically on German cultural production, the editors' main argument is that a focus on space as a theme permits us to reconsider canonical literary and cinematic works from a new perspective, pointing towards the suitability of, and need for, a wider mapping of spatially driven analyses of texts. Although several contributions to the volumes by Boscaljon and Fisher and Mennel detailed above take visual media as their source of study,[20] the richness of analyses of space in film comes to the fore in other books and edited volumes specifically on cinema.

Considering space in cinema

As an inherently visual medium, cinema is able to represent space in its multifaceted dimensions. Taking Buñuel's cinema as an example, we see that films are able to psychologise space, as in the postcard image of Paris which comes to life before Castin's delirious eyes in *La Mort en ce jardin*; they are capable of narrativising and reifying space, as in the pestilential symbiosis between human and environment in *Tierra sin pan*; and, intentionally or not, they aestheticise the locations that structure and form them through an aesthetics of beautification – surprisingly for the ascetic Buñuel, critic Pauline Kael labelled the *mise-en-scène* of *Le Journal d'une femme de chambre* as 'revoltingly "beautiful"' (1978: 274) – or austerity. In the past few decades, the influence of the spatial turn has emerged in academic studies of filmic representation of space, place and landscape from film scholars, geographers and philosophers.

Feeding into the idea of geography as an exporter of ideas and the interdisciplinary spatial turn, geographers Stuart Aitken and Leo Zonn turn to film to argue 'cinematic representation needs to be a key part of geographic investigation' (1994: 5), on the basis that film is mode of cultural production and a social text. They argue in favour of the symbiosis between cinema and culture, or as they phrase it, between 'real-life and reel-life':

> the way spaces are used and places are portrayed in film reflects prevailing cultural norms, ethical mores, societal structures, and ideologies. Concomitantly, the impact of a film on an audience can mold social, cultural, and environmental experiences. Clearly, a research direction focused on the production and consumption of space and place in cinema deserves serious geographic attention. (Ibid.)

The contributions that make up Aitken and Zonn's volume are heterogeneous, drawing on documentary film, Third cinema and British cinema, but all affirm the importance of the representation of space in film and the authors hold film to be influential in 'understanding our place in the world' (ibid.).

In his study of space in cinema, André Gardies points out that the analysis of narrative space has traditionally been overlooked in favour of that of time (1993: 9). His monograph is a serious attempt to reverse this trend. In classical narrative cinema – largely the realm of Buñuel's Mexican cinema – Gardies believes that there is frequently concordance between what the films tell the viewer and the viewer's own knowledge; that is, the 'anchoring-in-the-real' [*l'ancrage réel*] of the film by way of recognisable toponymy helps to build on a viewer's encyclopaedic knowledge (1993: 77). Buñuel is an interesting figure in this respect: we need only think of *Los olvidados* – arguably one of his most linear films which appears to borrow from the coetaneous wave of Italian neorealism – to see how Buñuel's depiction of space is always an ambivalent one. Set unmistakably in Mexico City, the unforgiving slums that form the characters' world are quite unexpected, coming as they do after the images of grandiose British, French and Mexican metonymy as Big Ben, the Eiffel Tower and the Zócalo in Mexico City flash across the screen in the film's documentary-like prologue. Gardies's approach is largely structuralist, frequently drawing on Saussure's linguistic theories as analogies and Christian Metz's writing on cinema, examining the transmission of information from the screen to the audience and the audience's perception of this.

Contrasting with Gardies's claim that analysis of film has traditionally favoured time over space is Wendy Everett and Axel Goodbody's assertion that 'it would be rare today to find any serious study of film that did not in some way take account of the importance of space' (2005: 9). Their aim is to explore the various ways in which spatial theories and theorists have influenced investigations of filmic space. As such, theorists of contemporary urbanity such as Michel de Certeau and Henri Lefebvre are prominent among the contributions that make up their edited volume. In many respects, the birth of cinema as a medium was coetaneous with the rapid expansion of cities and the redefining of the urban metropolis. Early cinema was perfectly positioned to showcase recent architectural achievements, such as the American Mutoscope and Biograph Company's *Panorama of the Flatiron Building* (1903), and to capture urban life in its totality, from the bright lights and showgirls of commercial Weimar Berlin to the sewers underneath the city in Walter Ruttmann's *Berlin: die Symphonie der Großstadt* (1927). Not surprisingly, the depiction of the city in film is a field of substantial research.[21] However, there is also an effort in Everett and Goodbody's volume to look beyond the urban to different conceptions of space, such as the idyllic spaces of tropical islands and the relationship between space and the male body as represented by actor Javier Bardem.

More recently, researchers in film studies have shown a renewed interest in the ways in which film can represent landscape. Graeme Harper and Jonathan Rayner show that, from its inception, cinema has functioned as a screen on which to bring the landscapes of far-flung places to audiences who may not have had the means to experience these first-hand (2010: 16). As an example of cultural production, film establishes a contract of sorts with the spectator, who is at liberty to interpret the images on screen in his or her own way. Harper and Rayner point towards the affective potential of spatial representation when they suggest that a filmic landscape is a 'mnemonic offering', and can be 'landscapes of the mind, offering displaced representations of desires and values' (2010: 18; 21). What Martin Lefebvre terms 'a form of spatial predicate' (2006: 51), filmic landscapes are the most readily aestheticised element of *mise-en-scène*. Landscape can either be an integral element of the plot and appear in a so-called narrative mode, or can be separate to plot, where the viewer is meant to contemplate the aesthetic qualities of the landscape independently of the storyline. This, Lefebvre terms the spectacular mode of landscape (2006: 29). I find Lefebvre's admission that there is much more research to be done on the representation of space in cinema particularly pertinent. Indeed, this book addresses Lefebvre's view that

> While setting concerns narrative representation, and narrative aesthetic representation, it is equally possible to represent space in more 'anthropological' terms. Indeed, space may be represented as pertaining to lived experiences other than narrative or aesthetic. This is the case, for example, with 'identity' and 'belonging' and the myriad ways of engaging with space that both can entail. (2006: 52)

This call for a wider conceptualisation of the possibilities of spatial representation in cinema, beyond aesthetic analysis and in particular with regards to lived experiences, has been taken up by architect Juhani Pallasmaa in his analysis of existential space in cinema and its representation in architecture. According to Pallasmaa, 'experiential images of space and place are contained in practically all films', given that '[a]rt articulates the boundary surface between the mind and the world' (2007: 7; 21). His twinning of cinema and architecture springs from his view that '[t]hese two art forms create and mediate comprehensive images of life. [...] Both forms of art define the dimensions and essence of existential space; they both create experiential scenes of life situations' (2007: 13). Pallasmaa looks at the work of four directors: Hitchcock, Tarkovsky, Kubrick and Antonioni; interestingly, though, he believes Buñuel's cinema is equally deserving of his philosophical analysis of architecture in film (2007: 8). His approach coincides with that of film researcher Murray Smith and philosopher Thomas Wartenberg, who ask more generally:

If philosophy is regarded as the attempt to think systematically about fundamental issues of human existence, it seems more plausible to regard film as capable of embodying such acts of reflection. For if philosophy names a range of concerns that are the common property of every thoughtful human being during at least some moments of his or her life, why should films not mobilize these concerns in ways that would count as philosophy in this sense? (2006: 2).

This book addresses both of these concerns, firstly by reading space in the films beyond issues of purely aesthetic and artistic representation and secondly by using Buñuel's Mexican films to pose deeper questions of what it means to be in place and to belong in a place, and in doing so, widening the scope of Buñuel studies. Beyond aesthetic or narrative concerns, filmic depictions of space, place and landscape are replete with displaced desires and values, and we can take these as explorations of metatextual metaphors and allegories beyond the surface level of plot. This is the thrust behind my reading of these films, and the broad approach considers how film is suited to depict issues of belonging and non-belonging within the interrelated fields of human geography and philosophy.

Notes

1 The Spanish term originates from Buñuel himself in reference to *La hija del engaño* (1951). See de la Colina and Turrent (1993: 61). Julie Jones uses the term 'studio potboilers' in noting how scathing Buñuel was in the early 1950s about his commercial films, quoting him as saying: '[a]rtistically, they are zeros. They made it possible for me to shoot the films I believe in' (2013: 84).

2 [una bomba [que provocó] un gran impacto en sus primeros espectadores]; [de ninguna manera exaltante].

3 [es admirable desde muchos puntos de vista pero es un Buñuel al que le han cortado las uñas]; [un cine 'descafeinao' [sic]].

4 [jugueteo intelectual y el ajedrez de fantasmas (ideas de personajes más que personajes)]. This point is echoed almost word-for-word by Gianfranco Corbucci. He argues that in Buñuel's late films ideas are unmediated, as characters appear as 'phantasms [...] direct representations of ideas', leading to what he sees as an intellectual game (1974: 41). [Bastano soltanto fantasma di personaggi che siano pure e semplici, dirette rappresentazioni di idee].

5 [une fraîcheur d'invention, une franchise du regard, une clarté d'expression].

6 [salvaguardar la imagen del autor en detrimento de los filmes, que permanecen ignorados]. There is a wealth of European and North American criticism from the 1950s to the 1970s on Buñuel's Mexican cinema, as more of the lesser-known films made there began to arrive in Europe. Most of this criticism falls foul of the trap that Gaston Lillo identifies. Jean Delmas arbitrarily discerns the 'Sunday-best Buñuel' and the 'everyday Buñuel' (1978: 193). The latter, of course, refers to his Mexican films. See also Milne (1965–66); Hogue (1976); and Rubinstein (1977).

7 [el sello de esta doble nacionalidad].

8 [estas fotografías también nos muestran […] una percepción de México, alejada de lo turístico y con una sensibilidad que aflora a menudo en pequeños detalles]; [sus fotografías [que] se refieren a paisajes sin gente].

9 [morfología y genealogía de lo feo].

10 [desnutrida minoría].

11 [Lo cierto es que al hacer aquí Buñuel la mayor parte de su filmografía, con varias de sus obras maestras, no le estaba haciendo un favor a nadie; ya basta de esa actitud mesiánica: si Buñuel hubiese ido a parar a otro país del continente no hubiera hecho nada, y que lo digan sus dos estancias en Estados Unidos, una antes de venir y otra para hacer *Robinson Crusoe* y *La joven* […] si no filmó todo lo que quiso, tampoco lo hizo ningún director mexicano ambicioso].

12 [Si l'exil physique s'achève, l'exil du regard, lui, se prolonge, car il est le véritable exil cinématographique. Dans la mesure où l'exil n'a jamais été chez Buñuel un sujet, mais toujours un lieu depuis lequel s'exerçait la mise en scène, et qui agissait donc sur elle, il demeure exil du regard en dépit de la fin de l'exil physique].

13 [Se invoca el psicoanálisis, se invocan los Misterios, se invocan los Episodios Nacionales. ¿Ha invocado alguien la generalidad de las generalidades: el hombre?].

14 Antonioni's films are included in a variety of relatively recent monographs and edited volumes on space in film. See, for example, Bernardi (2002) and Gandy (2006). Marko Jobst considers that for Wenders 'cinematic storytelling is, at its core, a spatial act' (2008).

15 [la decisión de conectarse con el mundo o de rehusar ese vínculo]; [Los personajes de Buñuel cumplen un sacerdocio: sacerdocio de las barriadas, del crimen, de las alcobas, del abandono, de las obsesiones, de las soledades. Viven una búsqueda del ser auténtico a lo largo y ancho de las selvas subjetivas y los océanos

sociales. La identidad del deseo personal y de la autenticidad del hombre en el mundo otorga un sentido superior al sacerdocio buñueliano].

16 [los lazos de una precaria comunidad o la esterilidad de un nuevo y definitivo aislamiento].

17 [la recherché de l'homme]; [s'il y a un trait commun aux hommes, ce n'est pas «l'immuable nature humaine», mais le fait d'être aliénés].

18 [Buñuel filme très souvent des personnages en déplacement qui semblent ne jamais vraiment réussir à habiter les lieux où ils se trouvent].

19 See Santa Arias (2010) for a useful overview of the spatial turn. Arias is a Latin Americanist whose work on colonial Latin America has been influenced by the spatial turn. She co-edited an interdisciplinary volume specifically on the resonances of the awareness of the importance of space in the arts and humanities, discussed in this chapter. See Warf and Arias (2008).

20 See, for example, Seamon (2013: 155–70) and Jacobs (2010: 381–95).

21 Among the numerous examples, see Clarke (1997) or Shiel and Fitzmaurice (2001).

Chapter 2
The Island Heterotopias of *Robinson Crusoe* and *The Young One*

n July 1954, Buñuel's adaptation of Daniel Defoe's *Robinson Crusoe* premiered in North America.[1] In terms of the mechanics of the film's production and its subsequent reception, *The Adventures of Robinson Crusoe*, to give the film its full title, constitutes a unique work among his films made in Mexico. It was his first colour production; Buñuel even went as far as to claim it was the first film made outside the USA to use the Eastmancolor process (see de la Colina and Pérez Turrent 1992: 92) which, when coupled with the aesthetically arresting *mise-en-scène* and shot composition by Buñuel's Canadian cinematographer and colour film specialist Alex Phillips, culminates in what Tony Richardson sees as man and environment in harmony, ultimately leading to the realisation of a 'mature and beautiful work' (1978: 135). *Robinson Crusoe* was aimed at the Anglophone, principally North American, market, the audience most likely to possess a more familiar grasp of the English literary canon, and as Marvin D'Lugo explains, of all Buñuel's films made in Mexico, none enjoyed a wider distribution or greater box office success (2004: 80).[2]

Six years later, Buñuel began work on *The Young One*, released in Mexico under the title *La joven*. In many ways this can be considered the companion film to *Robinson Crusoe*. As Buñuel's only English-language productions, the two have frequently been mentioned in conjunction with one another. Indeed, Buñuel writes about the two films together in his autobiography precisely for this reason (2003: 191–3). Beyond the question of the language of the dialogue, both films were inspired by literary sources. *The Young One* is a liberal adaptation of Peter Matthiessen's short story 'Travelin' Man', first published in 1957.[3] Matthiessen's story depicts the racial struggle between an escaped black convict who flees to Ocean Island, off the coast of the US Deep South, and the white man who resides there. Like *Robinson Crusoe*, this film is often omitted from the Buñuel canon. Unlike *Robinson Crusoe*, its unpalatable subject matter undoubtedly contributed to its decidedly tepid reception and subsequent moderate takings at the box office.[4] This is echoed in Jonathan Rosenbaum's appraisal of the film, though he ultimately attributes its commercial failure in the USA to the fact that Buñuel 'still hadn't become a "brand-name" director, a recognized auteur' (2004: 258). What little attention has been paid to the film, as Santaolalla affirms (2004: 97), has invariably been caught up in the film's treatment of racial tension in the Deep South prior to the Civil Rights Movement of the 1960s.

Lastly, both films are given as Mexican-US co-productions and both were projects involving the Canadian screenwriter Hugo Butler and American producer George Pepper. Butler and Pepper were blacklisted within Hollywood circles under McCarthyism and the Second Red Scare sweeping US institutions in the 1950s and their identities are disguised under pseudonyms in the films' credits. The pair had found work south of the border, in Mexico. According to Conrad, at the time 'Mexico [...] was courting American projects, partly to help offset rising production costs. "They *want* foreign production now," observed blacklisted screenwriter Dalton Trumbo in 1958, "and are laying out the red carpet for all kinds of politically soiled artisans"' (1994: 31). The spatial analysis I set out in this chapter will concentrate on what is arguably the most obvious of the parallels between the two films: the island as narrative setting. The importance of islands in these two films – and in Buñuel's cinema more generally – cannot be underestimated. Fresh readings of the films can be achieved through a discussion of the spatial characteristics of the films' island spaces, with a specific focus on the ways in which these islands can be seen as representative of an Other space whose identity is constituted in the islands' alterity. This state of alterity is a contestation of the everyday space we inhabit and is what allows Buñuel's island spaces to be viewed within Foucault's framework of heterotopias.

Buñuel and the island as setting

We do not have to look very hard for evidence of the significance of the island as narrative setting in Buñuel's cinema. *La Fièvre monte à El Pao* takes place on a fictitious island near a totalitarian South American state and the location for *Cela s'appelle l'aurore* (1956) is the Mediterranean island of Corsica. Additionally, the alternative title for *El ángel exterminador* in English was to be *The Shipwrecked on Providence Street*. The island as *mise-en-scène* was also intended to form part of *Ilegible, hijo de flauta*, the surrealist screenplay that Buñuel wrote with Spanish poet Juan Larrea in 1948 and modified in 1957, but which he never filmed.[5] In the two present films, Buñuel's preoccupation with what Fernando Gabriel Martín (2010: 742–45) describes as spaces of isolation drives him to emphasise the physicality of these spaces through cinematography, as I will show. Martín's term is pertinent here: the island trope as an insular prison is a symptom of the unresolved dualism of freedom and isolation identified by Carlos Fuentes and Michel in chapter one, which is the primary focus of the spatial readings I carry out of Buñuel's films in this book. D'Lugo (2004: 98) draws attention to the fact that the island as setting really begins with the arrival of the Mallorcans in *L'Âge d'or* and later continues as the Mexican Pacific coast forms the backdrop to a number of Buñuel's international co-productions, functioning as a blank canvas to morph from Crusoe's solitary home into the nondescript game-preserve of Miller in *The Young One*. Juan Luis Buñuel states that his father 'always liked the idea of people being separated from the rest of society and how they would react in this new ambience' (1978: 254–55). Punning in the original Spanish, the two-fold nature of the island as both a self-enclosed site (or prison) and a secluded environment yet to be touched by commodification is encapsulated in the pithy term *salón en la selva* [salon in the jungle]. This expression first arises in de la Colina and Pérez Turrent's conversations with Buñuel about *La Mort en ce jardin* (1992: 126–130), though it is easily reworked for other Buñuel films with literal or metaphorical jungles, such as *Robinson Crusoe* and *El ángel exterminador*. The duality between the commodification impulse and the island as a site of banishment underscores both *Robinson Crusoe* and *The Young One*, marking the island spaces of the narratives as Other, yet permeated by the cultural influence of the mainland societies to which these islands are bound. As I will explain, it is often the conflict between what can be considered opposing spatial modes that constitutes these islands as Foucauldian heterotopias.

Heterotopias

Outlined in a lecture given to architecture students in 1967, Foucault's concept of heterotopias has gained substantial currency in considerations of space in the arts and social sciences since its inclusion in a 1984 exhibition intended to stimulate the urban regeneration of West Berlin, and subsequent publication in 1986. The literal meaning of the term is 'other spaces' and postmodernist approaches within the discipline of geography have encouraged the use of the concept to support and affirm difference and resistance in feminist, postcolonial or queer strands of geography and their interrogation of hegemonic power structures.[6] Moreover, evidencing the trend I outlined in chapter one towards human geography as an exporter rather than an importer of ideas, Foucault's analysis and its elaboration by geographical researchers has bled into literary and cultural studies and is a potent and fruitful tool for analysis in the arts, given its wide-ranging applications to the analysis of space and the ways that this is produced. Indeed, according to Derek Hook and Michele Vrdoljak, although specific spaces can be considered as heterotopias, the term itself can be used as a mode of analysis, as a 'particular way to *look at* space, place *or text*' (2002: 207).

In Foucault's words, heterotopias are 'counter-sites, a kind of effectively enacted utopia in which the real sites, all the other real sites that can be found within the culture, are simultaneously represented, contested and inverted'. He prefaces his discussion of heterotopias with observations on utopias: both spaces are separated from the surrounding space and remain 'outside of all places', but whereas the latter are ultimately imaginary, impossible spaces, heterotopias are culturally specific, able to be located in reality and are a 'constant of every human group' (1986: 24). Peter Johnson has explored the relationship between heterotopias and utopias, affirming that the former are abortive utopias or, to be more specific, they are utopias 'come unstitched', sites with a utopian intent that fails in practice (2006: 85). I should make clear the relevance of Johnson's particular conception of spaces that can be considered heterotopias, for, more than any other definition, this speaks directly to Buñuel's anti-utopian cinematic impulse. It is clear that the island spaces of both films in this chapter are failed utopias. However, heterotopias are not necessarily dystopias, since according to Hetherington they transcend the utopia-dystopia paradigm by problematising the etymological and homonymic ambiguity of the Greek term utopia as both a *ou*-topic no-place and a *eu*-topic good-place, existing 'in this space-between, in this relationship between spaces, in particular between eu-topia and ou-topia' (1997: ix). Furthermore, they require the presence of another space, an outsider viewpoint from which the counter-site can be seen as a heterotopia, as these are established as such 'by their difference in a relationship between sites rather than their Otherness deriving from a site itself' (Hetherington 1997: 43). The islands in *Robinson Crusoe* and *The Young One* are caught within a network of relations with the off-screen mainland, which is conspicuous through its absence in both films. In addition, the films' protagonists attempt to constitute their own elements of utopia that are shown to fail, influencing their interaction with their environment.

Robinson Crusoe

Off the map: Crusoe's desert island

An island is, by definition, a site of isolation and exile. In many ways, however, it functions as a metaphysical aperture which leads to experiences of self-discovery or self-realisation, facilitated paradoxically by its very nature as an insular site, in a physical and a psychological sense. For director and screenwriter John Truby, the island as setting constitutes a 'laboratory of man, a solitary paradise or hell, the place where a special world can be built and where new forms of living can be created and tested' (2007: 160). His description clearly chimes with the island as an alternate space *par excellence* in the form of Thomas More's *Utopia*. Significantly, in film and literature islands have frequently been located outside the perimeters of traditional geographical cartography, with castaways often chancing upon an island rather than following a deliberate trajectory, as in William Golding's *Lord of the Flies* and its subsequent cinematic adaptation by Peter Brook in 1963, H. G. Wells's *The Island of Dr Moreau* and the film adaptation by Don Taylor in 1977, and Robert Zemeckis's film *Castaway* (2000). This element of contingency imbues an island space with a mysterious quality when we consider Foucault's opinion that contemporary space

> is defined by relations of proximity between points or elements; formally, we can describe these relations as series, trees, or grids. [...] Our epoch is one in which space takes for us the form of relations among sites. (1986: 23)

A site, then, is defined in terms of its spatial coordinates – for example, latitude/longitude – in order to relate it to neighbouring sites; however, an island's location in film and literature is regularly shrouded in mystery, augmenting the element of serendipity, or misfortune, in its discovery. This element of mystery underscores the opening sequence of Buñuel's *Robinson Crusoe*, as the precise position of Crusoe's island is never fully elaborated: it lacks any relationality from the very beginning. Following the opening credits, as the camera focuses on a copy of Defoe's novel and a rudimentary seventeenth-century map, the voice-over narration gives Crusoe's location as 'in the latitude of twelve degrees eighteen minutes' before he is swept off course by the storm. The contrasting spatial modalities that Buñuel gives us here – contingency versus cartography – leading to Crusoe's shipwreck and arrival on the island are important, as '[i]t is in this sense that many traditional island narratives start to reveal tensions regarding space and possible shifts in organization due to heterotopic elements' (Storment 2008: 10). Crusoe's island exists, yet paradoxically it lies beyond the parameters of traditional cartography, at least beyond those of the elementary map shown in the opening sequence of Buñuel's film. The very inclusion of the map in this sequence is interesting as it marks a point of departure from the realist, empirical world into the unknown. Given that the archetypal image of the desert island is of a quasi-Edenic, unspoiled site completely closed in on itself, its precise location matters little. What is being stressed in the film's opening is the romanticised theme of adventure associated with the desert island trope in seminal works such as Defoe's novel, or Robert Lewis Stevenson's *Treasure Island*, the kind of swashbuckling escapades on the high seas that Foucault himself alludes to in the conclusion to his original lecture on heterotopias, where he writes: 'in civilizations without boats, dreams dry up, espionage takes the place of adventure, and the police take the form of pirates' (1986: 27).

This is a decidedly romantic ideal, of course, and Walter de la Mare sees this. He suggests the entire globe can be viewed as a collection of islands, yet there is an intrinsic quality to the desert island in particular that 'invites the soul' (1932: 18). Paralleling Truby's opinion that the island represents a malleable space fraught with dangers and bestowed with hidden pleasures – namely, that it swings between utopia and dystopia – de la Mare writes:

> Short of the subterranean, the submarine, and the wild vacancies of space, however, the conditions of an ideal retreat from the tumult and artificialities of man are fulfilled – solitude, danger, strangeness, the unknown, the discoverable, the eventual means of escape – if our hermitage is an island (1932: 16).

In the light of Buñuel's choice to adapt *Robinson Crusoe* and the subject matter of *The Young One*, it is significant that de la Mare considers an island as a space of opposition to the institutions of modern civilisation. This resonates with Martínez Herranz's argument that Buñuel's selective adaptation of *Robinson Crusoe*, which focuses exclusively on the hero's time on the island, suggests that 'the castaway's exile was not a form of atonement but rather an opportunity to discover himself and rid himself of social and moral ties that prevented him from freedom' (2013: 284).

Nevertheless, liberty, as Buñuel clearly suggested, is a phantom. Quite how far Buñuel's Crusoe achieves freedom is questionable when we consider the film's representation of what I have termed contrasting spatial modes. It is clear that the island archetype, and its representation in Buñuel's film, is '[a space] in which an alternate social ordering is performed [...] that stands in contrast to the taken-for-granted mundane idea of social order that exists within society' (Hetherington 1997: 40). Turning again to literature, Hetherington illustrates these spaces using the Marquis de Sade's castle of debauchery and death in *One Hundred and Twenty Days of Sodom*, and Franz Kafka's *Castle*, a space of absolute bureaucratic authority. Hetherington views both spaces as heterotopic by means of their implementation of an alternative social ordering: in the former, a system based on unbridled sovereignty; in the latter, the supremacy of faceless bureaucracy. The point is that the respective spaces' heterotopic qualities therefore derive from their ability to contest the ordinary, everyday space that we inhabit, either by 'creat[ing] a space of illusion that exposes every real space, all the sites inside of which human life is partitioned, as still more illusory', patently the subversive space of de Sade's castle, or by 'creat[ing] a space that is other, another real space, as perfect, as meticulous, as well arranged as ours is messy, ill-constructed and jumbled', akin to Kafka's *Castle* (Foucault 1986: 27). Cinematically, Buñuel achieves both of these effects in *Robinson Crusoe*, as Crusoe's island comes to encourage a conflation of real and illusory spatial modes.

Crusoe's island as a simulacrum and heterotopia of illusion

Illusory spaces are a veritable trope in Buñuel's cinema and they come into their own during the more explicitly surreal and illogical sequences in his films. I think of the strange country inn that fosters incest and bondage in *Le Fantôme de la liberté*, the quasi-oneiric mansion of the Sénéchals in *Le Charme discret de la bourgeoisie* and the country-road walking sequences of the same film. In *Robinson Crusoe*, a contrast of spatial modalities underscores the narrative due to Buñuel's representation of the island space: the island both erases the world beyond its shores and is the place of its reconstruction in miniature. For island spaces in film and literature, it is fundamental to 'recognize and interpret the competing spatial regimes being juxtaposed upon [sic], contested, and renegotiated' in those spaces (Storment 2008: 14). The spatial mode marked most dramatically in this film is the island's cultivation of illusion. Referring to the opening sequence of the movie, D'Lugo contends that the shadow of Crusoe over the book and the map, and the disembodied narration 'affirms the Eurocentric cultural-economical position that relegates the New World experience to an object status' (2004: 87–88). His postcolonial reading certainly holds weight; however, this is precisely the paradigmatic schema of control as represented by and contained within the centre as opposed to the periphery that Buñuel problematises in *Robinson Crusoe*. The dominant cultural space in Buñuel's adaptation (England) remains unseen. Primacy is given to space on the margins. Concerning the Mexican co-productions of the 1950s, D'Lugo continues that the raft of shady characters that appear in these – plunderers, fortune seekers and political schemers among them – are on a trajectory of 'subversive travel'. These are characters who

> by virtue of the plotting of these films, are brought to the same essential site of primitive tropical space that leads in each work to an implicit critique – often more visual than verbal – of the presumed superiority of civilisation over the culture of the periphery. (2004: 85)[7]

In *Robinson Crusoe*, though, Buñuel arguably does more than question the dominance of civilisation over the culture of the periphery. In its exploration of the island as a heterotopia of illusion, the film poses a challenge to de la Mare's Edenic image of desert islands. The consequence of this inversion of cultural hegemony is taken to its extreme halfway through the film, where we see the reality of Crusoe's bitter despair and solitude as a vehicle through which the outside world, the supposedly dominant Eurocentric model, can be viewed as little more than an illusion, as I will show.

First, however, the term requires some explanation. As its name indicates, a heterotopia of illusion has the function of rendering 'every real space, all the sites inside of which human life is partitioned, as still more illusory' (Foucault 1986: 27). Foucault's example of this illusory counter-space is the traditional brothel. This is a self-enclosed site with a distinct social and moral ordering based on hedonistic rather than repressive drives. Though obviously dissimilar in their function, both the brothel and Crusoe's island-home subsume the surrounding space – all the sites in which human life is routinely carried out, as Foucault puts it – heightening the element of pleasure in the former and despair in the latter. Put simply, Crusoe's island-world becomes overwhelming in its totality. As its own self-contained world,

Disneyland can be considered as another such space. For David Shane, Disneyland as the apogee of utopian consumerism is a notable example of a heterotopia of illusion (Shane 2008: 259–71). Jean Baudrillard's writing on simulacra sheds more light on Disneyland's – and the island's – constitution as a heterotopia of illusion. Baudrillard's taxonomy of what he terms the order of simulacra helps to explain the way in which the proliferation of visual images – from analogue and digital media – distorts the boundary between the real and the illusory in the postmodern world through the creation of a hyperreality, acting as a simulation, rather than an inferior representation, of an original image or object. Disneyland belongs to the third stage of the sign, that is, '[the sign] masks the absence of a profound reality'. Disneyland, as a sign, as a place, is 'a play of illusions and phantoms'. It 'exists in order to make us think that the rest is real, whereas all of Los Angeles and the America that surrounds it are no longer real' (Baudrillard 1994: 6; 12). This theme is taken up also by Umberto Eco. According to Eco, in the culture of North America the absolute fake, the simulacrum, is invested with more meaning than the original. In this way, 'Disneyland not only produces illusion, but – in confessing it – stimulates the desire for it' (1987: 44). James Connor contends that Eco's voyage through the hyperreal derives from the collapse of the Platonic distance between image and thing, allowing Eco's hyperreality to unfold whilst 'enfold[ing] two ontological levels, collapsing the gap between illusion and reality' (1993: 71). This is precisely the effect that Buñuel shows to influence Crusoe on his island and which is compounded by the hero's solitude: in its total subsuming of all other reality, the island leads Crusoe to the brink of a profound ontological crisis.

Crusoe's existential crisis derives from his loneliness, of course. The theme of solitude figures within predictable pseudo-religious readings of Buñuel's film as 'a moral rebirth' (Durgnat 1977: 80). Freddy Buache takes this further, contending that from Crusoe's lowest ebb, as he runs into the sea screaming for help, he is 'devoid of cumbersome laws and rituals, and has emerged reborn' (1973: 71). D'Lugo avoids rehashing this parabolic reading by focusing on Buñuel's interesting use of sound in the film. He posits that sound is configured by Crusoe as a 'liberating power of acoustic imagination', as '[Crusoe's] response to his fear and loneliness is [...] acoustic. When he speaks within the diegetic space, for instance, it is invariably to fill the void of his solitude' (2004: 89; 86–87). Buñuel renders Crusoe's solitude as much through audio techniques as through visual techniques, and sound features prominently in the three sequences of the film that depict the nadir of Crusoe's loneliness. Rather than functioning as a liberating power, as D'Lugo suggests, the sound here points directly towards the dominance of illusion and hyperreality, whereby the island effectively becomes a totalising microcosm of the world at large. This is evident in three sequences in particular.

Following the death of his dog, Rex, Crusoe, in his desperation for the reassuring sound of another human voice, charges towards his so-called valley of the echo in order to recite Psalm Twenty Three. The sequence is visually arresting as the camera pans the vast green wilderness, interspersed with three-quarter shots and distance shots of Crusoe, suggesting not only a sense of scale in which Crusoe is dwarfed by his environment, but also his uneasy attitude towards his hyperreality where illusion, or simulacrum – here in the form of his own voice reverberating – has taken the place of reality. Disembodied vocalisation stands not as a comfort to Crusoe, but as a relentless onslaught, and the reverberations link with the camera's panning of the valley of illusion as if seeking the source of these utterances even after we have clearly seen Crusoe producing the sounds. The longed-for onslaught of disembodied vocal simulacra in the valley of the echo filmically evidences the principle behind Eco's view that, in announcing itself as illusion, Disneyland (and Crusoe's island) actually stimulates the need for that illusion. This sequence pre-empts Crusoe's profound ontological crisis. Later, attempting in vain to take comfort from his Bible, a remnant from his milieu, Crusoe indicates that space beyond the island has now been divested of all meaning. The dialogue switches here from Crusoe's diegetic utterances as he tries to make sense of the scripture to an extra-diegetic voice-over, used to communicate Crusoe's inner confusion, which laments: 'the scriptures became meaningless to my eyes. The world seemed like a whirling ball with oceans and continents of green scum. And myself, of no purpose, of no meaning.' This recalls the film's opening image of the map, highlighting the fragility of epistemological security as it unmasks this as an illusion. The switch from Crusoe's outer voice to inner voice is more than just a device for filmic narration. The island as a Baudrillardian third order simulacrum lacks any corresponding reality underneath; it is a subsuming totality that renders signs from elsewhere – Crusoe's Bible and spoken voice – insignificant, emerging as a heterotopia of illusion in its rendering of the world beyond its impassable borders as an even greater illusion. The following sequence, as Crusoe runs headlong into the roaring surf, is the representation of the height of Crusoe's dejection and in which, according to Fuentes (1993: 97), Crusoe's image becomes that of an anti-Prometheus, fleeing from the reality of his illusion into the sea, his torch, his voice and his hope drowned by the waves (see Figure 1). Therefore, at the culmination of Crusoe's despondency,

Figure 1: Fanning the flames: the anti-Prometheus running from the illusion. (Producciones Tepeyac/Ultramar Films)

his island-home succeeds in shaking the hero's worldview, dissociating the space beyond its borders with meaning by virtue of its uncontested hyperreality. The result is that Crusoe's despair is compounded by an 'exaggerated universe where nothing holds it back' (Doniol-Valcroze in García-Abrines 1956: 62).

Towards a heterotopia of compensation

There is a paradox at the heart of Buñuel's *Robinson Crusoe*, however. The island is the site of contradictory spatial modes that undermine its constitution as purely a heterotopia of illusion. Crusoe's island is also unchartered and mystified territory – a potential threat to the hero's survival – and he therefore feels compelled to establish a taxonomy of flora and fauna. Soon after his arrival on the island, Buñuel introduces a series of almost documentary-style shots of the variety of vegetation and wildlife as Crusoe narrates his findings. This can be considered the foundation of what Foucault terms a heterotopia of compensation, the space that Hetherington associates with Kafka's *Castle* and which, contrary to that of a heterotopia of illusion, is 'as perfect, as meticulous, as well arranged as ours is messy, ill-constructed and jumbled' (Foucault 1986: 27). The alternation of despair and resignation with the quest for knowledge and self-preservation is one example of what Durgnat terms the dialectics of Buñuel's cinema, 'in that every character, every event, is not an assertion of any one point, but is a synthesis between opposing polarities' (1977: 17). In this way, Crusoe's island is able to concurrently constitute both a heterotopia of illusion and a heterotopia of compensation. This duality of spatial modes is symbolised by Crusoe's attachment to certain objects on his island. We could contrast Crusoe's extinguished torch in the scene in which he runs screaming into the sea with his telescope that he uses frequently on top of his vantage point to survey his surroundings. Fittingly, D'Lugo suggests that empowerment for Crusoe is contained within 'the fetishism of the look' (2003: 99). To this end, the montage of the island's wildlife is presented in the style of an objective documentary and the voice-over narration seems like a quasi-zoological instruction rather than a free indirect discourse of Crusoe's uncertainty and existential crisis.

As the name suggests, then, a heterotopia of compensation acts to compensate and counteract the disorganised space in which our everyday lives are played out. These particular types of counter-spaces perhaps best display the characteristics of an effectively enacted utopic social order, one based on the enforcement of a system of organisation and regimentation that contrives to construct a place for everyone and to keep everyone in their place. Notable examples of such operational counter-spaces were the bishop Vasco de Quiroga's *república de indios* [Republic of Indians] in sixteenth-century colonial Mexico. De Quiroga attempted to establish the economic and political system of More's *Utopia* through the creation of so-called hospital-villages of Santa Fe, settlements founded on

> the common ownership of property; the integration of large families; the system-atic alternation between the urban and the rural people; work for women; the six-hour working day; the liberal distribution of the fruits of common labor according to the needs of the inhabitants. (Zavala 1947: 347)

Although de Quiroga's regime may have modelled itself on More's theoretical notion of his utopic good-place, it is necessary to signal that, viewed as a space of alternative social ordering, the hospital-village of Santa Fe acted as a Panopticon for social control through the natives' conversion to Christianity (Verástique 2000: 124). For Crusoe's part, his desire to demarcate the island space is driven by a desire to impose a sense of order and stability on fundamentally unpredictable space, a hierarchy which emulates the modern Western spatial model judged by Foucault to operate on a series of binaries – the division between public and private space, for instance, or between the space of leisure and that of labour (1986: 23). Crusoe is shown herding his goats into a pen, sewing corn seeds in a field and making pottery. He takes pride in his demarcation of spaces: 'I built a barn, so that I fancied I was lord of the whole manor, and had my country house and sea-coast house, too. In short, I learned to master everything in my island except myself.' Though obviously evidencing the bourgeois, mercantile attitude towards property, this differentiation of spaces is telling of Crusoe's endeavour to counterbalance the feelings of confusion and disempowerment associated with the island as a heterotopia of illusion. To this end, David Melbye argues that this film depicts a 'landscape allegory of the "Western megalomaniac" pitted against an exotic wilderness and its native inhabitants' (2010: 17), categorising this film as an imperialist allegory that underscores later films such as Werner Herzog's *Aguirre: The Wrath of God* (1972) and John Boorman's *Deliverance* (1972).

Crusoe's unexpected encounter with Friday also helps to counter the island's role as an illusory other space and, to a large extent, Crusoe's ontological crisis. Friday is effectively the other to Crusoe's same, a physical manifestation and reminder of the space beyond the insular landmass on which Crusoe has been trapped for eighteen years. Buñuel's treatment of the colonialist trope and portrayal of the subaltern in *Robinson Crusoe* has featured in numerous analyses of the film and I will not add to this discussion here.[8] However, the allusion to the colony is pertinent to Crusoe's move towards a heterotopia of compensation. Significantly, for Foucault, the paradigm of such an other space was the colony, specifically the seventeenth-century Jesuit colonies of the Americas. The layout of these villages was designed to replicate the sign of the cross, with the various buildings and areas clearly positioned within this symbolic plan (1986: 27). The ambivalent atheist Buñuel does not overstate the reference to the role of religion within the colony of mutineers who arrive on the island at the end of the film; his protestant Crusoe merely suggests that they live according to his instructions gained through his extensive knowledge of the island's ecosystem and how this can best be manipulated to avoid a 'sacrilegious waste'. Of course, even if it were successful, Crusoe's colony would act as such in a very loose sense, to mention nothing of the fact that the group of mutineers are all male, suggesting theirs will be an abortive endeavour. What is fundamental here, though, is that their existence is to be regulated spatially and temporally: the time to sew crops, how to care for livestock, the places of concealment for weapons and gunpowder.

Crusoe's island as heterochrony

It would perhaps not be an exaggeration to say that *Robinson Crusoe* is the film of Buñuel's most overtly concerned with the passage of time. The many scenes in which time is alluded to in Crusoe's dialogue, or via visual clues such as Crusoe's growing beard and changing attire, find their culmination in the last words spoken by the protagonist, as he sails away from his home of 'twenty-eight years, two months and nineteen days'. For Foucault, many forms of heterotopias were intrinsically linked to time. Indeed, that Foucault acknowledges the 'fatal intersection of time with space' is a precursor to what he later goes on to describe as heterochronies, places linked to time in its fluid, ephemeral aspect, such as the festival, or, alternatively, places concerned with the material accumulation of time, such as the museum or the library (Foucault 1986: 26). The colony, a heterotopia of compensation in its utopic ordering, was an exercise not only in spatial regimentation but also its temporal equivalent, organised around times of work, prayer and reproduction. Even before the appearance of Friday and the mutineers, Crusoe is shown constructing his own existence around spaces and activities of labour, as well as periods of spiritual reflection in an elementary colonial system.[9] The division of time according to various spheres of activity is an attempt to impose order on an unknown space, in much the same way as Crusoe's rigorous documentation of time is an attempt to catalogue it.

The documentation of time in the film is communicated principally through Crusoe's attachment to his date-post and his diary, and the numerous shots in which these two objects figure is testimony to their importance in the narrative. They are instrumental in driving the chronology and they function as a visual point of correspondence with the narrative voice-over. On a symbolic level their significance lies in their object status as physical manifestations of time and of the intersection of time with space. The composition of the various shots of Crusoe documenting his life on the island in his diary are identical, with Crusoe's book and hand filling the frame. Time and space are inextricably linked within the pages of the diary as Crusoe narrates his written words: 'My eleventh month. Days passed in hunting wild foal, preparing food, trips to my lookout hill in search for sight of ships, one day much like another.' More explicitly, his date-post acts as an accretion of time juxtaposed with space. Its plaque reads: 'I came on shore here the 30th of September 1659.' This object features in one of the most notable shot compositions in the entire film (see Figure 2). For all its significance in terms of my argument, this scene lasts a mere eight seconds. It follows the beginning of Crusoe's despair, as he laments that he is imprisoned by 'the eternal bars and bolts of the sea'. It is essentially a self-contained time-space montage, with the temporal metaphor of Crusoe's date-post twirling in the centre of the frame, superimposed on to a

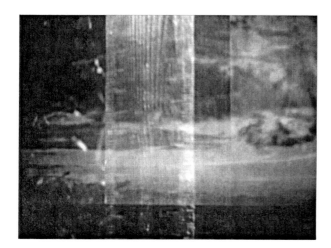

Figure 2: Superimposed
space-time. (Producciones
Tepeyac/Ultramar Films)

spatial backdrop of the island's coastline as the sun sets. When compared with other remarkable instances of superimposition in Buñuel's films, this scene may appear much less significant. Buñuel's superimposed images are often constructed as a mechanism to foreground a particular sequence within a surrealist aesthetic. In *Los olvidados*, in Jaibo's death throes, the superimposition of the advancing mangy dog is read by Libia Stella Gómez as a possible example of the Freudian uncanny (2003: 131). Similarly, the collective dream sequence in *El ángel exterminador* and its various superimposed images are unsurprisingly read as 'the interior world – thoughts, daydreams, nightmares – of the protagonists' (Poyato 2011: 161).[10] In *Robinson Crusoe*, this scene acts as a narrative device on the one hand, communicating the passage of time along with the accompanying voice-over. However, it also inextricably links time with space, especially when we consider the previous sequence in the film.

As Crusoe stares out to sea, he regrets bitterly his imprisonment on the island. The succession of shots of the roaring waves that follows and which leads to the time-space montage I have described above, makes clear that the ocean is a constant prison guard and suggests Crusoe's attempt to document his time spent on the island is useless. The numerous scenes in which the ocean figures in the film look towards *The Young One* and evoke Santaolalla's observation of this latter film as 'hysterically accumulat[ing] images of water' (2004: 107). As a symbol of stasis, the sea thus stands opposite Crusoe's adherence to Westernised time and its measurement in terms of days, weeks and years, evoked visually in terms of the date-post and diary, as well as aurally in the voice-over. Moreover, the makeshift grave of Crusoe's dog, Rex, inflects Crusoe's documentation of time ironically. This brief scene as Crusoe buries his companion shows the protagonist hammering the wooden headstone into the ground in close up, before the camera zooms out to frame Crusoe and the grave against the backdrop of the sea. The inscription 'Rex 1673' freezes this specific moment in time, opposing the ever-changing yet constant waves of the ocean in the background of the shot, the frontier separating the island from Crusoe's home milieu, in a spatial and temporal sense.

According to Foucault, the heterotopia functions at full capacity 'when men arrive at a sort of absolute break with their traditional time' (1986: 26). It is unsurprising, then, that Foucault deems the cemetery to be a heterochrony in that it symbolises both the end of life and death eternal. The links between the cemetery and Crusoe's island are clear throughout the film. Besides Rex's grave, Crusoe's effort to document his time spent on the island is both a testimony and a testament. Estranged from the outside world, Crusoe more acutely feels the accumulation of time and this is accentuated by his solitude. In an echo of island's constitution of alternating spatial modes, Crusoe's voiceover periodically suggests an indefinite sense of time, in the example given above, for instance, and later in the film when Crusoe likens the island to a tomb and a prison, belying his dogmatic categorisation of units of time. As the paradigm of the late seventeenth-century bourgeois male estranged from his social milieu, Crusoe's date-post and diary are vital tools in keeping alive a link with his culture while simultaneously attempting to impose a Westernised framework of time on a potentially perilous space. The tension between spatial regimes – the ordered reconstruction of the bourgeois labour/leisure dichotomy to counteract the island's potential to render all other space meaningless – therefore has its counterpart in the juxtaposition of static and transitory time.

The overall effect, then, of the desert island on Crusoe is ultimately the driving force of the narrative. At its simplest level, it is a documentation of a man's negotiation of his environment and space is at the heart of this film. The ambiguity contained within the portrayal of spatial and temporal modalities leads to the island being a space that 'exist[s] out of step and meddle[s] with our sense of interiority' (Johnson 2006: 84). This tension underlies the entire film. It therefore seems fitting that D'Lugo, commenting on the film's ending where Crusoe seemingly returns to his place and time, and his man-servant Friday is taken from him, views the conclusion as 'only a beginning for Buñuel, leading him to the subsequent series of films [...] that will enable him to rework that utopian myth' (2003: 100). Like *Robinson Crusoe*, *The Young One* is a film that accomplishes just this.

The Young One

An island of shame: undoing Eden

Recounting the critical reception of *The Young One*, Rosenbaum outlines the plot of the film and frames his introduction with a hypothetical scenario. He asks us to imagine that a daring film were made about racism in the Deep South, with a storyline that 'fairly sizzles', championing a brave Buñuel for 'taking on [these] volatile American materials'. But the scenario is not hypothetical and, breaking his rhetoric, Rosenbaum acknowledges: 'Buñuel did all the things I've mentioned in 1960, but hardly anyone noticed – and most of those who did were far from pleased' (2004: 257). In terms of the difficult thematic matter of the film – its depiction of a parasitic racism alongside the sexual abuse of Evvie, the film's teenage protagonist, at the hands of Miller, the older caretaker of the island game-preserve – Buñuel repeatedly affirmed his desire to eschew a Manichean stance and to avoid making a thesis film, stating that he wanted to 'understand – not defend – the racist characters' (de la Colina and Pérez Turrent 1992: 146).[11] The subject matter of the original story is no less provocative in spite of the substantial alterations made by Buñuel, Butler and Pepper. Though the character of Evvie and therefore the sexual exploitation of a minor was their addition to a narrative essentially concerned with a racial violence, Matthiessen's short story is littered with physical violence, more so than the film itself, with vivid descriptive passages exposing the latent bestial instincts of man and the human drive towards annihilation. Buñuel's predilection for the island as setting allows him to explore these tropes within a contained environment in *The Young One*. Rosenbaum encapsulates this idea:

> The island itself – where all the action, apart from a brief, early flashback, transpires – is a palpable, living presence [...] a character in its own right, closely identified with Evvie. Buñuel establishes this universe as elemental and predatory from the start. (2004: 261)

As shown in *Robinson Crusoe*, an island functions on a basic level as a microcosm of the world at large and can be both an extension of, and the opposite of, the mainland that governs it, working simultaneously on principles of mimetic representation and antithetical inversion. Additionally, the iconography of a secluded island is often imbued with poetic overtones in the vein of an Edenic shelter. Santaolalla evokes the allegory of the Garden of Eden when discussing the island game-preserve in

The Young One. For Santaolalla, the island of the film is Eden destroyed, a view that recalls the alternative English title of the film: *Island of Shame*. In contrast to the Biblical garden, Miller's island has never known innocence:

> This is no Garden of Eden – at least not one without irony. In fact, the man, woman and snake all reappear, but their part in the story modifies the Christian myth: neither does the snake whisper in the woman's ear (though it bites and kills her dog), nor is Evvie the defiant, seductive bearer of fruit personified by her namesake. (Santaolalla 2004: 101–02)

In addition to the Bible, Santaolalla considers that the island as setting, together with the film's depiction of 'patriarchal control, subordination and restitution', links *The Young One* with Shakespeare's *The Tempest* (2004: 109). Kara Zimmerman views the island on which the shipwrecked Duke of Milan and his cohorts find themselves as a heterotopia for the same reason that Foucault considers the garden as such. Zimmerman ventures that the heterotopia in *The Tempest* is, of course, the island itself, due to its position as a 'homogenization of two incompatible natures – utopia and dystopia – being created simultaneously in the same heterocosm' (2010: 38). That which to the subjugated Caliban is an autocratic dystopia is likewise to Traver, the black fugitive fleeing a lynch mob on the mainland after being falsely accused of raping a white woman, while both Shakespeare's Prospero and Buñuel's Miller attempt to constitute their own utopia as governors of their respective islands.[12] Crucial to an understanding of the significance of the island in *The Young One* is therefore the question of power.

'You can't keep a man cooped up on this stinkin' island!': Miller's island as a heterotopia of deviation

Exploring the relationship between modernity and the heterotopia, Hetherington analyses the influence of Foucault's discussion of Jeremy Bentham's Panopticon design for penal institutions. Sites reserved for members of society whose behaviour has attracted the label of 'deviant', such as mental institutes or prisons, are profoundly heterotopic, given the residents' or inmates' deviance from the behavioural norm and the consequent need for surveillance, as I explore here with regards to Miller. Hetherington asserts that the Panopticon 'was indeed an example of a heterotopic space associated with the alternate ordering of deviance, in contrast to earlier regimes of incarceration and punishment' (1997: 42). The advantage of the

Panopticon is its ability to move beyond the traditional observe/observed, subject/object dyad, as the observer, or penitentiary guard in Bentham's original design, possesses a unique vantage point, enabling them to watch their subjects without themselves being watched. The name is not euphemistic: it is clearly an exercise in omniscience and omnipresence. Indeed, the French title of Foucault's account of the historical development of the modern prison is *Surveiller et punir*, which has been translated as 'discipline and punish'.[13] The original French suggests that the notion of surveillance, or inspection, is intrinsically allied with castigation, itself necessitated by some form of deviant behaviour. With a specific emphasis on the character of Miller, I now examine the island game-preserve of *The Young One* specifically as a heterotopia of deviation.

For the caretaker of the game-preserve who plans to induct the barely adolescent Evvie into the world of adult sexuality, the island is the secluded environ that allows him to do so. Miller assumes the role of his own prison warden, permitting himself an authoritarian freedom on the game-preserve he guards, perhaps in an effort to counter-balance his ostensibly self-imposed exile. We could view his island in much the same way as the island on which Prospero has attempted to administer his own brand of autocratic utopia: Miller is a law unto himself, controlling who is permitted to visit and who is not. As acquaintances and representatives of the mainland, the racist boatman Jackson and the Reverend Fleetwood are allowed to stay on the island, while the clandestine Traver is shot at by Miller when he learns of his presence. As the game-preserve's caretaker, Miller's authority is challenged only by his boss, the owner of the island, Mr. Hargreave. When Miller's friend Jackson informs him that his presence is required on the mainland by Mr. Hargreave, Miller replies, 'If Mr Hargreave says come to town, I gotta come to town'. Although the game-preserve's owner is never seen throughout the narrative, the allusion to his influence evidences the precarious nature of Miller's longed-for utopia; Mr. Hargreave is one of several reminders throughout the film that the island's power system is intimately woven together with that of the mainland.

The sole link between the island and the mainland, a small motor-powered boat, comes only once per week, and throughout the course of the narrative Miller ventures to this off-screen space only once, although its presence is continually felt throughout the narrative. There are numerous verbal references to the mainland: Miller points out the educational opportunities available to Evvie had her grandfather, Pee Wee, who dies at the start of the film, opted to send her to school (an idea he abandons as his lust for Evvie increases); in addition, he remarks that, though she can 'be out here looking like a swamp rat', this is not the case in town, alluding to the island's nature as a space of alternate social ordering where normal rules do not apply. The unseen other space even becomes visible for an instant during Traver's flashback when he first arrives on the island in a rowing boat as he flees the mainland lynch-mob hunting him down for the false rape allegation made by a white woman. However, like the influence of the unseen Mr. Hargreave, it is the physical presence of visitors from the mainland to the island in the form of Miller's ultra-racist counterpart, Jackson, and the well-meaning but ineffective Reverend Fleetwood that recalls the silent influence of mainland society on the island's micro system of power. Though there is no denying the ideological differences between these two characters, ultimately they both function to a certain extent as external vehicles of surveillance, as Jackson scours the island, desperate for any trace of Traver, or, 'that dirty nigger', and Reverend Fleetwood admonishes Miller when he learns that he has sexually violated Evvie. Indeed, Santaolalla argues that 'the island of [Matthiessen's] original story obviously remained an appropriate location for a narrative about characters placed under scrutiny' (2004: 99). In the same way as the island can be seen paradoxically both as Miller's sanctuary and his prison, the outsiders Reverend Fleetwood and Jackson are akin to the invisible, scrutinising watchman of the Panopticon. What is more, this analogy is reflected in the name of the town on the mainland from which they come: Hammerville. Martín notes that this name 'must have been chosen with a certain intention' (2013: 768),[14] alluding to its relentless violence against Traver; though, as the instigator of his own space of deviation, Miller can also feel its force.

Foucault acknowledges the growing presence of heterotopias of deviation in modern society, providing examples such as the prison, the mental asylum, and even care homes. Given their purpose as spaces of confinement, the subject is placed there because their behaviour is deemed 'deviant in relation to the required mean or norm' (Foucault 1986: 25). While it is true that, to some extent, the island is Miller's refuge, it is dualistic in its function and serves simultaneously as a site of banishment. After Miller has forced himself on Evvie for the second time and Reverend Fleetwood asks him probing questions regarding his relationship with the girl, Miller, out of sheer exasperation, retorts: 'You can't keep a man cooped up on this stinkin' island! It had to happen!' That which becomes a heterotopia of deviation for Miller begins as an abortive pseudo-utopia where adolescent girls serve to alleviate the pent-up sexual desires of an alpha-male. With Miller's first violation of Evvie, as Traver unwittingly plays the clarinet outside the cabin, the island is transformed into a space of deviance, becoming further detached from the mainland by means of its alternate social ordering. The irony of this is not lost on the viewer, either. Traver, the persecuted black man innocent of the offence alleged against him on the mainland is unaware of the same crime being committed a few feet away from him by Miller, the white man privileged within the social system.

The rape of Evvie is a patent attempt on Miller's part to constitute his own form of social ordering in what he and, disturbingly, some early reviewers and scholars of the film, clearly view as his space. Writing during the film's showing at Cannes in 1960, one review in the Italian press centres on the theme of *lolitismo* as 'Ewie [sic] makes her guardian fall in love with her, provoking reactions in him that are far from favourable to the black man' (Press cuttings on *La joven* by Luis Buñuel, 1960-62, item 140).[15] It is even more perturbing that Buache is adamant that 'Ewie [sic] fully consented to make love and as a result the film does not [...] centre on a rape but on an act of love' (1973: 114). The film's original shooting script is revealing here, exposing the perversion and gender bias underscoring those patriarchal readings of *lolitismo*. This script, in the Buñuel archive at the Filmoteca Española, Madrid, includes a scene from the morning after Miller's first assault on Evvie, cut from the final version of the film. Miller approaches her menacingly:

> Miller: One thing, Evvie. What I said. How I acted. Don't tell 'em in town. Okay? [...] Because Evvie, if you do, I'm just liable to take that rifle, put it here [touches her temple] and pull the trigger. Hear me? Now hear me? (Buñuel and Addis 1960: 76)

In the final version of the film, after the close-up shot of Miller lying on top of the teenager, forcibly kissing her, the dawning of a new day is heralded by a dissolve into a high-angle shot of the island's coastline. The shift to the spatial aspect of the island is significant here; it emphasises the nature of the island as a space of alternate ordering for both Miller and Evvie, though albeit for different reasons, which I will come to explain. The dual aspect of the island for Miller, the liberation-imprisonment dyad, is what constitutes the island as a heterotopia; for Evvie, however, though it also represents a kind of confinement, it derives its heterotopic qualities principally from its function as a site of crisis.

'You're a woman now, Evvie': Evvie's island as a crisis heterotopia

Like *Los olvidados*, *The Young One* is also a film fascinated with life crises and both films could be said to deal with the difficult theme of failed adolescence. Durgnat believes Evvie is 'one of Buñuel's most haunting creations, innocent, therefore enigmatic; free, therefore calm. Physically she recalls Gin [sic] in *La Mort en ce jardin*. She might even be Gin [sic] before her corruption' (1977: 118). Likewise, Fuentes considers Evvie as a veritable *magna mater*, intrinsically linked to the sense of adventure that the island-environ presents (1993: 100). Though they are interesting, neither Fuentes nor Durgnat's considerations of Evvie capture the crisis that is so patently associated with her. Santaolalla is more perceptive of the turbulence facing not only Evvie, but the entire cohort on the island. She points out that many of the characters are undergoing their own transformations:

> Pee Wee from life to death, Evvie from childhood to womanhood, Traver from alleged guilt to proven innocence, and Miller, perhaps above all, from a high-handed sexual and racial mindset to greater sensitivity and moral awareness. (2004: 99)

Although it is certainly true that most characters in the film are faced with, and challenged by, stages of transition, in a biological sense it is Evvie who undergoes the most significant alteration.

Foucault's discussion of a crisis heterotopia is somewhat limited. He suggests that such categories of heterotopia featured more prominently in ancient societies, where the various biological stages of life were imbued with greater importance, and perhaps also viewed with greater suspicion, necessitating their temporary segregation from the mainstream, as in the case of menstruating women (1986: 24). Save a few examples such as the boarding school, or the early twentieth-century honeymoon trip, the crisis heterotopia has all but vanished in modern society. *The Young One*'s island game-preserve, I believe, constitutes for Evvie a crisis heterotopia, one in which her budding sexuality and adolescence are at once private and made public.

Evvie is first introduced sitting on a swing – a childlike activity – in the space directly in front of the two cabins, having just made the sobering discovery of her grandfather's dead body. She is initially described in the film script as 'blonde, thirteen, unkempt' (Buñuel and Addis 1960: 4). Throughout the film she is clearly more comfortable in her tomboy image despite her biological transition from girl to woman. This is demonstrated most acutely in the scene where Evvie, having just finished showering herself in the yard, meets Traver for the second time. Wrapped in a towel, Evvie's body is fragmented by the camera, first via a close up shot of her legs as she dries them and later via a point-of-view shot from Traver's perspective, who, no doubt aware of her age and the false accusations of rape made against him on the mainland, swiftly encourages her to better cover her pubescent body. The point-of-view shot seems to suggest that the young one's sexuality is confronted and constructed through Traver's male gaze, recalling Miller's discovery of her pubescence as she hands Miller an apple after dinner. This particular scene with Miller arguably marks the point at which her surroundings are transformed into a crisis heterotopia, as this is the point where Miller perceives her as 'beginning to bud out' (Buñuel and Addis 1960: 13). The reverse angle zoom shot, first showing Evvie's face and hair as she hands Miller the apple, then showing Miller's reaction as he sees Evvie in her dress, is unsettlingly suggestive. It is clear that Evvie's sexuality is projected onto her principally through Miller's gaze, though as a child she cannot – should not – fulfil what Laura Mulvey sees as the female's role in narrative cinema as erotic spectacle.

Mulvey's seminal theorisation of gender expectations within narrative cinema contends that the female character represents 'to be looked-at-ness' on an increasing scale: by the camera, by the male protagonists and by the audience. By means of identification, the (male) viewer vicariously possesses the female through the male protagonist (1975: 17). Though Mulvey's theory certainly has its limitations – most notably, her neglect of female and queer spectators' positions[16] – it is perhaps the barely pubescent female abused by an older male and the unpalatable repercussions this has for spectatorship that led to the early sexist, reactionary and, quite frankly, misogynistic reviews of the film that I have discussed. Indeed, Mulvey suggests that the female connotes castration with her lack of penis and that, as a defence mechanism, the male unconscious can devalue and punish the female or fetishise her to neutralise her threat (1975: 13–14). To this end, Marion Löhndorf writes that Evvie's biological transition is rendered filmically as 'an uncomfortable, taboo-evoking combination of innocence and seduction, childhood and sexuality' (2008: 70) through motifs such as the shot of her lower legs as she skips in high heels on the jetty.[17] Nevertheless, Mulvey's critique of what she terms 'the determining male gaze project[ing] its phantasy on to the female figure, which is styled accordingly' (1975: 11) and the (heterosexual male) spectator's identification with this gaze is interrogated early in the film's narrative and remains a point of contention throughout the film.

After Evvie hands Miller the apple at dinner, he tries to kiss her. She runs away and sits on the bed before running over to the other side of the cabin. At this point, the camera cuts from its position inside the cabin to outside the window, looking in, where we witness Miller coercing Evvie and picking her up to carry her to the bed. The *mise-en-scène* here suggests a meta-cinematic comment on voyeurism as the window acts as a visual frame whilst rendering Miller's dialogue inaudible, giving primacy to the image. Moreover, the camera appears in subjective mode, attempting to track Miller and Evvie as they move out of the frame, as in a point-of-view shot. Throughout this sequence as a whole, however, the focus of the camera's gaze is Miller rather than Evvie, as the viewer sees him wrestling with his desire while Evvie remains largely off screen. After Miller's advances, Evvie rushes into her cabin, locking the door. There is no attempt to eroticise Evvie when she is alone in her cabin, which makes the reactionary Lolita narrative read by critics of the film even more surprising: the low-key lighting here acts in contrast to the high-key lighting of Miller's cabin and Evvie deliberately ruffles up her hair, preferring the so-called 'swamp rat', non-sexualised appearance chided by Miller earlier. In fact, the entire sequence is foregrounded in Miller's deviant gaze, which by nature highlights the artificiality of Evvie's sexuality as it recurs throughout the narrative, triggering her crisis life-stage, since she cannot willingly fulfil the role of an object of erotic desire that Miller forcefully projects onto her.

On a spatial level, the heterotopic qualities of the island for Evvie are linked to her crisis life-stage. The fade-in shot of the island's coastline following the first night she spends in Miller's cabin is significant not only for its delineation of the insular space; for Evvie it marks the conflation of her waning childhood with her premature arrival to adulthood. Buñuel leaves the viewer in no doubt as to Miller's action here. The close-up shot of the faces of Evvie and Miller as the latter forcibly kisses the girl as she lies on the bed is striking. Significantly, Evvie opens her eyes when she feels Miller's touch, breaking the fourth wall as she gazes, horrified, into the camera and directly at the audience, again blurring the boundary between spectatorship and voyeurism, and highlighting Miller's deviant act. It is a moment of believable terror and Buñuel explained that, in this scene, when Zachary Scott (Miller) delivered his line 'Don't be afraid, Evvie', the actor 'said that more to the actress than to the character because the girl was really afraid' (de la Colina and Pérez Turrent 1992: 147). This is the juncture that forces Evvie to behave differently in her surroundings; whereas prior to Miller's indecent act the viewer comes to associate Evvie with nature, placed as she is so frequently in the island's natural *mise-en-scène* – among the trees, petting the deer kept in the yard between the two cabins – afterwards she is often confined within, or just outside, the cabins, augmenting the sense of claustrophobia. For Santaolalla the two cabins are 'the most conspicuous emblems of Evvie's entrapment' (2004: 102). Miller's cabin is the locus of transgression for Miller, just as it is the locus of the limit-experience for Evvie. According to Foucault, an experience is 'something you come out of changed', suggesting a degree of self-discovery and a heightened self-awareness (Foucault 1991: 27). He explains that the perception of experience shared by writers such as Nietzsche, Bataille and Blanchot attempts to 'reach that point of life which lies as close as possible to the impossibility of living, which lies at the limit or extreme', or a limit-experience. This concept of experience is categorised by the detachment of the subject from itself in order that it may arrive at its own annihilation and dissociation (Foucault 1991: 31). As Martin Jay explains, this radical experience by necessity 'undermines the subject [...] because it transgresses the limits of coherent subjectivity as it functions in everyday life, indeed threatens the very possibility of life – or rather the life of the individual – itself' (1995: 158). The links to sacrifice here are obvious, and for Bataille, the limit-experience is intrinsically linked to human sacrifice and to death, though, importantly, it also finds representation in various liminal states such as madness and sexuality (Hetherington 1997: 44). Significantly, a substantial number of the sites Foucault names as heterotopias have the function of 'containing' the sufferers/perpetrators/former subjects of just such liminal states: the mental asylum, the prison and the cemetery. Hetherington contends that 'in one important sense heterotopia are the sites of limit-experiences, notably those associated with the freedoms of madness, sexual desire and death in which humans experience the limits of their existence and are confronted by its sublime terror' (1997: 46).

The island, and more specifically its kernel in the form of the cabins in which the characters reside, are similar in their function to the mental asylum or punitive institution for they both conceal the limit-experience and make it possible in the first place (see Figure 3). In his transgressive act, Miller brings himself consciously to the limit of his desire where we can understand transgression as 'carry[ing] the limit right to the limit of its being; transgression forces the limit to face the fact of its imminent disappearance, to find itself in what it excludes' (Foucault 2000: 73). In other words, the transgression implicit in Miller's act facilitates his own limit-experience during which the subject gravitates towards a seductive, but ephemeral, self-annihilation. This bent towards an egocentric nihilism that finds its culmination in the transgression of the limit is a trait embodied – and enacted – by a good number of Buñuel's protagonists: I am thinking of *Él* and Francisco's attempt to throttle his wife, Gloria, atop the bell tower; the slitting of

Figure 3: Cabin fever. (Producciones Olmeca)

the eye in *Un Chien andalou*; or the 'desperate call for murder' inherent in Gaston Modot and Lya Lys's fervent attempts at fornication in *L'Âge d'or*.[18] Needless to say, Buñuel presents such characters without prejudice, remaining impartial to (and perhaps occasionally even revelling in) their exploits.[19] In fact, with specific reference to *The Young One*, M. K. S. of the *Monthly Film Bulletin* contends that 'the seduction of the minor [...] is in fact presented with a quietness and lack of sensationalism' (1962: 19). Although this reviewer acknowledges Evvie as a minor, the dubious reference to her 'seduction' – something Buñuel himself is guilty of – echoes the reactionary readings of the film with regards to spectatorship that I have detailed above.

As a figure of surveillance from the mainland, Reverend Fleetwood prevents Miller from continuing his abuse of Evvie. After he has arrived on the island with Jackson, as he and Evvie are preparing his sleeping quarters in Evvie's cabin, he discovers the true nature of her relationship with Miller and his dismay is palpable. Responding to the Reverend's comment that she is a child and will have to share a room in the children's home on the mainland, Evvie repeats in parrot-fashion Miller's words: 'I am not a child. Mr Miller told me yesterday I wasn't.' The zoom shot that follows her words clearly fixes the Reverend's look of dismay with a paradoxical lack of sensationalism highlighted in the film review above.[20] With these words Evvie betrays her crisis, sealing her fate as Reverend Fleetwood feels compelled to remove her from the island and to bring the social mores of the mainland to bear on Miller's behaviour. However, her eventual move to the mainland is ironic: in taking up residence in the children's home, according to Foucault (1986: 24) one of the few remaining examples of a functioning institutional crisis heterotopia, she is merely perpetuating her crisis life-stage and continuing her experience at the limit of society.

Trespassers will be shot: the open-closed island

Although an island is segregated from the space that surrounds it, it can be approached from any angle. It is at once an open and closed site. This system of opening and closing is the paradox that, for Foucault, is often integral to heterotopias and which allows us to further consider the heterotopic qualities of island game-preserve in *The Young One*. The emphasis on the demarcation of the island and an obsession with its borders within the film is confirmed in the very first shot of the opening scene: a tracking shot from the shore is focused on a small boat cautiously approaching the island. As Traver traverses the island's border, the suggestion is of vulnerability and it is clear that for him the island, given the sign erected on the beach – 'Private game-preserve. Trespassers on this island will be prosecuted to the full extent of the law' – is foreign territory. The wording of the warning sign betrays the island's penetrability while affirming that the island functions along an open/closed dichotomy that welcomes certain groups and excludes others.

In his discussion of the peculiar opening/closing mechanisms of heterotopias, Foucault maintains that, generally, these do not grant the visitor free access. He explains that 'either the entry [to the heterotopic site] is compulsory [...] or else the individual has to submit to rites and purifications. To get in one must have a certain permission and make certain gestures' (1986: 26). This has led scholars to propose such organisations as the Freemasons as heterotopic, though Foucault himself refers to the Muslim hammin and the Scandinavian sauna.[21] Perhaps not so dissimilar to the selective and esoteric Masonic lodge, the game-preserve is presented as a closed space to the uninitiated such as Traver. Initiation comes in the form of approval by the autocratic Miller and unsurprisingly is dependent on conformity to his personal social model, in its turn derived from the gun-toting patriarchy of 1960s Deep South rural society that renders most forms of difference dangerous. Even after Traver's presence becomes known to Evvie and Miller, to the latter he remains effectively persona non grata, unwelcome at Miller's dinner table. The antithesis to Traver is Jackson, who follows Miller's social

Figure 4: 'Private. Keep out. Trespassers will be shot'. (Producciones Olmeca)

model with even more zeal than Miller himself. That Jackson is permitted access to the island without repercussion is evident in his manner of negotiating the space that surrounds him with confidence and ease. Following Miller's only trip to the mainland, a distance shot shows his arrival back on his territory. The unremarkable jetty is the official entrance, the true site of opening/closure, to the island for the initiated: as Miller disembarks on to the jetty after returning from town the warning sign intended for would-be trespassers looms large in the shot, obscuring a considerable part of the skyline, and, most significantly, reinforcing the inclusion/exclusion dyad (see Figure 4). In the scene prior to this, Traver can be seen peering through the trees from a concealed stretch of beach as he watches Miller's arrival, an obvious contrast with his own.

Finally, the island's function as a game-preserve and resort can cast further light on the impact of the spatial dialectics of the island on Evvie and Traver. When Jackson informs Miller that a decision has been made to construct a clubhouse on the island to attract more guests, Miller boasts that '[they] gonna fix me up, too. Butane, hot runnin' water. Be like livin' in a hotel'. Nonetheless, behind this façade of modernity, the island's heterotopic qualities would continue to exist, although in a different form. In his discussion of heterotopias, Foucault employs the analogy of the American motel. The motel is a kind of placeless place, under the radar of society and social convention, where 'a man goes with his car and his mistress and where illicit sex is both absolutely sheltered and absolutely hidden' (1986: 27). The island, and more specifically Miller's cabin, functions in the same way as it shelters and hides his lust towards Evvie. Moreover, the frequent positioning of hotels and their derivatives on the outskirts of cities is significant. With a focus on the etymological roots of the words 'hospital' and 'hotel', Kari Jormakka contends that:

> Since the late Middle Ages, for example, heterotopias such as hospitals and hotels were situated at the edge of towns as sites of indefinite social identity. The reason is clearly written in the etymology of the words 'hospital' and 'hotel'. Together with the words 'host' and 'guest', they derive, via the Latin *hospes* 'guest/host', from the Indo-European *ghotis*. From the same root we also get the Latin *hostis*, 'stranger/enemy' [...] and *hostia* 'sacrifice/victim.' (1998: 44)

The hotel, through its very function as a site of hospitability, necessitates a deconstruction of the inside/outside friend/stranger binary. In *The Young One*, the spatial dynamics of the island as a secluded environment and a future commercial venture collude with the characters' social backgrounds and biological transitions to underpin a perverted triad of *hospes*, *hostis* and *hostia*. Miller is an autocratic *hospes*, Evvie's ambiguous biological transition – she is, in Miller's words, a 'wild thing' – renders her *hostia* and the ethnic outcast Traver is *hostis* to the social model. In this respect, the originally planned ending according to the film's shooting script is striking: following their climactic scuffle on the beach, Traver is actually killed by Jackson as the latter strikes him with a rock, recalling Jaibo's murder of Julián in *Los olvidados*. The disturbing image of Traver as 'blood stains the whole front of his white shirt, trickles thinly from his mouth' leaves Miller alone in the film's final shot on a non-descript beach, calling out in vain to the travelling man (Buñuel and Addis 1960: 129). Traver's planned passage off the island from its unofficial exit was intended to cost him his life.

Conclusion: failed utopias

My consideration of *The Young One* and *Robinson Crusoe* as companion pieces is in part pragmatic. These two films constitute the sole English language productions in the director's catalogue. Both are adapted from literary sources and both are set within the confines of an island. In these films, according to Fuentes, Buñuel adheres to the conventions of Hollywood cinema 'in order to subvert them from within', in a similar way to his subversions of popular Mexican film genres in his commercial films of the 1950s (1993: 96).[22] Fuentes contends that while both films can be read innocently, they each conceal a darker message and this is where we find evidence of Buñuel's more personal cinema (ibid.). The supposedly neat, happy resolutions of both films are undoubtedly haunted by the spectre of the oppressed and the repressed. Friday returns to Western civilisation with Crusoe as his servant first and friend second, while the sound-image incongruity as Crusoe stares back at his island and hears the phantom barking of Rex complicates the triumphalist narrative resolution. Evvie returns to the US mainland with Reverend Fleetwood as an orphan and Traver returns as a second-class citizen; while the former has undergone a serious ordeal, the latter, according to the intended ending of the film's shooting script, was never meant to leave the island alive.

Both island spaces derive their heterotopic qualities ultimately from their spatial dynamics. The geographical characteristics of an island can translate into psychological characteristics of insularity through the island's physical and psychological state of alterity. However, Buñuel does not show alterity positively here, as a space of resistance. The vulnerable and the subaltern characters in the films remain subjected to the influence of the respective dominant cultures on their islands: Traver is almost killed by the racist Jackson and Friday is forcefully 'civilised' by Crusoe. Neither island-space remains uncontested. Although the dominant spaces of mainland America and Britain are not given visual representation in the respective films, their presence is markedly felt throughout both narratives. For D'Lugo, Crusoe's island becomes the site of impulse for commodification, leading him to attempt to appropriate nature and transform it into objects for possession that mimic the 'closed order of the world he left behind in England' (2003: 98). In a similar manner, the space of the US mainland pervades the island game-preserve not only through dialogue but also via the commodification impulse. In one notable scene, perhaps in repentance for taking advantage of Evvie, or some misguided attempt to woo her, Miller promises to return from the mainland with some perfume for her. Later, as the film reaches its conclusion and Evvie is about to leave the island, we see her transformed, sporting a hat, dress and high-heeled shoes.

Not only space but also time is fundamental in the narrative of Buñuel's Crusoe. The contrast between the transit and the stasis of time is marked throughout the film as Crusoe attempts to impose his own system of time onto a space alien to the customs of his milieu. On the one hand, the time setting of *The Young One* is clearly depicted through its all-too-real depiction of racially motivated violence in the Deep South. Indeed, in a more immediate and visceral way than any of Buñuel's other films, this film forms part of the cultural zeitgeist: in her astonishing review in 1961, Louise Corby indignantly wrote: 'after espousing practically every form of degeneracy in his films for thirty years, Luis Buñuel espouses the Negro in this one' (1961: 111). On the other hand, the game-preserve remains a largely non-descript place which seeks to emphasise its spatial and temporal distance from the mainland, as when Jackson scolds Miller for not accompanying him on the 'long, cold trip' to fetch reinforcements to search for Traver. Referring to the duality established in this film via the persecuted and the persecutor, the former representing the city and the latter the country, Fuentes writes, 'the circular shape of the island, with its symbolism, imposes its turns on the thread of the narrative, which splits into two: dissimilarities and similarities' (1993: 99),[23] though such a statement could easily apply to the idea of time in the film. In each, modernity appears marginalised, reduced largely to commodities, such as Evvie's high-heeled shoes or the gold coins that Crusoe gives to Friday, explaining that they are of no use to him. To take the point further, we can consider the island spaces as heterotopias of crisis. Clearly, the game-preserve is a site of crisis for Evvie and Traver, just as it is for Crusoe in relation to his solitude and metamorphosis. For both Crusoe and Evvie, their crises entail more than solely a biological alteration and are arguably just as psychological as they are physical. A psychological crisis could be seen to involve a break with traditional perceptions of time, and as Foucault suggests, the heterotopia functions at its peak when there is a break with traditional notions of time.

Ultimately, for Johnson, heterotopias, perhaps like Buñuel's cinema, 'offer no resolution or consolation, but disrupt and test our customary notions of ourselves. These different spaces, which contest forms of anticipatory utopianism, hold no promise or space of liberation' (2006: 87). Two other films from Buñuel's Mexican period which can be said to hold little promise of liberation and which can be fruitfully examined from a spatial perspective are *La Mort en ce jardin* and *Simón del desierto*. Although the settings of these movies are the jungle and the desert respectively, like the companion films discussed in this chapter they evidence Buñuel's preoccupation with characters 'in their longitudes and latitudes, their climates – their spaces' (Rubinstein 1978: 247). Moving from an analytical framework of heterotopias to one of liminality, I will examine the jungle and desert spaces to suggest that the protagonists in each of the films are located in the interstices, and will show how a spatial reading can inform and inflect existing criticism on both works.

Notes

1 The film was actually filmed quite early in Buñuel's Mexican career, after *El Bruto*, which debuted in 1953. Victor Fuentes tells us that the Mexican première of *Robinson Crusoe* came in 1955 (1993: 177).

2 Despite being his first English-language film, Buñuel shot a version of the same film in Spanish. See Martínez Herranz (2013).

3 See Matthiessen (1990: 37–56).

4 For a detailed account of the film's production and reception, see Conrad (1994: 28–31).

5 See Juan Larrea and Luis Buñuel (2007).

6 For a detailed account of the way in which the term has been used by scholars in these fields, see Hetherington (1997: 9–54).

7 Of the twenty-one films that Buñuel made within the Mexican film industry, six were international co-productions: in addition to the two Mexican-US co-productions, *La Mort en ce jardin* and *La Fièvre monte à El Pao* were Franco-Mexican co-productions, *Cela s'appelle l'aurore* was a project involving Mexico, France and Italy, and *Viridiana* was a Mexican-Spanish co-production.

8 See, for example, Conrad (1978: 332–51) or D'Lugo (2004: 90–2).

9 Distinguishing his adaptation from Defoe's novel, Buñuel consciously monitored the number of Biblical references in the film, as, in his words, 'to put in more quotes from the Bible would have seemed too much to me' (de la Colina and Pérez Turrent 1992: 89).

10 [el mundo interior – pensamientos, ensoñaciones y pesadillas – de los protagonistas].

11 On this point, see also Buñuel (2003: 224–5).

12 Prospero's utopia is at the expense of others, as is Miller's. Speaking of the enslaved Caliban, Prospero says 'we cannot miss him; he does make our fire / fetch our wood, and serves in offices / that profit us' (Shakespeare 2011: 1.2.312–14). Similarly, Miller barks his orders to Evvie: 'Go on over to my cabin and build me a fire. That stove's as cold as a dog's nose. Go on, get!'

13 See Foucault (1979).

14 [debió ser elegido con cierta intención].

15 [Ewie [sic] fa innamorare di sé il custode, provocando in costui reazioni non certo favorevoli al negro].

16 Linda Williams outlines the challenges to Mulvey's argument in subsequent feminist film criticism. For Williams, it is problematic that 'activity and passivity have been too rigorously assigned to separate gendered spectator positions with little examination of [...] the mutability of male and female spectators' adoption of one or the other subject position and participation in the (perverse) pleasures of both' (1989: 206).

17 [eine unbequeme, an Tabus rührende Verbindung von Unschuld und Verführung, Kindheit und Sexualität].

18 Echoing Buñuel's own words about *L'Âge d'or*, his sons Juan Luis and Rafael Buñuel invoke this term in their afterword to the edited collection of their father's writings. See Buñuel and Buñuel (2000: 265).

19 André Bazin highlights Buñuel's objectivity in two of the director's most ostensibly cruel films, *Tierra sin pan* and *Los olvidados*, and warns that we cannot 'reproach Buñuel for having a perverse taste for cruelty'. Buñuel's cruelty, he affirms, 'is entirely objective; it is no more than lucidity' (1978: 197–98).

20 The lack of sensationalism is due in part to the absence of non-diegetic music in this film. Aranda quotes Buñuel on his opinion of non-diegetic music: 'Personally, I don't like film music. It seems to me that it is a false element, a sort of trick, except of course in certain cases' (Aranda 1976: 91). In this respect, the adventure score of *Robinson Crusoe* provides a point of contrast with *The Young One*.

21 For a discussion of Freemasonry as a heterotopic organisation, see Hetherington (1997: 72–108).

22 [para subvertirlos desde dentro].

23 [la figura circular de la isla, con su simbolismo, impone sus vueltas al hilo del relato, el cual se desdobla en dos, disímiles y afines].

Chapter 3
Betwixt and Between: Liminal Space in *La Mort en ce jardin* and *Simón del desierto*

I n 1956 Buñuel adapted the Belgian novelist and playwright José-André Lacour's *La Mort en ce jardin* for the cinema. A politicised tale of suppressed uprisings against the fascist regime in a backwater diamond-mining village in an unspecified Latin American state, the film had drawn relatively little criticism until recently. Buache posits the narrative as another example, alongside *The Young One*, of Buñuel's penchant for eschewing a Manichean stance, though unlike in the latter film, in *La Mort en ce jardin* 'nothing either begins or ends [...]. Everything is transitory' (1973: 81). More disparagingly, Harcourt views Buñuel's input into the film as fairly minimal, lamenting what he considers the director's 'artistic fatigue' (1967: 12). As I outlined in chapter one, recently the film has featured in Stone and Gutiérrez-Albilla's companion volume to Buñuel and my inclusion of the film in this book continues its reappraisal. Due to the film's political theme, its status as a co-production and the language of the dialogue (French, not Spanish), comparisons have inevitably been drawn between this relatively minor work and two other lesser known Buñuel films which give focus to a discourse of political idealism in the face of fascist oppression, *Cela s'appelle l'aurore* and *Le Fièvre monte à El Pao*.[1] One point of criticism in relation to *La Mort en ce jardin* is in response to the disproportionate amount of time spent on showing the miners' revolution in the village at the expense of the later, and irrefutably more personal, part of the film where a motley crew of Buñuelian archetypes – including a priest, a prostitute and a deaf-mute girl – flee into an endless jungle to escape the army police.[2] I do not subscribe to Harcourt's view of this film, given that, even when mentioned in passing, the film's indelible Buñuelian stamp is often highlighted. For José Agustín Mathieu, for instance, *La Mort en ce jardin* 'possesses an unequivocal Buñuelian sense' (1980: 162; 166) in contrast to several other of the director's more conventional Mexican melodramas, such as Buñuel's Mexican adaptation of *Don Quintín el amargao*, released in Mexico under the title *La hija del engaño*.[3]

Almost a decade later in 1964, Buñuel reunited with producer Gustavo Alatriste and his wife, actress Silvia Pinal, to direct the ultimate film of his Mexican period, *Simón del desierto*, released in 1965. Buñuel drew inspiration from the legend of Saint Simeon Stylites, a fifth-century ascetic who withdrew from the world to live atop a pillar in the Syrian desert, from which he would preach to those who made the pilgrimage to see him. According to the director, Saint Simeon had been a source of humour and fascination among his peers at the *Residencia de Estudiantes* in Madrid, especially Lorca, who 'especially prized this description: "Shit flowed down the column like wax drips from candles"' (de la Colina and Pérez Turrent 1992: 177). The germ of this film had been long implanted and irrevocably rooted within surrealist soil. Although the film's depiction of a naive ascetic seems to recall the narratives of *Nazarín* and *Viridiana*, Kael sees *Simón del desierto* as a truly unique film in the director's corpus, a charming 'shaggy saint story' with an 'almost jovial' tone that distinguishes it from Buñuel's more complex and potentially obtuse ruminations on quixotic and misguided saint-hood in the two former works (1978: 273). Nonetheless, against Buñuel's two full-length features of Simón's contemporary peers, this film about the Syrian ascetic is something of an oddity in the filmmaker's corpus at forty-five minutes long. Although Buñuel originally conceived of *Simón del desierto* as a feature-length picture, producer Gustavo Alatriste's funds ran out before the film was finished and Buñuel was forced to cut the film short (Baxter 1994: 273). In spite of production setbacks, however, *Simón del desierto* remains one of Buñuel's more striking films of his Mexican cinematic career and, crucially, one which Ulrich Gregor stresses 'should also offer Buñuel specialists and exegetes a wealth of material with new meanings' (1965: 592).[4]

It is in the spirit of developing new readings of two relatively overlooked films that I continue in this chapter. It is quite obvious that *La Mort en ce jardin* and *Simón del desierto* seemingly have little in common on a narrative level. Moreover, from a technical perspective, the two refuse any overarching parallels: *La Mort en ce jardin* is a Franco-Mexican co-production, a genre film which adheres largely to the traditional syuzhet of the Western or adventure narrative, and was Buñuel's second colour feature after *Robinson Crusoe*; *Simón del desierto* is an entirely Mexican production over which Buñuel arguably had more creative control, was shot in black and white and is neither a feature-length film nor a short. However, I propose that the pair are ideal companion films, independently of established interpretative paradigms in Buñuel scholarship that could quite feasibly set them apart. As spaces that not only provide the striking scenic backdrop to the films' narratives, but also assume an active role in the characters' confinement in a transitional, transitory zone, the jungle and the desert locations of the respective films are examples of liminal spaces. My focus here will be on examining these liminal zones of the jungle and the desert in the respective films, in order to explore the ways in which these spaces act as interstitial arenas in which structure and order are suspended in such a way as to create and perpetuate the protagonists' uncertain physical and psychological states.

La Mort en ce jardin

Liminality and the mining settlement of *La Mort en ce jardin*

Although *La Mort en ce jardin* has a running time of 99 minutes, it is only the final third of the film's narrative that is played out in the jungle alluded to in the title. Though my principal focus is the jungle space and how this is theoretically and physically an 'in-between' space, some discussion of the mining village is first necessary, because it is here that the characters' position and condition as interstitial migrants is foregrounded. The film opens with an unremarkable scene of labour as the diamond miners down tools for lunch. The site of the diamond mine – similar to the labour camp on the island of Ojeda in *La Fièvre monte à El Pao* – appears nondescript, as a paltry stream meanders through the striking yellow boulders.[5] However, this scene is really an introduction to the rather complex politics of place in the film. The diamond mine and the nearby village are merely a kind of transitory home for the miners, part of the Francophone diaspora who have settled in a country in the Americas to seek their fortune. As the labourers sit down to lunch, a rather aged man, Castin, nostalgically reminisces about the culinary delights of home, telling his workmates of his desire to open a restaurant in Marseilles. Significantly, France will come to function as a marker, an ideological and idealistic construct used to frame first the space of the mining village and later the interstitial space of the jungle. Castin is interrupted by a group of soldiers who have appeared to evict the miners from the site. Their obfuscated legal jargon tells us that the diamond mine of the fictional Guluva valley is scheduled to be nationalised and this takeover of the mineral-rich diamond mine by the corrupt fascist state is the catalyst for the miners' disquiet and subsequent revolt.

The increasingly intriguing politics of place is amplified through the miners' unrest, and through their abortive coup the structure of their community, or lack thereof, becomes apparent. Following the soldiers' announcement that the mine is to come under state administration, Buñuel inserts a brief but pertinent shot of the workers entering their seemingly remote village of Cachazu, on the edge of the jungle. Here, and in the early scenes of revolution that follow, the viewer is given to understand that this is a dystopian diaspora in an unspecified South American nation close to the Brazilian border. In fact, in interview, Lacour, the author of the original novel, stated that the scenes in the mining village were filmed on location in an abandoned village 200 kilometres from Mexico City (Press cuttings on *Jardin*, ABR-1981, item 53). The village appears dilapidated, as if nature is encroaching on civilisation even before the group flees into the forest. When considering the Francophone mining settlement and, later, the jungle as liminal spaces, their interstitial position is key. Cachazu's exact location remains undisclosed and its interstitial position is highlighted early in the narrative, as the two principal referents flanking the village on either side are France, the birthplace and *patrie* of the labourers, and Brazil.[6]

Liminality as a concept was first introduced by the German-born anthropologist Arnold van Gennep in 1909 as a theoretical framework to analyse rites of passage and initiation ceremonies within tribal societies. The etymological root of the term comes from the Latin *limen*, or threshold. Van Gennep postulated that passage rituals share a tripartite structure. The first stage, where the person undergoing the passage rite is separated from their social group van Gennep names the preliminal stage; the liminal stage is where the passage rites are administered; finally, the post-liminal stage marks the re-incoporation of the subject back into their society (1960: 21). He believed that all rites of passage included a central, liminal phase, one in which the initiate, or the liminar, was suspended in an intermediate stage between the realms of the profane and the sacred worlds (1960: 1). Though he was primarily concerned with liminality as human experience, van Gennep nevertheless did allude to its spatial dimension by evoking the so-called neutral zones of classical antiquity:

The same system of zones is to be found among the semi-civilised, although here boundaries are less precise because the claimed territories are few in number and sparsely settled. The neutral zones are ordinarily deserts, marshes, and most frequently virgin forests. (1960: 18)

Crucially, van Gennep's singling out of deserts, marshes and virgin forests is particularly relevant in terms of the wild spaces that are the interstitial arenas of the two films I discuss in this chapter. He goes on to explain that, because of the subjective 'pivoting of sacredness', the neutral zone appears sacred to those on either side of it, but to those within the neutral zone, the adjacent territories are sacred (1960: 18). It is the passage from one adjacent territory to the other which gives the subject his or her interstitial position and liminal state; in van Gennep's own words, the subject 'wavers between two worlds' (1960: 18).

However, the liminal dimension of the mining village derives not only from its location between the reveries of remembered France and the Brazilian border, but also from the breakdown of structure within the town itself. In the local saloon, a place of proletariat solidarity against the fascist oligarchy, the rowdy miners lament their circumstances, and, despite a trite maxim courtesy of Father Lizardi, the local missionary – 'the mightiest one day shall stand weakest the next' – the group outlines its position against the autocratic governors. Although Buñuel clearly has the workers pitted against the soldiers, the oppressed-oppressor dyad is not as simple as this: characters oppressed by the military government, such as the amoral prostitute Djin, the macho adventurer Chark and tradesman-turned-pimp Chenko in their turn bully the more naive Castin and his deaf-mute daughter, Maria. In this way, they bear similarities with ambiguous (anti)heroes popular in the Western genre and the scenes in the mining village before the group flees into the jungle not only establish place, or a lack thereof, but also characterisation and the film's supposed imitation of generic conventions. Leahy (2013: 328–30), for instance, notes that French actress Simone Signoret (Djin), for example, had previously been a character actor, known for playing *garces* (bitches). She also points out that the film employs Mexican and Spanish tropes such as melodrama and picaresque, as well as borrowing conventions from the Western and the Hollywood adventure film. While the scenes of rebellion and the copious shootouts that follow might not look out of place in a Western, they are a palpable political commentary on despotic South American states, a theme to be later reprised in *La Fièvre monte à El Pao* and through the immoral Rafael Acosta, ambassador of the fictitious banana-republic of Miranda in *Le Charme discret de la bourgeoisie*. This commentary has been read by Fuentes as an allegory of the Spanish Civil War (2000: 129). Interestingly, responding to a suggestion that the film could be read as a political metaphor, Buñuel himself commented that the movie was 'a little anarchistic' but did not push this any further (de la Colina and Pérez Turrent 1992: 128). Fuentes goes on to note that the filming of *La Mort en ce jardin* coincided with a period of changing attitudes and values towards Latin America, particularly in Western society, when the continent's romanticised image as a far-flung 'El Dorado' for immigrants after World War Two gave way to a succession of dictatorships, civil unrest and package holidays for Europeans (2000: 135). The repressive state in this film finds itself at this exact juncture: the days of carefree opportunism are over, to be replaced by oppression and totalitarian dominance. The miners' rebellion is thus a refusal to accept the rigid, unjust structure imposed on them by the fascist governors; in a manner of speaking, it is a move towards anti-structure in anticipation of a new, fairer structure.

Liminality, as defined by Turner, following on from van Gennep, is equated with the temporary suspension of structure; that is, it is essentially an 'interstructural situation' (1967: 93). It is in the interstructural situation that the all-important transformation associated with the liminal state of the liminar occurs. The liminar is betwixt and between, a notable phrase from Turner's essay, for the period of the ceremony. According to him, the eradication of traditional structure within passage rites facilitates a sense of community and solidarity among liminars, a state that Turner terms 'communitas', defined as

> a relational quality of full unmediated communication, even communion, between definite and determinate identities, which arises spontaneously in all kinds of groups, situations, and circumstances. It is a liminal phenomenon which combines the qualities of lowliness, sacredness, homogeneity and comradeship. (1978: 250)

Communitas, then, is akin to anti-structure, though for Turner this is invariably a positive state in its fostering of comradeship. Indeed, as Arpad Szakolczai highlights, Turner's 'rediscovery' of van Gennep's concept of liminality in the late 1960s, further to the optimism he sees in communitas, has become synonymous with 'the happy celebration of anti-structure and difference' whilst 'the dangerous, troubling, anxiety-generating aspects of uncertain periods of transition, conflict, and crisis were simply ignored' (2009: 142). Despite the portrayal of proletarian solidarity in this film, Buñuel's depiction of the Francophone mining village's lurch towards revolution lacks a positive spin, as does the dissolution of structure when the persecuted group subsequently flees into the jungle. Conrad, for instance, sees the group's jungle ordeal as a vicious cycle that shows they are unable to establish any structure in the liminal period: 'what finally condemns most of them is their dependency [...] upon the very civilization which has cast them out and which they are unable to re-establish in miniature even for their own safety' (1978: 343). Also, as a possible allegory of the Spanish Civil War, the miners' revolt is indisputably a period of liminality, though the constructive connection to communitas is swiftly bypassed in favour of a more permanent deconstruction of the miners' micro-society, in what ultimately seems likely to become a schismogenic state, a term coined by anthropologist Gregory Bateson. According to Bateson (1935: 179), contact phenomena between two groups within a specific culture can result in the elimination of both groups, the assimilation of the weaker group into the stronger, or the persistence of both factions in dynamic equilibrium within the same society. It is perhaps the third of these outcomes which most closely resembles the schismogenic state of Buñuel's mining village in the film. Furthermore, Bateson distinguishes between 'complementary schismogenesis' and 'symmetrical schismogenesis'. The former is closer to Buñuel's own vision, functioning on a dominant-dominated paradigm in the vein of the workers' struggle against fascist autocracy and avarice, a struggle that will lead to a 'progressive unilateral distortion of the personalities of the members of both groups, which results in a mutual hostility between them and must end in the breakdown of the system' (Bateson 1935: 181). This point is neatly echoed by Szakolczai, and his choice of words is certainly pertinent to *La Mort en ce jardin*: 'societies can maintain themselves in such situations of oppression and violence for a long time, without returning to normal order, if stable external reference points are absent' (2009: 157). As I have explained, for its residents the mining village appears to lack stable reference points, finding itself between an absent France and an equally absent Brazil.

Although the liminal state was originally conceived in anthropological discourse as the physical or psychological state of the liminar during a rite of passage or initiation, its potential pertinence to the discourse on space has not gone unnoticed. With a focus on Turner's work, Bjørn Thomassen affirms:

> liminality refers to any 'betwixt and between' situation or object. [...] Speaking very broadly, liminality is applicable to both space and time. [...] Liminal places can

be specific thresholds; they can also be more extended areas, like 'borderlands' or, arguably, whole countries, placed in important in-between positions between larger civilizations. (2009: 16)

Thomassen's comments resonate clearly in the modern world where movement outranks stasis and where substantial numbers of asylum seekers, migrants and exiles (Buñuel included) have long been in flux. The transformation of the space of the mining settlement in *La Mort en ce jardin* into a liminal zone is twofold, for its geographical location betwixt and between absent spatial referents is compounded by the process of revolution taking place there. As Dag Øistein Endsjø (2000: 357) signals, interstructural areas were for Turner imbued with a quality of liminality via a transition taking place there, while for van Gennep such spaces had their liminal meaning projected onto them by the various cultures that contemplated them. Writing about the *eschatia*, or geographical periphery, and how this represented a liminal space in the ancient Greek worldview, Endsjø argues that, further to Turner's assumption that interstitial spaces (here, the mining village) were impregnated with a liminal quality due to the ritual taking place there, certain spaces can be considered to possess a more autonomous liminality independent of human agency (2000: 357). Similarly, Naficy utilises the concept of liminality to investigate the representation of tropes common to exilic cinema, such as displacement and border crossings, as well as the interstitial modes of production of such films. In the context of this cinema, Naficy considers airports and seaports to be liminal spaces of transition (2001: 243–48). As vast, virtually unpopulated spaces removed from the Western cultural sphere, the blank spaces of the jungle and the desert in *La Mort en ce jardin* and *Simón del desierto* as Buñuel presents them to us possess a certain autonomous liminality, though meaning is undeniably projected onto them by the exiled group fleeing for their lives and the ascetic monk in his self-exile from society.

The endless jungle

The liminal period in which the fugitives find themselves is therefore inscribed spatially, and, as their liminal experience is elongated through time, so is its spatial equivalent. In the bar scene, as the miners discuss their revolt, Father Lizardi asks about the route that the tradesman and town pimp Chenko takes with his boat in his trafficking of prostitutes to and from the village. The bartender replies that Chenko's trajectory takes him to the Marqués plantation, close to the Mambuti river and the Brazilian border. Having broken out of the local prison where he has been held on suspicion of committing a robbery in a nearby town, Chark takes advantage of the extended skirmishes between soldiers and miners to make his escape. For his part, Castin takes shelter from the riot in Djin's bordello, and, discovering that a price has been put on his head as a supposed instigator of the riot, persuades the mercenary madam to flee with him and his daughter Maria, entrusting his diamonds to her as proof of his love. Hunted by the authorities, Castin, Maria, Djin and Father Lizardi board the boat in the dead of night, with the surprise addition of Chark, to flee unnoticed upstream towards Brazil. Various characters claim in their turn that crossing the Brazilian border will bring salvation, supposedly putting an end to their interstitial position. However, this deliverance proves harder to obtain than first envisaged, as the group has to abandon the boat and enter the foreboding mass of the jungle.

The jungle now becomes the primary locus of liminality in the film. Intuiting that this is for the director the more personal of the two halves of the film, Barbáchano (2000: 184), writes: 'here […] Buñuel finds himself in his element: a few characters adrift, in a limit situation, hounded by hunger and insanity'.[7] Barbáchano's choice of phrasing is most definitely pertinent to the spatial situation of the protagonists, encapsulating their figurative position adrift, in an ostensibly perpetual fruitless search for definite spatial referents. In typical Buñuelian style, time and space are liberated from their objectivist constraints within the liminal junglescape, and relativity acquires new meaning. As the group takes shelter in a cave during their first night in the rainforest, Djin mocks Castin's proposal to navigate by the position of the sun, as it is 'impossible to know which way is which with all this twisting and turning', while a desperate Castin is told by Chenko that the Mambuti river and Brazil could be anything from a three day hike away to a twenty day gauntlet – 'it depends on the jungle'. Moreover, the visual representation of the jungle emphasises its intrinsic liminal quality. Significantly, the coming of each new day is marked by a high-angle shot of the seemingly endless canopy of trees, repeatedly reinforcing the liminal quality of the rainforest with no beginning and no end (see Figure 5). The cinematographic depictions of the endless tree canopy have their aural counterpart. From the moment the group enters the jungle its soundscape is inescapable. This is undoubtedly one of Buñuel's films in which the diegetic sounds of the characters' surroundings are prominent to a striking degree, more so even than the comparable sounds of the wilderness in *Robinson Crusoe*. In this way, the blanket of sound can be said to function as an aural indicator of the group's spatial liminality, immersed

Figure 5: The unfurling jungle. (Producciones Tepeyac/Film Dismage)

in the jungle. This aural and visual onslaught allows the jungle, as a site removed from the Western cultural sphere, to become a place 'which seems to manage to create its own planes of reality, to alter consciousness, to trigger madness' (Midding 2008: 26), as the mental and physical states of the trekkers deteriorate.[8]

Corporeal and cohesive disintegration

As a physical counterpart to the dissolution of communitas, the desperate and disparate group suffers corporeal disintegration. The irony is almost laughable as, following the Lieutenant's comments that Chark and the gang will be eaten alive by the jungle as his men endeavour to pursue them into the undergrowth, there is a brief sequence in which Maria is shown trapped in an overgrown bush, her hair consumed by its branches and brambles. However, Maria is not the only character to be injured in the jungle: Djin limps miserably after twisting her ankle and Castin's head wound incurred during the miners' uprising in the village is exacerbated. Moreover, not only does spatial disintegration and lack of structure have its corporeal correlative, it also exerts its influence on the psychological state of the characters. Durgnat pays more attention to this aspect of the film, pointing out that 'from the moment Chark's band enters the jungle, the film has an atmosphere of dream, as it prepares the inner disintegration of the characters' (1977: 108). Djin's regression to an infant-like mentality is the first marker of this. Perturbed by the inhospitable terrain and her twisted ankle, she lashes out at the good-natured Castin, her would-be suitor, and is scolded by Chark for sobbing as the group stoically attempts to sleep despite the heavy rain. As Szakolczai states, 'we become "children" again when we leave behind a fixed role, status, or identity; when we re-enter a liminal situation' (2009: 148). Undoubtedly, though, the main instance of the spatial liminal's influence on the characters' mental states is Castin's abrupt descent into madness. We can again look to Turner to clarify this aspect of liminality. He explains that 'liminality may be the scene of disease, despair, death, suicide, the breakdown without compensatory replacement of normative, well defined social ties and bonds. It may be anomie, alienation, angst, the three fatal alpha sisters of many myths' (1982: 46). As is evident in *La Mort en ce jardin* and in many other of Buñuel's films – in the ending to *Simón del desierto*, for example, or *El ángel exterminador* in its entirety – anomie, alienation and angst become a Buñuelian triptych, colluding with the spatial dislocation of the protagonists to devastating effect. For his part, Castin is not only physically trapped between two ideological and physical spaces, he is also in a state of hysteria – arguably between sanity and insanity. It is telling that, as he receives superficial comfort from the gold-digging Djin, who tells him that his dream of opening up a restaurant in Marseille will become a reality, he responds by exclaiming 'there will be nothing!', a nihilistic outburst that is an indication both of his delirium and their indefinite position in the never-ending jungle.

Tricksters in the Transandino aeroplane wreck

Just when the wanderers are at their lowest ebb, having unwittingly traced their own steps back to their campfire from the previous evening and failed to navigate the endless junglescape, they find temporary salvation in the wreckage of an aeroplane that has crashed in the jungle. Before Chark returns with a suitcase of luxury supplies pillaged from the passengers' luggage, the human trekkers are turned almost fully feral, digging up plant roots with a machete and eagerly devouring them. Critics have invariably viewed the intrusion of the aeroplane wreck in the jungle space as the symbol of a ubiquitous consumerism, commenting occasionally on the auterist significations of the group's surreal discovery;[9] this is arguably the site which allows Buñuel to develop a more personal cinema via the principle of contradiction. The jungle is at once a liminal space of ambiguity in which all spatial referents are abolished and, for Ado Kyrou, it is also the space in which the affirmative cry of man finds its enunciation (1956: 27). Kyrou reads Buñuel's film, not surprisingly, as yet another of the director's critiques of religion, and the affirmative cry of man is pitted bathetically against religious mysticism, of little use in the jungle. Kyrou focuses almost exclusively on the character of Father Lizardi and the degenerative effect on the group as a whole, and the active, rather than passive, role of space in their degeneration are given little mention, and his reading is comparable to that of Buache, who believes that the man of the cloth is the character most appealing to Buñuel. Buache's reading is anchored firmly in the interpretive Buñuelian bedrock, as he continues: 'Buñuel is once again pointing to the total pointlessness of Christian faith in adversity' (1973: 86). In exploring the spatial significance of the group's miraculous discovery and the way this is represented filmically, we can consider alternative readings of this key sequence, independently of surrealism or religion. I hold that the plane wreck is not their salvation; rather, it is a trick that reveals the inherently liminal condition of the party.

The half-destroyed aeroplane and its contents seemingly provide the group, and the viewer, with a focal point: it is a clearly delineated spatial area within the uniform jungle and it offers salvation by way of the goods strewn around the crash site. Furthermore, it is by the side of the fictitious Lake Topochapa and supposedly close to the Brazilian border. It is ostensibly the focal point that Castin's photographs of Paris that he burnt on the group's campfire the previous night fail to be: his lament that 'there will be nothing!' has yielded something. The sequence begins with a focus on a suitcase in the trees, before the camera pans to show the decimated aircraft. There follows a distance shot of Djin, incredulous, framed on one side by a tree trunk and on the other by the plane's propeller. This brief shot recalls the earlier, striking mid-distance shot of the group trekking through a swamp, framed on each side by a tree trunk in a *mise-en-scène* redolent of a theatrical proscenium. The implication here is that the products of the wreckage are a locus of spatial and cultural identification for the gang. It is a reconfiguration of Crusoe's salon in the jungle, but while Crusoe's salon serves to compensate for his isolation, the group in *La Mort en ce jardin* rely on the wreck to mask their collective sense of uprootedness.

The consequences of the group's find also have an effect on the narrative and the viewer. As Chark and Djin talk against the picturesque backdrop of the lake, the genre and gender codes and iconography seemingly established at the start of the film when Djin sleeps with Chark in her bedroom convey a traditional romantic reconciliation at the culmination of an adventure quest narrative. Suddenly concerned about her appearance, Djin says, 'I'm ugly, right?'. With Chark's less-than-chivalrous response ('You don't look good'), they leave to take a bath in the lake. It appears that the group has been saved and Chark has got the girl. Leahy's interpretation of this particular scene is interesting. She argues that it is Chark who is eroticised, with the key lighting coming from the left of the frame and highlighting his tanned skin, while Djin, on the left of the frame, remains with her back to this light (2013: 335–36). I argue that subsequently it is Djin who undergoes the most dramatic physical transformation back to the sexualised vamp. The following scenes depict this superficial transformation of the group, except the delirious Castin who continues to bear the somatic effects of the jungle in his festering head wound: besides Djin, who is shown in an expensive black gown and ruby red lipstick, Father Lizardi is dressed once again in his priestly garb, Maria is scolded by Lizardi for collecting the jewellery of the crash victims. This supposed narrative resolution is swiftly undercut by Buñuel; indeed, the logo on the aeroplane chassis is suggestive of its failure. In the shot of Djin making herself up, the viewer can make out the plane's logo – *Transandino* – on a piece of machinery behind her (see Figure 6). Like the fugitives, the plane is forever lost in its transitional Andean transit, not managing to successfully navigate the jungle, and is an ironic reminder that their salvation within this closed world is not guaranteed.

The group's physical transformation from 'rags to riches' is significant in revealing their true nature as Tricksters. The Trickster is a key figure in liminality, as Agnes Horvath and Bjørn Thomassen explain. Traditionally, the Trickster

> is a vagrant who happens to stumble into the village, appearing as if he came out of the blue. He tries to gain the confidence of villagers by telling tales and cracking jokes, thus, in the most elementary manner, by provoking laughter. (2008: 13)

The Trickster figure can, in the breakdown of political and social structures, assume control, perpetuating the liminal situation for his or her own gains. Given his status

Figure 6: Djin as a Transandino trickster. (Producciones Tepeyac/Film Dismage)

as an outsider in the mining village, Chark would appear to be most closely approx-imated with the Trickster. Indeed, Carlos Rebolledo believes that Chark is char-acterised by a 'non-belonging to the Buñuelian universe', given that the character's 'presence reveals the political and social repercussions of all the characters, although he never participates in their conflicts' (1964: 108).[10] The counterpart to the Trick-ster, however, is the Master of ceremonies, traditionally the member of a tribe leading the liminars in their interstitial period and who 'maintains order once the stabilities of everyday life are dissolved' (Horvath and Thomassen 2008: 13). As the finder of the plane and the leader of the group, as well as an outsider, Chark's role is thus problematised: is he a Trickster or a Master of ceremonies? The discovery of the aircraft is really a catalyst for revealing the entire group as a collection of Trickster figures. Importantly, the Trickster superficially mimics the behaviour of others, rather than unconsciously imitating it; as Horvath and Thomassen put it, the Trickster is simply 'a good mime' (2008: 15). The characters' superficial consum-erism is evident in their dressing up. Though they all appropriate the crash victims' belongings, minus Castin, this superficial consumerism is particularly evident in the narcissistic Djin whose blonde curls, crimson lips and mercenary demeanour cast her as a vampish Marilyn Monroe.[11] The act of dressing up here is significant. Szakolczai highlights Turner's consideration of theatre performance as a liminal ritual, noting that in a condition of permanent liminality 'individuals are required to identify with the roles they are supposed to play all the time, all their lives, and their role will *become* their life' (2000: 222). Indeed, Evans's observation that '[f]aced with the certainty of death, Djin makes a statement about life, gesturing colourfully and defiantly against the fate that awaits all' (2004: 144), points directly towards the exuberant, ostentatious *mise-en-scène* around her performance: on the verge of tears after declaring her love for Chark and dressed in a figure-hugging black ball dress and lavished in jewels, a point-of-view shot as Castin prepares to shoot her shows Djin lighting her cigarette with a large piece of wood from the campfire. Following the discovery of the aircraft, Buñuel's characters, as critics such as Fuentes have signalled, revert to type, perpetuating their 'roles' whilst paradoxically exposing the mechanics of the theatrical mode and the superficiality of identity (2000: 138). As Hayward phrases it with reference to Djin's soiled-to-sultry transformation: '[t]he masquerade is nearly complete' (2004: 127). Put simply, the Tricksters are tricked by the aeroplane wreck.

At the same time, the viewer's expectations that the discovery of the plane and the lake in the quest narrative will reach its fulfilment in the group's salvation are undermined through cinematography and sound. After Castin has murdered Djin and Father Lizardi, Chark hides with Maria overnight. The establishing shot the next morning is of the lake rather than the jungle. Yet the shot composition reveals that this is no less a liminal space than the endless canopy of trees. The only distinguishing feature of the lake is a small island; the expanse of water stretches to the horizon and the distant hills. Furthermore, as Chark kills Castin and sets out down river with Maria on the dinghy, the soundscape of the jungle is still heard.

An ambiguous reaggregation

It has been common to read the ending of *La Mort en ce jardin* in a relatively positive light, encouraged perhaps by Buñuel's comments when discussing the film.[12] According to the director, the unlikely couple Chark and Maria are 'saved' because of their respective cold-blooded pragmatism and innocence, roughly foreshadowing *Viridiana*'s relationship with Jorge in *Viridiana* (de la Colina and Pérez Turrent 1992: 130). Certainly, following the decimating effects of Castin's madness on the group as a whole, Chark and Maria are the sole survivors, though from a spatial perspective the two have not escaped their interstitial position; they remain betwixt and between. As mentioned above, the final shot of the film – a long distance shot of the pair floating down the Mambuti river – eschews positive interpretation as much as it does negative; it is in its ambiguity that the liminal is perpetuated.

Echoing Kyrou's comments regarding the subversive structure of Buñuel's manipulated documentary *Tierra sin pan*, Durgnat (1977: 108) believes that *La Mort en ce jardin* functions according to a 'yes, but' Buñuelian dialectic: before the group can cook the snake they have killed for food, it is miraculously resuscitated before Father Lizardi's eyes, swarming with thousands of red ants; the wreck of the aeroplane, a contemporary reconfiguration of Crusoe's 'salon in the jungle', offers the tantalising promise of corporeal reintegration through the acquisition of the material belongings of the deceased passengers, yet does not deliver; Chark and Maria's journey downriver seems to suggest salvation, but, as Buache asks, 'will they survive? And for how long?'. Buache ultimately circumscribes the theme of ambiguity, which he identifies as being at the heart of this film, within a theological narrative: the 'biggest sham of all', according to him, is God (1973: 85; 81). Contrastingly, Jean Fac posits a heroic salvation narrative that concords with Buñuel's own opinion that Chark and Maria are saved, and points to a reading of the film coloured by expectations of the character-driven adventure genre (Press cuttings on *Jardin*, ABR-1981 item 68). Teasing out the spatial resonances of ambiguity exemplified through the concept of liminality, the reading of the film I have elaborated here offers a thematic inflection on this salient trope, avoiding allegorical interpretations to focus precisely on the film's inconclusive conclusion. It is precisely from the ambiguous middle ground, betwixt and between the 'yes' and the 'but' that the liminal quality of both the characters and their milieu arises.

Simón del desierto

Simón's desert

In spite of its relatively short running time, the unexpected and impromptu finale of Buñuel's final Mexican film, *Simón del desierto*, has attracted much attention from critics and Buñuel scholars who have remarked upon the ways in which it disturbs the spatio-temporal continuity of the film's narrative in a move which anticipates the episodic structure of *La Voie lactée* and Buñuel's later films. What is more, Buñuel himself reinforced the connection between these two films, even suggesting that Simón could feasibly feature among the eclectic episodic encounters of the two pilgrims in *La Voie lactée* (Buñuel 2001: 283). Together with *El ángel exterminador*, Buñuel's penultimate film produced in Mexico, *Simón del desierto* can be seen as closer in style to the director's first two surrealist movies, *Un Chien andalou* and *L'Âge d'or*, than to more commercial works made in Mexico and, as Acevedo-Muñoz contends, is an appropriate conclusion to Buñuel's Mexican corpus, representing 'the logical conclusion, the closure, of that period of Buñuel's career' (2003: 7). Through an analysis of the spatial properties of this film, I suggest that, although *Simón del desierto* may be a fitting finale to Buñuel's Mexican period in that it coincides with the move towards more independent, avant-garde cinema in Mexico between 1964 and 1965, as Acevedo-Muñoz points out (2003: 13), like *La Mort en ce jardin* it is a film whose spatial liminality renders any conclusion inherently problematic.

As the credits roll during the opening sequence of the film, the viewer is confronted with a vast expanse of desert space. The high-angle camera first pans the landscape, picking up nothing more than a handful of arid cacti before settling on a group of pilgrims and monks chanting a haunting *Te Deum*, trickling through the dunes. Having reached Simón's column, the hooded monks and the following crowd appear insignificant as they are shown from above, among the dunes, interspersed with ground level, medium shots that frame the crowd against the distant hills of the desert. From the initial sequence of the film the isolation and extension of the desert are emphasised. This space is integral to Buñuel's humorous portrayal of the monastic life of Saint Simeon Stylites, one of the most notable figures in the early Christian tradition of the desert fathers. Writing about the desert as a space of monastic retreat and contemplation in late antiquity, Claudia Rapp states that, 'beginning with the late third century, the Egyptian desert was populated by the pioneers of the desert life, the desert fathers' (2006: 97). The desert is a transcendental space, at once everywhere and nowhere, a void that is impossible to fill, as Rapp signals, admittedly from a generalised Western viewpoint: 'the desert [...] symbolizes an empty and threatening space, devoid of people and far removed from all the advantages and achievements of human society' (2006: 94).

In the same way as the open landscapes of Mexico's Pacific coastline were transformed into the liminal jungle in *La Mort en ce jardin*, here the parched landscape of El Valle del Mezquital, in the Mexican state of Hidalgo, becomes the fifth-century Syrian desert. As with Buñuel's portrayal of the jungle in *La Mort en ce jardin*, it is apparent from the start of the film that traditional aesthetics were not of great concern to the director. The spaces of the jungle and the desert are not exoticised or beautified. In fact, Buñuel highlights the ambiguity, even the banality, of such landscapes, as opposed to, for example, the artistic aerial panoramas of rolling desert dunes of Death Valley in Antonioni's *Zabriskie Point* (1970). Just as with the filming of *Tierra sin pan* some thirty-two years previously, Buñuel had once again chosen a space on the margins, inhospitable and industrially underdeveloped. Felix Martialay makes the connection between the landscape of *Simón del desierto* and that of *Tierra sin pan*, positing a pathetic fallacy in their depictions: '[a] desert. Landscape scorched by the sun. A landscape-character in many of Buñuel's films, as if the calcination of Las Hurdes had conditioned that miserable, parched, inhospitable "being"' (1969: 8).[13] This parched and inhospitable area was actually home to the Otomi Indians, as Eduardo McGregor, the Spanish actor cast as Daniel, the naive young monk ordered in one scene by Simón to abandon the monastery and not to return until he has grown a beard, recalls (2000: 37).

The desert of *Simón del desierto* is as much a blank canvass as is the jungle of *La Mort en ce jardin*, then, both peripheral spaces which become central to the narratives of the respective films. The term 'blank canvas' refers to the liminal characteristics of both locations that are derived from their position on the margin and their homogenous form. The two are portrayed filmically as boundless expanses of open space in which spatial referents or geographical coordinates are ambiguous. However, as opposed to the interstitial position of the mining village and jungle in *La Mort en ce jardin*, that is, their position between the ideological spaces of France and Brazil, Simón's desert is more problematic in this respect. Unlike in the former film, here the bulk of the narrative takes place around Simón's column in the desert and the viewer is not privy to any other locations off-screen. The throng of pilgrims at the start of the film, for example, comes from such an unseen off-screen space which, presumably, is where the monastery that is home to the monks who periodically visit Simón is located. It is, nonetheless, enough simply to acknowledge that a space beyond the desert exists. After all, the film's title is the protagonist's alignment with a seemingly vacuous, marginal space writ large. Simón is characterised immediately by his removal from society and the title alludes to the possibility that his may be an irrevocable detachment. Furthermore, the concept of van Gennep's comments regarding the territorial delineation of neutral zones in classical antiquity is pertinent to Simón's spatial liminality. In this era, where each country was separated from another by a sort of no man's land buffer zone, the desert became an archetypal neutral zone, set aside for potential battles (van Gennep 1960: 17–18). The act of passing between one country and another through such a neutral zone is, for van Gennep, essentially a transition during which the subject 'wavers between two worlds' (1960: 18), precisely the in-between location in which Simón anchors himself.

If the topography of Simón's scrubland is indicative of the ascetic's horizontal liminality, the pillar on which he stands serves to suspend him in a vertical interstitial position, too. For Durgnat, Simón, 'lost in the wild blue yonder', is the embodiment of 'the first astronaut, alone on a Space Platform' (1977: 138). The opening scenes of the film show Simón relocating from his modest pillar to a gigantic, profoundly phallic column that has been specially constructed for him by a pious benefactor. Gleaning the irony in the preacher's promotion, Wood suggests 'even in the realm of renunciation there are opportunities for professional advancement' (2009). Wood is also one of the few critics to remark upon a further patently Buñuelian sardonic irony: Simón's 'promotion' occurs after he has been on his first pillar for precisely six years, six months and six days – 666, the number of the Beast in the Book of Revelation, an ominous portent which undoubtedly heralds the later appearances of the Devil, played by Silvia Pinal, as she taunts Simón. The change of pillar is indicative of the protagonist's desire to distance himself from earthly concerns through an increased propinquity to God, albeit by a few metres. The short sequence as Simón walks among his followers from one pillar to the other is the only incidence of the desert father's feet on *terra firma*; abjuring all things earthly in his naive quest for seraphic benediction leads him to reject even his own mother, a possible incarnation of the long-suffering Virgin as she camps out at the foot of her son's pillar in the hope of filial affection. Before he climbs the ladder to take up his place on top of the higher pillar, he hugs his mother for the final time, telling her that 'my love for you must not come between my Lord and his servant'. In his deliberate positioning of himself between the celestial and the terrestrial, Simón's liminal location is two-fold, in a so-called neutral zone and between two supposedly opposing planes. The cinematography is also key in perpetuating and giving visible representation to his liminal location. A myriad of high-angle shots depict the solitary figure of Simón against the vast expanse of sky in addition to distance shots which frame him and his column against the endless desert, for example. Additionally, shots such as the high-angle, low-angle reverse shot during Simón's conversations with his regular visitors (the monks, the dwarf goatherd and the Devil), as Catherine Dey indicates, are also utilised to exaggerate the physical and emotional detachment of Simón from his contemporaries (1999: 239).

Within the vast scrubland, the only definitive landmark is Simón's pillar — ironically, all roads lead to the indefinite liminar. Perhaps the most significant indication the viewer obtains of the ascetic's liminal position is through his three encounters with the Devil. Pinal's voice is heard off-screen before we first see her appear from behind Simón's former, shorter pillar, wearing an early twentieth-century schoolgirl's outfit and rolling a hoop. Durgnat reads the hoop as a symbol of eternity, without beginning or end (1977: 138), a visual metaphor for the indefinite interstitial position of the protagonist as well as an allusion to the cyclical nature of the diegetic world, an idea I will come to shortly. As the Devil-schoolgirl finishes her little ditty about Simón's supposed penchant for scrubbing his teeth with Syrian urine, the two engage in an apparently banal conversation:

Simón: What are you doing here?
Devil: Playing.
Simón: Where did you come from?
Devil: Over there.
Simón: And where are you going?
Devil: Over there.

This is the first instance of a series of essentially meaningless adverbial locutions of place peppered throughout the narrative. Though the Devil's responses to Simón

Figure 7: Neither here nor there. (Producciones Gustavo Alatriste)

may appear glib, they confirm that the space in which Simón dwells is betwixt and between indefinite spatial referents, in the middle of here and the unseen there, from which there is no escape (see figure 7). And it is not only the Devil who provides indefinite expressions of place; during the course of his satanic ordeals Simón frequently utters the exclamation 'get thee behind me, Satan!'. Unfortunately for the ascetic, the Devil's continued appearances throughout the film suggest that there is no going backwards or forwards in a world so bleakly uniform it is almost oneiric. Indeed, the Devil's retort to Simón during her third and final appearance before the pair are whisked to a New York nightclub that ends the film indicates this: as an increasingly weary Simón issues a rather feeble 'get thee behind me, Satan!', the Devil asserts 'not behind, nor anywhere else'.

The desert as smooth space

My exploration of the spatial liminal is also informed by Gilles Deleuze and Félix Guattari's concept of smooth and striated space. This supposed binary pair is elaborated via a number of models to provide analogies to what is a rather abstract concept. Smooth space, the antithesis of striated space, is one in which 'the points are subordinate to the trajectory' as opposed to the traveller's movements through striated space in which 'lines or trajectories tend to be subordinated to points: one goes from one point to the other' (Deleuze & Guattari 2004: 474). As such, the distinction between the two is visible in the randomly arranged fibres of felt and the striated form of imbricated woven fabric in a so-called technical model, or the contrast between the smooth vector and the striated point in the navigation of the seas (or the desert) in a maritime model. The spatial paradigm of striated-smooth, then, can have its counterpart in a sedentary-nomadic binary. Deleuze and Guattari posit that '[i]n striated space, one closes off a surface and "allocates" it according to determinate intervals, assigned breaks; in the smooth, one "distributes" oneself in an open space, according to frequencies and in the course of one's crossings' (2004: 481), which goes some way to explaining why smooth space is a space of 'affects, not belongings, haptic, not optic' (2004: 479). Fittingly, the ocean, steppe, and desert belong to this category of space as their topography invites a nomadic way of life and sensory negotiation. On the other hand, the archetypal striated space is the city, highly regimented and grid-like, its verticality to be negotiated optically. Despite his rigid degree of fixity to his column, Simón is patently a Buñuelian (and a Deleuzian) nomad, as '[w]e can say of the nomads, following Toynbee's suggestion: *they do not move*. They are nomads by dint of not moving, not migrating, of holding a smooth space that they refuse to leave' (Deleuze and Guattari 2004: 482).

In his self-imposed liminal state, then, Simón is holding his nomadic smooth space, not moving from point to point but existing permanently in the trajectory, in the vain hope of a spiritual epiphany. Deleuze and Guattari point out that '[t]o think is to voyage' (ibid.), and in his thoughts Simón is perpetually waiting for a metaphysical manifestation, 'waver[ing] between two worlds' (van Gennep, 1960: 18). Furthermore, a key aspect of the traversing of smooth space, and one that provides a link with the concept of liminality as proposed by Turner, is the degree of 'becoming', to use Deleuze and Guattari's expression, that this act entails: '[v]oyaging smoothly is a becoming, and a difficult, uncertain becoming at that' (2004: 482). For Turner, the liminal state is 'transition [...] a becoming, and in the case of *rites de passage*, even a transformation' (1967: 94). This means that any physical, psychical or ethical metamorphosis should occur in liminal – in this sense, we could perhaps also read smooth – space. Although Simón's desert home is certainly a liminal zone, the transformative potential of this spatio-temporal area is forever occluded through his refusal to acknowledge his innate connection to the earth plane.[14] Simón, therefore, is forever stuck in a potential becoming not yet begun.

Despite its apparent rigidity, however, the smooth-striated space pair does not in practice function within a dichotomy; its nature is fundamentally cyclical and dialectic. Deleuze and Guattari make clear:

> Smooth space is constantly being translated, transversed into a striated space; striated space is constantly being reversed, returned to a smooth space. In the first case,

one organizes even the desert; in the second, the desert gains and grows; and the two can happen simultaneously. (2004: 474–75)

To give an example, just as the city is the archetypal striated space, so the sea is the smooth equivalent. Even so, the oceans were the first to be subjected to the desires of Western civilisation for striation, with the latitudinal/longitudinal grid being superimposed on the seas to aid navigation (2004: 479). In her discussion of the desert as the chief arena of nomadism in Arab cinema, Laura Marks writes: 'the more we examine the relationships between the smooth and the striated in desert space, and the relations of life and death that their movement describes, the more difficult it is to distinguish them' (2006: 126). For Marks, desert space is contested space, at once smooth and striated, as 'a true cinema of the desert sees the desert in relation to the outside forces that shape it' (ibid.). This is not the case in *Simón del desierto*. Notwithstanding the obvious differences between the contemporary Arab road movie and Buñuel's depiction of what is supposedly the fifth-century Syrian desert, in Buñuel's film the outside forces that shape this space remain unseen: the viewer never sees the monastery, home to the monks that provide Simón with food and water, nor the town from which the pilgrims journey to witness his miracles. The smooth-striated-smooth cog has ground to a halt in *Simón del desierto*, never rotating beyond smooth, at least for the protagonist. This interruption in the system is what permits the spatial-smooth to transpose itself onto the ontological-smooth, as it were; the ascetic's spatial liminality has suffused his mental detachment. This is evident in particular in Simón's dream sequence, before the appearance of the Devil-schoolgirl, which shows him running and playing at the foot of his pillar with his mother before resting his head on her lap as she asks him whether he ever thinks of her. Letting a handful of sand slip through his fingers, he replies: 'Hardly ever, mother. I don't have time.' It is possible to live striated on the dunes, just as it is equally feasible to occupy a smooth space in the most striated of spaces – the city – though this is not the case for Simón. He is a nomad, an occupant of smooth space, by dint, as I have explained, of *not moving*.

The desert as Deleuzian originary world

Furthermore, the smooth and the liminal – and, therefore, Simón's desert – bear a clear relation to Deleuze's idea of the originary world in his writing on cinema. In *Cinema 1* Deleuze focuses his attention on the movement-image. He argues that the cinematographic medium provides us not with 'an image to which movement is added, it immediately gives us a movement-image' (1992: 2). Cinema is in a unique position to show the continuity of movement, and 'the essence of the cinematographic movement-image lies in extracting from vehicles or moving bodies the movement which is their common substance, or extracting from movements the mobility which is their essence' (Deleuze 1992: 23). The term 'movement-image' does not denote a singular image; it is an umbrella term that Deleuze uses to encompass the specific varieties of movement-images he goes on to identify in cinema, one of which is the impulse-image. This type of image is located between two major components in his taxonomy of cinema: the affection-image and the action-image. The affection-image is often represented by a close-up shot of the face while the realism of the action-image is most often depicted by the medium-shot. As Conley explains: '[a]ffective images are found in *lieux quelconques* or "any-places-whatsoever," and they are charged with emotion while action is given to "determinate milieus" and "behaviors" appropriate to them' (2008: 46).

The affection-image works to 'abstract [the object of the close-up shot] from all spatio-temporal co-ordinates' (Deleuze 1992: 96) within an any-space-whatever, a particular space which appears fragmented and lacking in homogeneity. Simón's desert is quite clearly not an any-space-whatever, resisting fragmentation through its bleak uniformity. The action-image, however, 'is the domain of realism, of qualities and powers actualized in a concrete, specific space-time' (Bogue 2003: 85), the model on which the hegemony of US narrative cinema is based. There is a preponderance of distance and low- and high-angle shots in *Simón del desierto*, which depict neither the affection- nor the action-image: just as the preacher's perpetual existence atop the pillar is related to his surrounding environment cinematographically, rather than being abstracted from this as in the affection-image, so his surrounding environment, through its incessant uniformity and unspecified location, cannot be considered a concrete, specific space-time, as in the realist action-image. Before the derived milieus begin to assert their independence to become the arenas of action in which '[a]ffects and impulses now only appear as embodied in behaviour, in the forms of emotions or passions which order and disorder it' (Deleuze 1992: 141), they are the locus of a 'degenerate affect' or an 'embryonic action' (Deleuze 1992: 123) contained within an impulse. This is where Simón's desert is located.

As opposed to the action-image, which is a marker of cinematic realism, the impulse-image has its roots in naturalism, an aesthetic mode which, according to Deleuze, 'is not opposed to realism, but on the contrary accentuates its features by extending them in an idiosyncratic surrealism' (1992: 124). Inherent to this naturalistic cinema, and underscoring in a subliminal vein the more realist geographical and historical milieus within the diegesis, is the originary world, a place regulated by base drives. About this world Deleuze writes (and here he is worth quoting at length):

> The originary world may be marked by the artificiality of the set (a comic opera kingdom, a studio forest, or marsh) as much as by the authenticity of a preserved zone (a *genuine desert*, a *virgin forest*). It is recognisable by its *formless character*. It is pure background, or rather, a without-background, composed of uniform matter, sketches or fragments, crossed by non-formal functions, acts, or energy dynamisms which do not refer to the constituted subjects. Here the characters are like animals: the fashionable gentleman a bird of prey, the lover a goat, the poor man a hyena. This is not because they have their form or behaviour, but because their acts are prior to all differentiation between the human and the animal. These are human animals. And this is indeed the impulse: the energy which seizes fragments in the originary world. (1992: 123–24, my emphasis).

Deleuze goes on to categorise both the jungle of *La Mort en ce jardin* and Simón's desert as originary worlds (1992: 125).[15] Given the formless character of the originary world, this bears the hallmark of smooth space, which is essentially 'amorphous', and with 'no background, plane, or contour' (Deleuze and Guattari 2004: 477, 496). Indeed, it is not difficult to see how the arid plains of Simón's desert can be considered formless in appearance. As regards the function of these originary worlds, Paul Sandro explains that these worlds extract impulses from modes of behaviour in the determinate milieus and give rise to the fetish object, simultaneously present in the real milieu and originary world which underlies it (2003: 37). Such is often the case in Buñuel's cinema, replete with fetishised objects. As evidence of this we might think of the animated postcard, the re-animated snake and the entire aircraft wreck in *La Mort en ce jardin*, the fixation of the dwarf goatherd on his goat's udders in *Simón del desierto* and the Chinese urns-turned-toilets in *El ángel exterminador*.

One of the primary proponents of naturalistic cinema according to Deleuze is Buñuel. Examining the themes of confinement and dislocation in the Buñuel's cinema, and how these plot devices give rise to the Deleuzian impulse-image, Sandro maintains that 'Buñuel, like Zola, subjects his characters mercilessly to the pressures and demands of their social settings, their *milieux*' (2003: 36). As

Deleuze explains, '[t]he originary world is [...] both radical beginning and absolute end', both of which are linked by what he terms 'a line of the steepest slope' (1992: 124). The slope acts as a bridge between the real milieus and the originary world, underscoring it and encouraging an entropic degradation; as Bogue has it, 'a cruel passage from primal origin to ultimate destruction' (2003: 83). The slope is therefore inextricably linked to chronology, as 'it has the merit of causing an originary image of time to rise, with the beginning, the end, and the slope' (Deleuze 1992: 124). Most significantly, the bestial impulses of the originary world are said by Deleuze to coalesce in what is the ultimate degradation: 'a great death-impulse' (ibid.). The relevance of this slope of degradation to *Simón del desierto* underscores the allegorical readings of this film; that is, that Simón ends up in the hellish disco. Deleuze encourages the viewer to question this deceptively neat interpretation. Buñuel's, he says, is a particular brand of naturalism; his line of steepest slope is not actually a slope at all. The radical beginning in Buñuel's cinema often occurs at the end of the narrative: the group fleeing though the originary world in *La Mort en ce jardin* is (re)turned to the bestial, while the incredible conclusion of *Simón del desierto* suggests a perpetuation of the protagonist's self-imposed exile, albeit in the Big Apple of the swinging sixties. The point is really that Buñuel's cinema operates cyclically, as 'in Buñuel [...], entropy was replaced by the cycle or the eternal return' in which the saintly and the malicious find themselves indiscriminately (Deleuze 1992: 131). The trope of repetition returns us to liminality. As an interstructural situation, liminality forms part of a cycle whereby structure dissolves to leave anti-structure before subsequently giving way once again to a redefined structure (Turner 1995: 94–130). The open, ambiguous endings of both films discussed in this chapter, however, do not suggest the re-imposition of structure. Instead, Buñuel prefers to continue his repetition in the originary world/liminal space, which, I will show, conditions both of the films discussed in this chapter.

From desert to disco

The Devil's final appearance heralds the protagonist's spatial dislocation as he is magically transported through time and space to end up in a nondescript discotheque in modern New York City. This begins with a medium close-up tracking shot of a coffin, apparently self-propelled through the desert scrubland. The weary Simón clearly knows what the ominous object contains, crossing himself and asking for divine succour. The coffin lid opens and out steps the Devil, this time clad in a revealing toga. The ascetic's Hail Marys are of no use to him now, she warns, and instructs him to prepare himself for a long voyage, the destination of which will be a place where he will witness 'the gaping red wounds of the flesh'. This description has undoubtedly given rise to various critics' allegorical readings of the translocation between the desert and nightclub at the end of the film as a movement towards a postmodern hell. As the Devil states 'they're coming for us', Buñuel cuts to a shot of an aeroplane traversing the sky above what is supposedly fifth-century Syria; the film's oneiric dimension is never more apparent than in the leap from late antiquity to modernity as the following dissolve shows Simón's empty pillar become the pulsating megalopolis of New York. These readings are summed up most succinctly by Fuentes, who states that Simón falls from 'the peak to the abyss […]. In two frames we have gone from expectations of a transcendental flight to a *descensus ad infernos*' (1993: 157).[16] It should also be said that Buñuel's own envisioning of the *mise-en-scène* of the nightclub sequence appears to toy with such an allegorical reading: the name of the band playing in the nightclub is *The Sinners* and the film's shooting script suggests that anyone viewing the scene for the first time 'would think themselves a toy in a nightmare' (Buñuel and Alejandro 1964: 75).[17] However, Deleuze's comments on the cyclical impulse in Buñuel's cinema disavow this interpretation and here I propose an alternative.

The footage of New York opens with disorientating aerial shots of the cosmopolitan centre before the camera moves to street-level, framing the high-rise blocks from an extreme low-angle, read by Durgnat as a multitude of modern columns (1977: 138). The camera then pans the interior of a nightclub, passing over a writhing corporeal sea before settling on Simón and the Devil, both of whom are dressed fittingly in more modern attire. Indeed, while Wood (2009) believes Simón's appearance to be reminiscent of a French intellectual, and in the shooting script he is described as resembling The Beatles (Buñuel and Alejandro 1964: 76), what is important here is that he remains a Deleuzian nomad, holding his smooth space. There is once again a brief but telling exchange between the Devil and Simón. Responding to his decidedly languid 'get thee behind me' [*vade retro*], Pinal delivers with gusto a decisive 'get thee gone', or *vade ultra* in the original Latin. With this rebuttal, the viewer realises that, while the (post)modern *ultra* may have triumphed over the archaic *retro*, the rules of the game remain the same: the continuation of the ambiguity surrounding spatial referents confirms that the striated space par excellence, the city, is ultimately a smooth space, a postmodern desert, and the decadent nightclub is anything but an oasis of tranquillity. In this way, the dialogue anticipates the view of cultural theorists such as Szakolczai (2000: 215–26), namely, that modernity can become equated with a perpetual liminality, where social structures can collapse beyond repair.

Also apparent is that behind – or rather beneath – the disco's shimmering façade of hedonistic rock and roll lies an originary world as liminal as that of the desert. This originary world, this time underscoring a place of self-indulgence in the twentieth century, is both radical beginning and absolute end, to echo Deleuzian terminology. Simón cannot leave to go 'home' as another alienated ascetic has begun his own tenancy in the desert, and the Devil informs him that he will have to stay forever. The modern-day Simón is misled by the Trickster figure of the Devil, being brought not to a reaggregation into society, but forced to exist in the disorientating urban jungle of 1960's New York among a mass of bodies to which the individual must capitulate. Conley's (2008: 47) observation that, '[f]or the director [Buñuel] the originary world carries the bonus of being a site for caustic reflection that goes well beyond the time and space in which it is placed', points directly to the transcendental, limitless quality of the realistic milieu of the nightclub. Furthermore, the frenetic floundering of the partygoers' limbs is a dance aptly-titled *radioactive flesh* and is, the Devil says, 'the latest dance, the final dance', the absolute end to Simón's radical starting point of forever (see figure 8). The dancers' gestures are described in the shooting script as 'disquieting, gestures at times funny, at times obscene, contortions, attitudes and movement imitating monkeys, dogs, chickens', before the script calls for such eclectic dance-styles as 'chicken back', 'cheetah the monkey' and 'watusi' (Buñuel and Alejandro 1964: 75).[18] We should remember that the originary world is prior to any division between human and beast. Here, then, the originary world of the desert is conflated with that of the disco. They are contiguous planes of formless character underscoring their respective milieus in which actions are neither human nor animal. In this way, the nightclub is much less an allegorical hell than it is an interstitial, uncertain purgatory; to read it as the former is to over-simplify its connection to the desert and to impose a neat, teleological discourse on what is ultimately shrouded in ambiguity. The fundamental difference between allegorical readings of the film's ending as a modern hell and my own is one of directional planes; that is, a vertical (allegorical) reading versus a horizontal (spatial) reading: Simón's 'fall' naturally implies a definitive ending-place (hell), yet I argue his nomadic existence gives primacy to the unfurling horizontal. In this vast, formless expanse the smooth, the originary and the liminal lie.

Figure 8: The latest dance. The final dance. (Producciones Gustavo Alatriste)

Conclusion: liminal teleologies – starting from zero

The endings of both films are, as I have noted, deeply ambiguous, on a psychological and spatial level. Although *La Mort en ce jardin* ends with a distance shot of Chark and Maria as they sail down the Mambuti river, anchoring the narrative in a realist (albeit fictional) place, the intrepid survivors find themselves in as ambiguous a space as ever. Similarly in *Simón del desierto*, the ascetic appears in a nondescript yet believable nightclub setting in New York City. On the surface, the characters of both films appear to have escaped their 'in-between' locations – for better or worse – thanks to an apparent narrative *telos*: by dint of her innocence and his pragmatism, Maria and Chark are spared death; because of his weakened spiritual resolve, Simón is transported to what appears to be hell. If we posit a teleology in these and other of Buñuel's films, we certainly facilitate an ethical or thematic reading of these. According to Cristiana Malaguti (1993: 25), although Buñuel's characters appear to operate from a self-determinist perspective, 'in Buñuel the dynamism around the text always unfolds in a teleological manner'.[19] Ironically, however, Buñuel's own teleological model often functions to *negate* any notion of design, at least any design which is neat in its conclusion, through Deleuze's idea of cyclical return. Even in the most open-ended of his films, Malaguti notes, there is not a trace of certainty or of redemption (1993: 26). In applying a neat *telos* to these two films we are therefore dulling their ability to unsettle the audience beyond the end of the narrative. In addition to the two films I have paired together here, we might think of the ending to *Le Charme discret de la bourgeoisie*, where the characters tirelessly continue their perpetual walk through a non-descript countryside space as the camera zooms out, or the final distance shot of Ramón Vázquez after he has freed the chained prisoners in *La Fièvre monte à El Pao*, for which he will presumably face execution. The expectations and obligations of the individual following the suspension of the liminal period is exactly the conclusion of certitude denied by Buñuel's narrative *telos* that works towards an end of ambiguity.

Malaguti highlights this ambiguity in Buñuel's cinema. That Buñuel's narratives are constructed cyclically does not escape her notice and she echoes Deleuze's comments on this point: 'in Buñuel time assumes the mythical dimension of the eternal return, the predominant rhetorical figure is that of *repetition*'. Such repetition is made possible because Buñuel's work features

> a resetting [*azzeramento*] of narrative time, especially in the presentation of the characters themselves, who usually lack any historical roots or any referent outside of the economy of Buñuelian discourse; in general this concerns orphans, such as the protagonists of *Susana* and *The Young One* (1960), or individuals who interpose a rift between present and past, and between present and future (the religious men of *Simón del desierto* (1965) and of *Nazarin* (1958)). (1993: 25)[20]

The resetting of time is clearly pertinent to *Simón del desierto*, given that the ascetic finds himself permanently on the limen between present and future, but it is also palpable in *La Mort en ce jardin*. Within the jungle space, both the temporal and spatial dimensions shift from their objectivist matrix to become anchored in subjectivity. If that were not enough, the ending of the film sees Maria orphaned as her father, Castin, descends into insanity, murdering Djin and Father Lizardi, and is subsequently shot dead by Chark. In this way, Maria finds her liminal period compounded; she is between a past with her father and a future alone, or possibly with Chark. This is Deleuze's cycle of return in action, a constant intrusion of liminality in the temporal aspect of the narrative.

Finally, a concern with space, although not often acknowledged in any sustained way, underpins both of these films. Writing about *Simón del desierto*, Annie Goldmann asserts that the film's primary thematic is a comment on the lack of *place* for a man such as Simón, as 'in its admirable simplicity this film poses the difficult question of the place of the believer in the modern world' (1969: 465).[21] Hers is a nihilistic reading of the film, suggesting that in the twentieth century there is neither God nor Devil, and Simón has no reason to exist. In this regard, the film can be read as a comment on a lack of place in the modern world, not only for believers but for almost anyone. Similarly, Acevedo-Muñoz writes that *La Mort en ce jardin*, along with Buñuel's other French language co-productions of the 1950s, features 'geographically isolated settings and characters that are foreigners, exiled, detached from their origins, and immersed in situations that they cannot escape, control, or understand. They struggle to *find their place*' (2013: 359, my emphasis). If the Buñuelian impulse against cinematic utopianism, as I suggested in chapter two, has its manifestation in the heterotopic island spaces of *Robinson Crusoe* and *The Young One*, his commitment to ambiguity finds its most overt visual representation in the liminal spaces of *La Mort en ce jardin* and *Simón del desierto*. Spatial concerns are also at the heart of what are arguably Buñuel's two most auteurist productions of the 1950s, *Los olvidados* and *Nazarín*, as I will show in the following chapter. Set in the city and countryside respectively, a focus on the body in place can serve to unite the two films, independently of their depictions of typologies of external spaces, and reveal once again how a spatial reading of the two films can enhance and inflect existing criticism on the films and open up new avenues of analytical exploration in the field of film studies.

Notes

1 See, for example, Durgnat, who discusses *Cela s'appelle l'aurore* in terms of this film's role as the introduction to a 'revolutionary triptych' in which each film represents 'a study in the morality and tactics of armed revolution against a right-wing dictatorship' (1977: 100).

2 Carlos Barbáchano (2000: 184) for instance, declares the first half of the film too long-winded.

3 [posee un inequívoco sentido buñueliano].

4 [Dieser Film dürfte auch den Buñuel-Kennern und -Exegeten reiche Materie zu neuen Deutungen bieten].

5 Susan Hayward (2004: 125) explains that Eastmancolor, a system of colour cinematography that was used for the first time at the beginning of the 1950s and with which Buñuel made *La Mort en ce jardin*, was able to accentuate the three primary colours through the use of filters to add or subtract colour. For her, the augmented yellow hues of the rocks in this initial scene are a reminder of human frailty, just as the green tones of the forest are later in the film.

6 Interestingly, Leahy (2013: 324–39) contends that the film itself is liminal within the director's corpus in her analysis of the film's production and the use of French actors in a Latin American setting.

7 [aquí [...] Buñuel se encuentra en su medio: unos pocos personajes a la deriva, en una situación límite, acosados por el hambre y la demencia].

8 [Zugleich ist der Dschungel ein Ort, der seine eigene Realitätsebene zu schaffen scheint, das Bewußtsein verändert, Wahn auslöst].

9 See, for example, Fuentes (2000: 138), who considers the protagonist's discovery of the aircraft wreck '[a] homage to surrealism within Latin American magical realism' and that the consequence of the characters' find is that they return to consumer society. [[un] homenaje al surrealismo dentro ya del mágico-realismo latinoamericano].

10 [Shark [sic] n'est déterminé que par sa non-appartenance à l'univers buñuelien]; [Sa présence révèle les incidences politiques et sociales de tous les personnages, bien qu'il ne participe jamais à leurs conflits].

11 Going further, Hayward (2004: 126) suggests that Djin's red lips and prominent teeth evoke the Freudian/surrealist image of a vagina dentata.

12 Fuentes, for example, contends that Chark and Maria possess 'an aspect of salvation' (2005: 163) [una dimensión salvífica].

13 [[u]n desierto. Paisaje quemado por el sol. Un paisaje-personaje en muchos films de Buñuel, como si la calcinación de las Hurdes se hubiera condicionado ese «ser» miserable, reseco, inhóspito].

14 Simón's refusal to recognise and give countenance to the Other forms the backbone of many readings of the film. Dey, for example, argues that Simón's disavowal of his ethical obligation to approach others in order to bring himself closer to the deity he serves is his ultimate downfall (2000: 238–45).

15 Although Deleuze proposes that the jungle of *La Mort en ce jardin* is an originary world characterised by its studio artificiality, this appears a mistaken assumption. Baxter (1994: 247) writes that the shoot took place on location near Lake Catemaco in Veracruz, Mexico.

16 [la cima a la sima [...]. En dos planos hemos pasado de las expectativas de un vuelo de transcendencia a un *descensus ad infernos*].

17 [se creería juguete de una pesadilla].

18 [inquietantes, los gestos a veces graciosos, a veces obscenos, las contorsiones, las actitudes y el caminar imitando a monos, perros, gallinas, etc.... todo ello, contribuyendo a formar una alegoría inquietante de nuestra época].

19 [in Buñuel il dinamismo all'interno del testo si risolve sempre in chiave tele-
ologica].

20 [in Buñuel il tempo assume la dimensione mitica dell'eterno ritorno, la figura
retorica predominante è quella della *ripetizione*]; [un azzeramento del tempo
interno del racconto, innanzitutto nella presentazione stessa dei personaggi, per
lo più privi di una qualsiasi matrice storica o di un qualche referente esterno
all'economia del discorso buñueliano; in genere si tratta di orfani, come le
protagoniste di *Susana* e di *Violenza per una giovane* (1960), o di individui che
interpongono una frattura tra presente e passato, e tra presente e futuro (i relig-
iosi di *Simon del deserto* (1965) e di *Nazarin* (1958))].

21 [dans son admirable simplicité ce film pose douloureusement la question de la
place du croyant dans le monde moderne].

Chapter 4
The Body-self in Place: The Place-worlds of *Los olvidados* and *Nazarín*

I n late 1950 Buñuel released what has become one of the most notable works of his entire corpus. The unflinching depiction of the Mexican underclass via a gang of Mexico City street children in *Los olvidados* is a point of departure from Buñuel's first two Mexican films, *Gran Casino*, a musical which 'clearly sought to emulate the success of Golden Age musicals' (Leen 2010: 101), and the comedy *El gran calavera*. Despite the unequivocal failure of *Gran Casino* at the box office, the relative success of the subsequent *El gran calavera* meant that producer Óscar Dancigers – who would work as a producer on ten of Buñuel's Mexican films produced under his company Ultramar films – allowed Buñuel to undertake a more original project of his choosing. Because of its depiction of disenfranchised youths and its unremitting focus on the everyday reality of life in the slums, *Los olvidados* has been likened to both Nikolai Ekk's *Road to Life* (1931), a Soviet drama concerning wayward youths, and Italian neorealism.[1] Bazin holds that *Los olvidados* distorts the myth propagated by Ekk's paradigm – namely that 'misery makes an evil counselor, and redemption comes through love, trust, and hard work', whereas Buñuel seeks to show 'the evil objective cruelty of the world' (1978: 195-96). Sebastiaan Faber suggests that, rather than poetic tragedy, the film can be seen as adhering more closely to naturalism, as '[the] characters' fate, after all, seems completely determined by the famous triad of milieu, moment and race – that is, their environment, historical moment and genetic make-up' (2003: 236).[2] To a certain extent, this is indeed true. The deluge of violence and criminality may appear gratuitous and 'forced', as Aranda (1976: 143) would have it, but, as Buñuel was keen to point out, was based on his own research into of the lives of the dispossessed within the slums of Mexico City, consulting details of the criminal trials of young people as well as making trips over a period of six months to observe life in impoverished areas of the capital (de la Colina and Pérez Turrent 1992: 53-54). This pseudo-documentary quality, Xavier Bermúdez argues, is exactly what drives its importance as a challenging film, so much so that in 2003 it was included in the UNESCO Memory of the World programme to safeguard its artistic heritage. Bermúdez argues:

> It was and it continues to be necessary that cinema reflects as unflinchingly as possible the misery of a world, as the only and desperate way/as a last resort to eliminate the poverty of that world, or at least as the only way not to justify it or praise it. (2000: 112)[3]

Eight years later, Buñuel began work on *Nazarín*. Like *Los olvidados*, *Nazarín* proved successful at Cannes, receiving the International Prize. Based on Benito Pérez Galdós's novel of the same name, the narrative depicts the (r)amblings of the quixotic priest Father Nazario, also known as Nazarín, as he drifts indiscriminately about the Mexican countryside accompanied by two unlikely female 'disciples', Ándara and Beatriz, while attempting to bring comfort to the diseased and the dying.[4] Foreshadowing Viridiana and Simón, the aloofness of Nazarín here is the cause of his naivety. Indeed, just as Edwards posits that Buñuel's first three films constitute a surrealist triptych, so Gregor proposes a grouping of *Nazarín*, *Viridiana* and *Simón del desierto* predicated on a thematic and ethical reading of these films, as in each it is the protagonists' submission to a Christian morality of self-negation and sublimation that brings about their downfall (Gregor in Aranda 1976: 225). The film's enthusiastic reception by Catholic institutions also highlights the difference between *Nazarín* and the later *Viridiana*: while the latter was decried in the Vatican newspaper *L'Osservatore Romano*, the former, as Durgnat (1977: 111-12) points out, came close to being awarded the Prize of the International Catholic Cinema Office.[5]

Whereas in the previous chapters of this book I have taken two films on the basis of their shared spatial characteristics – heterotopic islands and liminal desert and jungle spaces – in this chapter I will shift the analytical emphasis somewhat from typologies of external space to focus more specifically on the body (and, by extension, the self) in space as read through *Los olvidados* and *Nazarín*. While

Buñuel, in early press interviews for the film, described *Los olvidados* as a social documentary,[6] effectively creating an affinity between this and the earlier *Tierra sin pan*,[7] with regards to *Nazarín* he resists any similar such claims to documentary realism, stating: 'I didn't aim to make a film portraying that kind of believability, but rather one about an exceptional priest' (de la Colina and Pérez Turrent 1992: 132). *Los olvidados* is set against the backdrop of a Mexico City undergoing rapid but disproportionate modernisation during the presidency of Miguel Alemán (1946-52); the setting for the itinerant *Nazarín*, however, is given less importance. Galdós's novel is recast in the countryside of Mexico under the authoritarian president Porfirio Díaz around the turn of the twentieth century. Certainly, the respective settings of the films are important here; however, I am not building my argument upon a premise of the urban as opposed to the rural. Rather, I give consideration to the filmic depiction of the body's being-in-space – independently of the category of space this is. Both films reveal much about Buñuel's treatment of the body and its interaction with its surroundings. Key to this chapter, then, will be how the relationship between the corporeal and the psychological, and the places that the characters encounter, is represented filmically. As a framework for investigation, I draw extensively on the philosopher Edward Casey's concept of the place-world.

The place-world

Casey's work centres on the relationship between what he calls the geographical self; that is, a combination of the corporeal and the psychological as located in place, through the convergence of geography and philosophy. For Casey, 'the self has to do with the agency and identity of the geographical subject; body is what links this self to lived place in its sensible and perceptible features' (2001a: 683). Casey is of course not unique in his emphasis on the body and its relationship to the lived environment; as Phil Hubbard and others signal when they suggest that '[i]t seems logical [...] that any understanding of the spatiality of society must examine the geographies of the body' (1998: 97). They make clear that the body's emergence as a central factor in the discipline of human geography is a relatively recent one.[8] Like Casey, they attribute the disregard of the body in part to the Cartesian modality of mind and body as discrete entities, privileging ontology over epistemology. In an attempt to reconcile the body and the psyche with the world in which we live, Casey attempts a more nuanced explication of the linkages between the human subject and place. He argues that this relationship:

> is not just one of reciprocal influence (that much any ecologically sensitive account would maintain) but also, more radically, of constitutive coingredience: each is essential to the becoming of the other. In effect, there is *no place without self and no self without place*. (2001a: 684)

Place and self, Casey holds, are discrete entities that nevertheless play an integral role in the actualisation of the other: the central tenet of his argument is that the self is always implaced.[9]

The place-world of the geographical self derives from the self's 'inhabitation of places in a circumambient landscape', where place is taken to be 'the immediate environment of [the] lived body – an arena of action that is at once physical and historical, social and cultural' (Casey 2001a: 684). The place-world, then, corresponds to the immediate lived and enacted world of the self. In the cases of the street gang of *Los olvidados* and the wandering Nazarín, the place-world is contained within the claustrophobic slums of Mexico City and the open bucolic vistas of the Mexican countryside respectively. Casey proposes three distinct ways in which we engage with the place-world; these mediatrices between self and place, to use Casey's terminology, are habitus, habitation and idiolocalism. In this chapter, I show how each of these facets of the self-place relationship are shown in these two films. Moreover, in considering the two films in this chapter through the lens of Casey's spatial philosophy, I show how the fields of philosophy and human geography can inform the discipline of film studies and the act of film spectatorship. Before moving on to the films themselves, however, Casey's three terms require some initial explanation.

In employing the term habitus, Casey acknowledges his debt to sociologist Pierre Bourdieu, and in particular Bourdieu's *Outline of a Theory of Practice* in which Bourdieu introduces the habitus as 'the universalizing mediation which causes an individual agent's practices'. Habitus, Bourdieu says, is a 'system of durable, transposable *dispositions*' generated by the structures of a particular type of environment or condition (for example, social class), and through the re-enactment of which we are able to comprehend our environment (1977: 79; 72). Linking Bourdieu's concept more directly to space, Casey affirms that 'a given habitus qua settled disposition or "habitude" is thus the basis for action in any given sphere – indeed, in any given place' (2001a: 686). If habitus is the scheme that conditions the way in which we act in any given environment, then habitation, the act of holding place – Casey evokes the Latin root of the verb *habere* (to have, hold) – is 'the primary way in which the geographical subject realizes its active commitment to place' (2001a: 687). We can say, then, that habitation is a product of the systems of behaviour, 'of taking the habitus that has been acquired and continually re-enacting it in the place-world' (ibid.). Idiolocalism, as opposed to habitation, shifts the focus from the body in place to place in the body. Through idiolocalism, the persistence of place in the body and, by extension, the psyche is explored – that is, the ways in which places mark their subjects, be it ephemerally or permanently.

My investigation of the construction of what we can take to be the respective place-worlds of *Los olvidados* and *Nazarín* is in dialogue with the previous two chapters of this book. Like these, the guiding principle is that space is far from a passive container of the narrative, but is also a vehicle of representation in itself. Like Casey, I generally maintain the space/place distinction whereby space is the more generalised, less personal component of spatiality while place is the more intimate, lived aspect of space. Here, then, as opposed to the external configurations of island heterotopias and jungle/desert liminality, I am moving towards a more philosophical elucidation of space and place through their relation to the body and the self. It is an approximate move from the outside in, and it approaches the more intimate concept of a home-place and the ways that Buñuel's Mexican cinema problematises what it means to be at home, the subject of the following chapter.

Los olvidados

The metonymic opening sequence

The opening sequence of *Los olvidados* is an incongruous prologue to the rest of the film. The pseudo-documentary style of the sequence as the viewer is shown stock footage of the cities of London, Paris and New York, together with the voice-over narration, recalls the openings of *La ilusión viaja en tranvía* and *El río y la muerte* (1954), with their similar documentary aesthetic and focus on Mexico City. Suddenly, however, in this film the focus shifts solely to Mexico. The voiceover narrator leaves the viewer with little doubt as to the setting of the narrative; city and country share a metonymic bond as we are told that Mexico is a 'large modern city'. Just as the city is a microcosm for the nation, so the individual is representative of a larger section of the general population, both on a national and international level. Even before the viewer is introduced to the street gang, then, their link to the downtrodden classes who are 'doomed to criminality', according to the voiceover, is forged. Buñuel himself highlighted the artificiality of this opening in conversation (de la Colina and Pérez Turrent 1992: 59), which was added later in a bid to disarm Mexican audiences accustomed to what Fuentes has termed '[the] ideologised, triumphalist vision of the Mexico of the institutionalised revolution' (1991: 275) within their national cinema by resituating the reality of wanton poverty within a global context.[10] Miriam Haddu sees the film as departing from the *arrabal* [slum suburb] subgenre through its rejection of the tragi-comic elements common to films of this type, in particular Ismael Rodríguez's *Nosotros los pobres* (1948) or Alejandro Galindo's *¡Esquina, bajan...!* (1948). For her, the slums of *Los olvidados* are 'place[s] full of misery and anger, of frustration and violence' (2007: 128). Despite this ostensibly globalist opening, however, Julia Tuñón argues that the film is definitively Mexican in character, given what she sees as its reliance on melodramatic paradigms. For Tuñón, the documentary-style undertones of the film – its rawness – means that it is an 'atypical melodrama',[11] where emotion does not become a spectacle (2003: 75).

The street children are first seen immediately following this opening of the film. Although this short sequence serves mainly to introduce speculation surrounding the character of Jaibo, recently escaped from a correctional facility, it immediately creates a link between them and their environment. The establishing, mid-distance shot frames Pedro and the group of youths as they engage in child's play on the street against a backdrop of derelict and dilapidated buildings that will become one of the film's most visible motifs. The group is absorbed in a game as they mimic the actions of a bullfight complete with a makeshift cape and sword. This is an indicator of their underlying childlike innocence prior to the shocking scenes of theft, brutality and child murder that will occur later in the narrative, effectively disarming the audience. However, their horseplay is significant here for another reason, as it serves to connect the body-self with place in a deeper, more nuanced way, and it does so through habitus.

Habitus and the body techniques of the street children

I have already briefly commented on the dual nature of habitus as generative and generated: it is, in Bourdieu's words, 'structured structures predisposed to function as structuring structures' (1977: 72). This means it is a system of enacted dispositions and is part structure, part agency. For Bourdieu, our actions are shaped by and in turn perpetuate the particular social structure of which they are part (he suggests that class is one possible common denominator in habitus, though this is not to limit the habitus solely within a Marxist framework). We act, in turn, within a given 'field'; that is, the social (placial) arena in which we are placed, both physically and hierarchically (Hillier and Rooksby 2005: 22-24). Our actions within a specific place are a demonstration of habitus, and Marcel Mauss undertakes an explication of human action in the form of body techniques, or 'the ways in which from society to society men know how to use their bodies' (1979: 97). He maintains that body techniques are culturally specific and socially inscribed, and offers the example of the act of digging. According to his observations during the First World War, British soldiers struggled to use French-made spades, and, as a consequence, could only work productively with British spades (1979: 99). For Mauss, like Bourdieu, our body techniques are a product of sociality. The particular corporeal habitus of a given culture is therefore acquired through education, which, Mauss avows, is ultimately a form of imitation: effectively, mimetic representation of the body, which he describes as 'man's first and most natural instrument' (1979: 104). Mauss's theorisation of body techniques underscores more overtly than does Bourdieu the role of the body in the generation of structures and codes through which members of a particular social group can understand one another, but, as interesting as Mauss's theorisations of bodily movement are, they remain flawed through their gender bias and occasional anecdotal basis. I suggest Mauss's writing on body techniques is better understood as a point of departure from which to examine in more detail the body's movement through space.

The body techniques of the street gang in *Los olvidados* are striking. Most conspicuous of all in the opening scene, perhaps, is the imitation of bestial behaviour during the make-believe bullfight. The extreme close-up shot of the toothless boy, grimacing and grunting like a bull, extends Buñuel's anti-aesthetic stance from shot composition to the presentation of the body within the shot. There are parallels to be drawn here between this extreme close-up and similar shots of the impoverished Hurdanos in *Tierra sin pan*. This is more than a mere allusion to Buñuel's earlier film, as Jones (2005: 25) would have it; it forms the basis of a noticeable link between the two films as the boundary between human and animal becomes increasingly blurred throughout the narrative. In terms of *Los olvidados*, animal imagery is pertinent to my exploration of the place-world within the film and I will return to this point in my discussion of the psychological persistence of place within the body. There follows a shot of a smaller boy, known in the script simply as Chamaquito,[12] as he dexterously scales a column, monkey-like, in the courtyard before we see Jaibo, newly-escaped from the correctional facility, as he swiftly vanishes into the crowd on the street to evade the patrolling police. In the vein of Bourdieu's habitus as a structured and structuring set of dispositions, the gang's corporeal adroitness is both a product of their disadvantaged place-world of Mexico City's slums and a perpetuation of their place within its hierarchy.

A key feature of the children's behaviour in the film is hurried motion. The boys' rapid movement suggests their agility and intimate knowledge of their place-world, and is indicative of the youths' body techniques and how these are used to their advantage in place. More so than in other of the director's films in this period, especially those in urban settings such as *El Bruto* or *La ilusión viaja en tranvía*, the characters' actions unfold at an often frantic pace. We can think of the mid-distance shot of Pedro, Jaibo and Pelón sprinting back towards the marketplace after they have savagely beaten the blind beggar Don Carmelo, the high-angle shot of Pedro running away from home after stealing his mother's bread and meat, or Jaibo's flight from the police officers that leads them to shoot him at the end of the film. For the disenfranchised boys of *Los olvidados*, hurried motion is part of their criminal world and crime is an artisan practice. After their unsuccessful attempt to steal Don Carmelo's bag as he sings in the marketplace, the boys' adroit criminality is evident in one striking scene in which the teenagers accost a legless man wheeling himself along in a trolley, stealing his wallet and jacket before lifting him out of his vehicle and kicking it down the street. The cinematography in this sequence demonstrates the actualisation of the boys' habitus of criminality within their environment at the same as it augments the viciousness of the attack. The establishing shot tracks the disabled man as he pushes himself along the pavement, before this cuts to a high-angle depicting the gang as they emerge from outside of the frame. After the man refuses to give the boys his cigarettes, the camera remains at an objective distance, documenting the youths in their co-ordinated display of artisan criminality. Stealing his jacket and cigarettes, they leave the amputee powerless on the pavement before running out of the frame in various directions. Their familiarity with criminality simultaneously reflects their position within the micro-structure of the slums and their own role in perpetuating this structure. Habitus, as Bourdieu indicates, is '*lex insita*, laid down in each agent by his earliest upbringing, which is the precondition not only for the co-ordination of practices but also for the practices of co-ordination' (1977: 81). In a similar vein, Javier Vargas writes that the film's exterior locations – the marketplace, the square, the avenue – represent 'the violent motherland that feeds with a cruel condescension the fortuitous union of intentions that the adolescents *practice*' (2003: 95, my emphasis.).[13] As evidenced in the gang's assault on the legless man and underscoring the narrative more generally, a practice shown to be firmly entrenched in the youths' habitus, which is cruelly encouraged by the State that fails them, is the denigration of the body.

'Broken body-broken city'

Here, I am thinking primarily of the disabled/disintegrated body and the ways in which Buñuel's examples of these bodies are positioned within the place-world of the slums. Tuñón highlights Buñuel's focus in his cinema on what she terms the 'broken body',[14] evident already in the infamous eye-slitting close-up three minutes in to *Un Chien andalou*. For Tuñón, the pattern is duplicated at the start of *Los olvidados* with the medium close-up of the toothless grimace of the boy pretending to be the bull (2003: 78). It should come as no surprise that corporeal perfection is untenable within the slums, but Buñuel shows us that corporeal integrity is similarly unlikely: Don Carmelo is blind; the unknown man in the wooden trolley is legless; the mother of Meche and Cacarizo is permanently prostrate in agony.[15] Even the bodies of the street children themselves are fragmented cinematographically: ironically, in the scene where the gang accost the legless man, Jaibo's legs are introduced into the frame as the amputee wheels into him; Marta and Meche are similarly cut off at the waist in two separate scenes as the camera focuses on their bare legs as they wash; Julián's lifeless legs protruding from behind a bush communicate to the viewer his death as Jaibo clubs him with a branch; Pedro is cut off at the shoulders as he peers under the bed to be met by the bleeding body of Julián in the dream sequence. Bikandi-Mejias (2000: 24) notes that this kind of somatic dismemberment via the lens is common in Buñuel's cinema, and is an example of the grotesque mode, itself part of the carnivalesque tradition. This observation is especially relevant to *Viridiana*, with its gargantuan pastiche of da Vinci's *The Last Supper*, though Bikandi-Mejias is certainly not incorrect when he points out the links that this dismemberment of the body has with the modernist art tradition of the collage (2000: 24).

Tuñón suggests that the broken body has its counterpart in the broken city. For her, the two are inextricably linked, as 'the city that Buñuel presents seems more like a broken city, disintegrated, sick and weeping, like the bodies of various characters in the film' (2003: 80).[16] We can therefore glean a symbiotic relationship between the place-world and its inhabitants predicated on the inescapable presence of the spatial and corporeal Other. The visibility of the deformed-disabled-disenfranchised body in the protagonists' place-world is augmented by the ubiquitous yet disintegrated nature of that place-world itself. Discrete locations such as the marketplace, the domineering skeleton of the social security hospital under construction and Cacarizo and Meche's family's stable, surface repeatedly as 'snapshots' of this place-world and its various appendages. Indeed, the editing of the film, passing back and forth between discrete and fragmented – though familiar – locations, is reminiscent of the collage technique that Bikandi-Mejias writes about. On both occasions that Pedro is outside of the slums – the sequence in the upmarket district of the city in which he is approached by a paedophile, reminiscent of the scene in the bicycle market in Vittorio De Sica's *Ladri di biciclette* (1948), and the scenes that take place in the farm school he is sent to after being falsely convicted of stealing a knife from his boss during his apprenticeship in a blacksmith's shop – his presence seems incongruous, and he will ultimately return to his place.

The abject and the idiolocal

In considering the ways in which the abject manifests itself within Pedro's place-world, I am shifting my focus from habitus and the body to idiolocalism and the self. Idiolocalism is based on reciprocity; that is, how the self is marked by the places it has been in, and the ways in which the self sets out to meet places (Casey 2001a: 688).[17] The abject, as theorised by Julia Kristeva, is rooted in Freudian and Lacanian psychoanalysis and implies a dissolution of corporeal and psychological boundaries. The experience of abjection, for Kristeva, is a necessary primer of human culture, bound up in part with the feeling of revulsion in order to protect us from that which threatens us. Faeces and the human corpse are the prime examples of the abject due to their rupturing of somatic and psychological boundaries:

> These bodily fluids, this defilement, this shit are what life withstands, hardly and with difficulty, on the part of death. There, I am at the border of my condition as a living being. My body extricates itself, as being alive, from that border. Such waste drops so that I might live, until, from loss to loss, nothing remains in me and my entire body falls beyond the limit – *cadere*, cadaver. (Kristeva 1982: 3)

Kristeva's recourse to Lacanian psychoanalysis, in particular the induction of the infant into the world of the symbolic as it begins to learn language, and its distancing from the maternal via the father, suggests that the female – and more accurately/acutely – maternal body is inherently abject. Although abjection is a defence mechanism to protect us from threats to our sense of self, importantly, Kristeva makes clear that there is pleasure [*jouissance*] within the abject, an ecstasy which derives from our loss of self in a pre-Oedipal state and to which we must not submit (1982: 9).

The abject in *Los olvidados* is communicated primarily through the maternal body, that of Pedro's mother, Marta. However, it is also discernible on a spatial level, and forms part of the street-boys' place-world. Evans has convincingly argued that Freud's notion of the uncanny is palpable in this film. This feeling of uneasy familiarity, manifests itself in the spatial as well as the corporeal, arising 'from the projection of unconscious fears and desires onto one's surroundings and the people with whom one comes into contact' (1995: 81). Likewise, Casey stresses that the feeling of alienation we may experience in place is a psychosomatic symptom of displacement and that, at the heart of our implacement, there is always the threat of the *unheimlich* – literally, the unhomely (2009: 34). I would argue that the abject is also present, permeating the matrix of self and place through idiolocalism. For Kristeva, the abject is 'essentially different from "uncanniness," more violent, too', due to the fact that 'abjection is elaborated through a failure to recognize its kin; nothing is familiar, not even the shadow of a memory' (1982: 5). Besides the allusion to the uncanny nature of dwelling, Casey makes no reference to the abject within the place-world, yet it is pertinent when we consider David Sibley's comments on exclusion and the Other. Sibley is concerned with the socio-spatial exclusionary practices of cultural hegemony against the Other – gypsies, the poor, racial minorities – and he proposes that, to understand these practices of exclusion, it is important to understand abjection (1995: 11). The social, spatial and economic divide between affluent suburbs and poor inner-city slums is an example of strongly classified spatial units. According to Sibley, clearly delineated boundaries are used to minimise the threat of contagion or pollution – literal as in disease or figurative as in a threat to the power structure – and strong classification serves to reinforce the process of abjection (1995: 80-1). Kristeva suggests that the condition of the abject resides in the spatial:

> The one by whom the abject exists is thus a *deject* who places (himself), *separates* (himself), situates (himself), and therefore *strays* [...]. Instead of sounding himself as to his 'being', he does so concerning his place: '*Where* am I?' instead of '*Who* am I?' (1982: 8)

The slums Buñuel depicts in *Los olvidados* are a clearly characterised by the abject, as they are by Pedro's search for identity, and the two come together in Pedro's nightmare.

As an exploration of the fantastic within a predominantly realist narrative, critics have often used Pedro's dream as a springboard for a discussion of Buñuel's depiction of Freudian iconography. Like Evans, I consider the *mise-en-scène* here key to any psychoanalytical reading of the film, and Evans's is a particularly sharp reading. The focus, as he rightly identifies, is on the feminine (Marta). Indeed, he acknowledges the links that Pedro's mother has to the abject. In the dream, Marta appears as 'the monstrous-feminine [...] castrator and not, following classic Freudian theory, as castrated, as dreaded agent, as victim of mutilation' (1995: 85). One aspect of *mise-en-scène* that Evans touches on is perhaps the most obvious: the domestic setting. Pedro's dwelling provides neither rest nor emotional or physical sustenance. Here, it acts as the arena in which the dangers of the outside world are played out; thus, Julián is subjected to another agonising death under Pedro's bed while Jaibo, in stealing the chunk of meat offered by Marta, usurps the affection that Pedro craves and reinforces the prophetic bond between the pair. The ramshackle abode is foreboding in its familiarity, a feeling that disquiets the viewer who has seen it before, though not quite as dark as it is now. Neither has the viewer seen Marta as she now appears: the abject mother, seductive and repulsive.

We could suggest a corollary between Marta's body and the city here. Victoria Rivera-Cordero argues that in *Los olvidados*, the parallels between the motherland and the mother are clear: both fail their children (2006: 315). Buñuel's film is also nourished by historico-mythical Mexican archetypes of the treacherous female – La Malinche – the indigenous Nahua translator for the conquistador Hernán Cortés who became his lover and mother of his son.[18] As Casey clarifies, 'idiolocality invokes the subject who incorporates and expresses a particular place' (2001a: 688-89). The body of the mother becomes idiolocalised in Pedro's imagination – that is, Marta becomes a cipher for her son's place-world, expressing the *idios* not only of the slum but of the nation. Through the figure of Marta in the dream, the tenacity of place for Pedro is revealed. To this end, Vargas's view that 'the violent motherland [...] feeds with a cruel condescension the fortuitous union of intentions that the adolescents *practice*' (2003: 95) obtains special significance. As mentioned, numerous Buñuel scholars have referred to Paz's *Labyrinth of Solitude* to underscore Marta's relationship to the Mexican paradigm of La Malinche. By positioning the character of Pedro's mother within a national narrative of female

Figure 9: Feeding the
violent habits.
(Ultramar Films)

betrayal, the violence of the patriarchal nation is implicitly feminised: through the figure of Marta, the *idios* of 'the violent motherland' is expressed, and her disdainful attitude towards her son encourages Pedro's delinquent acts. Furthermore, Vargas's use of the verb 'feeds' is conspicuous: the culinary metaphor resonates with Kristeva's discussion of food-stuffs as abject – a point I come to now – as well as recalling the chunk of gristle that Marta offers her son in his dream. Blood as a visual trope is key here: the bloody flesh symbolises the giving of life between mother and child (snatched by Jaibo) at the same time as it points to Jaibo's murder of Julián as he reappears, bleeding under the bed (see Figure 9).

Casey explains what he terms the 'incoming' aspect of idiolocality, whereby the self bears the traces of the places it has been (2001a: 688). This psychologically-rich resonance of the place-world is important here. In the dream sequence, Marta is the incoming, exiling, castrating, abject mother who horrifies her son not with her lack, but with her abundance. The bloody slab of flesh that she offers her son could be read, as Evans (1995: 86) says, as her torn vagina, an instance of oral pleasure and loss of self, given that 'food is the oral object (the abject) that sets up archaic relations between the human being and the other, its mother' (Kristeva 1982: 75-76). This torn vagina, essentially formless and without border, as is the abject, is the symbol of a perverse gestation-generation that has its links with the nascent modernisation of the protagonists' place-world. The recurring example of this supposed modernisation is the uncanny iron skeleton of the unfinished social security hospital that forms the backdrop to several key scenes of violence within the film, most notably Jaibo's murder of Julián and the gang's assault on Don Carmelo.

The unfinished hospital should stand as an example of modern Mexican infra-structure under President Alemán's modernisation project, yet it, like the vagina, remains formless and abject, bound up with criminality and murder. For Pedro, this is a specific place within his environment that has indelibly marked his self through trauma. Casey (2001a: 688) explains that trauma experienced in a particular place engraves that place in our psyche. Pedro wishes to stay with Marta – the familiar/familial – but he cannot, and is condemned to a life beset by abjection, in a state of exile, looking for his place, rather than his self. His search for his mother, in this sense, is re-enacted in his movement through the dense place-world of the slum. The viewer, too, is often made to wonder as to Pedro's location: when he awakens in the garbage heap and is hounded by two vagabonds; when he finds work at the shabby fairground; when he is approached by a paedophile in a commercial district; and when his corpse is tossed into the rubbish dump at the film's climax. He is, to quote Kristeva, an exile asking himself 'where?'. Furthermore, the film's ending is Pedro's irrevocable transformation into the abject. The image of his corpse rolling down the hill into the garbage heap, itself an abject space, indicates that Pedro has ultimately been subsumed by his place-world, forever taken over by the abject.

Finally, that the suburb is filled with animals is relevant, both in terms of the abject and the idiolocality of place. Animals link the inhabitants of the slums: Pedro's mother breeds chickens; Meche and Cacarizo's family have a makeshift stable filled with chickens, goats and donkeys; Pedro and Ojitos are followed by a pack of stray dogs in the marketplace at night; the double exposure technique used during Jaibo's death throes superimposes the image of a mangy canine. Besides the pertinent symbolic link between humans and their animal counterparts in the film, animals are also metaphors for the traumatic effects of place on the characters. The cockerel that bears witness to the boys' savage beating of Don Carmelo in front of the imposing frame of the unfinished hospital has its parallel in the dog in the frame in the high-angle shot of Jaibo and Pedro speaking to Julián on his worksite prior to the latter's murder which, in turn, has its parallel in the donkey in the stable where Jaibo kills Pedro. In short, the trauma of the slums is animalistic. Where the *idios* of place comes tenaciously into the body, Casey speaks of an *impressionism* of place, whereby 'this presence is held within the body in a virtual state, ready to regain explicit awareness when the appropriate impression or situation arises' (2001b: 415). Thus, in the chicken coup shortly after Pedro's arrival on the farm school for delinquent boys, he clubs a chicken to death in the same fashion as Jaibo beats Julián and Marta beats the cockerel earlier in the film. Although it is

Figure 10: A bestial reproduction of life in the slums. (Ultramar Films)

only shown briefly, Pedro's etching on the wall of the isolation room immediately after this incident further represents this. It depicts one bird clubbing another to death – the impressionism of place represented via the bestial self (see Figure 10). This etching acquires an even deeper significance when we consider that, as Polizzotti notes, the cocky Jaibo is identified in the film script as 'the bully [big rooster] of the group' (2006: 59).[19] The threat of life in the slums is reified for the viewer through the conflation of man and beast, and the *idios* of place therefore evokes the habitus of violence even when Pedro is away. Furthermore, the animalistic is a form of the abject, as Kristeva points out: '[t]he abject confronts us, on the one hand, with those fragile states where man strays on the territories of *animal* (1982: 12). Her use of the word 'territories' is interesting here as the children in the film are not simply shown to be acting on animal impulses; their own *territory* is rendered abject through its connection to the bestial, evident already from the opening scene and the toothless boy's bovine-like mimesis.

Nazarín

An unlikely hero

Octavio Paz commends the artistic vision of *Nazarín*, writing:

> These films [*L'Âge d'or*, *Los olvidados*, *Robinson Crusoe*, *Nazarín*] can be enjoyed, and judged, as works of cinema but also as something belonging to the broader

and more permanent universe of those works, each one of them valuable, that have the aim of both revealing human reality to us and showing us a way to transcend it. (2012: 41)[20]

I share Paz's sentiments regarding the transcendental nature of *Los olvidados* and *Nazarín*, both in relation to their poetic nature as well as their profound humanism, but without subscribing to the dismissive view that the bulk of Buñuel's more commercial Mexican features have little of worth to show us. Edwards posits a degree of similarity between the two films in that they share a straightforward storyline. In terms of the subject matter, however, Edwards affirms that *Nazarín* differs from *Los olvidados* in its more complex, episodic structure. In the latter, perspective is limited as the viewer almost always sees the same group of characters whereas the former is much more 'panoramic', in Edwards's view, representing 'Nazarín's journey along the highway and byways of life' (1982: 135). This can be applied to my spatial reading of the two films. I will continue in the same geographical-philosophical vein to investigate the extent to which Nazarín's habitation is successful. In addition to the question of habitation and how this is given representation in the film, my reading will be informed by another aspect of the place-world suggested by Casey: that of landscape.

The film's opening sequence centres on the squalid tenement block, on the top floor of which Nazarín has taken up lodgings. Ironically, this dilapidated block is named *Mesón de los Héroes* [Lodge of Heroes], a title that parodies its eclectic mix of residents: working-class labourers, groups of children playing in the courtyard and a gang of heavily made-up prostitutes. Although the narrative begins in the city, as a point of contrast with the various locations within the impoverished neighbourhoods of Mexico City in *Los olvidados*, the initial action in *Nazarín*, before the protagonist sets out into the world, is contained almost solely within this housing block. Shortly afterwards, Nazarín calls to señora Chanfa, the hardened landlady of the *Mesón*, as he has been robbed yet again. The interior of his apartment is sparse; in the shooting script it is described as 'bordering on poverty' (Buñuel 1958: 9),[21] a description that even holds back somewhat from the ascetic *mise-en-scène* as shown on screen. The spatial dynamics already at play in the opening sequence are significant: not by chance has Nazarín taken up residence on the upper floor of the building, removed from those around him. The similarities between Buñuel's pair of preachers, Nazarín and Simón, are patent: both are removed, to varying degrees, from the sphere of everyday life, and thus this opening sequence is to be understood in terms of its role as a prefiguration of what is to come as Nazarín sets out on his peripatetic path. Furthermore, in terms of habitation, the film immediately foregoes any connection between character and place, for Nazarín happily leaves behind his place in the city in favour of a life roaming the countryside after the prostitute Ándara has set fire to his room. Nazarín tells his stupefied friend and fellow priest, Don Ángel, that he wishes to accept alms and move to the countryside, 'where I will feel close to God'. Settled dwelling here is not a home as such and place becomes mere location, and it is telling that in their conversation with Father Nazario, the engineers at the beginning of the film who are working to connect the tenement block to the power grid conclude of the priest that he is 'not trying to better [his] position', an insight which invites both a socio-economic and a literal (spatial) interpretation.

The events that unfold in the tenement block communicate the protagonist's detachment on a spatial level but they also reveal more about his detachment from the realities of the body in one scene in particular. Following her brawl with Carmella, another prostitute, Ándara arrives at the priest's quarters in the middle of the night with a grisly flesh wound on her shoulder. The two then begin the first of several theological discussions. Ándara wishes to know if the dead have any realisation of their passing; Nazarín responds, 'your soul knows it, and it's immortal'. Though they will later attempt to emulate Nazarín's way of living, this is the first indication that the viewer gets of the chasm between the priest and his two female followers who, unlike their messiah, exhibit a patent preoccupation with the flesh. Echoing Evans' reading of the bloody chunk of meat in Pedro's dream sequence in *Los olvidados*, Fuentes sees in Ándara's flesh wound a visual marker of her sex (1993: 131). Similarly, his second 'disciple' Beatriz is immediately depicted as obsessed with the carnal through her sporadic convulsions brought on by her vivid, erotic fantasies. During Ándara's fight with Carmella, a close up shot of Beatriz's face, blinking rapidly, signals her first reverie, where she fantasises about her *machista* ex-lover Pinto and bites his lip in a paroxysm of sadomasochistic erotic frenzy until he bleeds. As I will suggest, both Ándara and Beatriz's integral connection to the corporeal serves to anchor them both in a more functional place-world through habitation. This connection is alien to Nazarín.

Nazarín's habitus, conditioned by the spiritual, leads to his disengagement with place, much like Simón. However, unlike Simón, his detachment from his surroundings is made all the more notable given that the protagonist is constantly confronted by place and by people. After Ándara has set fire to his apartment to remove all traces of her stay there, he sets out into the world. During Nazarín's trajectory, the viewer witnesses his brief stint as a manual labourer laying a train line in the countryside, his attempt to cure Beatriz's feverish niece in her home village, his willingness to come to the aid of the moribund members of a plague-ridden town, his arrest on the outskirts of a third town and his humiliating march along with other prisoners back to Mexico City. What is striking here is that, against the ever-changing backdrop to the film, Buñuel's protagonist remains the same. For instance, as Nazarín passes Beatriz in her home village, the latter is astounded that, having left the city, the two have once more crossed paths, proclaiming the serendipitous reunion to be a miracle. Nazarín's deadpan response, 'Why, child? The world is very big', betrays the priest's disengagement with the material plane, of which place is a fundamental aspect, bound up with corporeal awareness. As Joseph Grange writes, '[w]e sense vastness because our body feels its own limits and thereby grasps the "feel" of voluminous space' (1985: 74). It appears that the priest has not grasped the feel of voluminous space, as the world seems for him a plane of unremarkable encounters. To this end, it is also fitting to note Nazarín's repeated use of the term 'road/way': when abandoning the job he has just been given among the labourers laying the train track he excuses himself by saying 'I am on my way'; later, he encourages the dying woman in the plague-infested town to think that life 'is only a road'. In effect, a physical-metaphysical binary pair forms around the idea of the road and the journey, ironically undermined through the protagonist's disengagement with place, and the myriad travelling shots of Nazarín and his female followers are offset by the priest's solely figurative use of the word 'road'.

Nazarín's unsuccessful habitation

Don Willis offers a pertinent analysis of *Nazarín*, shedding light on the social – rather than the spiritual – repercussions of Nazarín's estrangement. For Willis, '[t]he primary polarity in *Nazarin* is not faith/lack of faith or even theism/humanism, but passion/detachment'. Though not inherently concerned with the spatial, Willis's argument is conducive to an exploration of the protagonist's habitus:

> Nazarin is mild, likeable, unprepossessing, and has a slight self-consciousness of movement that seems to come from self-effacement. But his subdued and matter-of-fact manner, although it effectively stifles self-importance or self-righteousness, also unfortunately stifles in him the possibility of spontaneity or responsiveness to others. (1978: 7)

The impossibility of spontaneity of response is ultimately a stumbling block to the protagonist's contemplation of his place-world and his implacement within it. In effect, we can say that Nazarín is defined from *without*. In his discussion of the identity of places and the dialogue between this and our personal experience of place, Relph posits that we can experience place as an existential outsider. By this, he intends 'a self-conscious and reflective uninvolvement, an alienation from people and places, homelessness, a sense of the unreality of the world, and of not belonging'. Relph writes, '[f]rom the outside you look upon a place as a traveller might look upon a town from a distance; from the inside you experience a place, are surrounded by it and part of it' (1976: 51; 49). Fittingly, Relph illustrates the concept of outsideness through the analogy of a traveller approaching a distant town, as Nazarín does several times throughout the film as he flits from village to village. Most telling, though, is the third town, where Nazarín and Ándara are arrested by the local police for the fire in Nazarín's former tenement block. Here, both Ándara and Beatriz are shown to be actively engaged within the town's social fabric: a tracking shot depicts Ándara begging for alms on residents' doorsteps where she meets her admirer, the dwarf Ujo – played by Jesús Fernández, the same actor who appears in *Simón del desierto* as the goatherd – while Beatriz is shown at the communal water fountain, intending to wash the group's dirty clothing when she is accosted by her ex-lover, Pinto. Ándara and Beatriz come into contact with *place* and with *people*; despite their nomadic existence with Nazarín, the two women are seen to be more successful in their habitation of place – they are engaged from within. By contrast, Nazarín is shown to be an existential outsider. He is never shown in the town; he remains among the ruins of a former edifice on a nearby hill, his elevated position negating his active implacement and encouraging his conscious state of existential outsideness.

As opposed to the frenetic movements of the children in *Los olvidados*, Nazarín demonstrates little commitment to physical action. His stint as a railroad labourer is short-lived; he does not protest his arrest, and when he is later locked in a cell with other prisoners, he does not defend himself against the brutish criminal accused of parricide. He simply cannot be seen to *hold* place through his docile body, which suggests a disjuncture between the protagonist and the various locations of the narrative. Explaining the changing nature of the place-world – as is the case in *Nazarín* as the group moves from town to town – Casey says that, as we journey through this, 'we live out our bodily habitudes in relation to the ever-changing spatiality of the scenes we successively encounter' (2001a: 687).

Nazarín's failure to demonstrate the required bodily habitudes indicates his disengagement with situation, a term I use to encompass both location and the action that takes place there. The sequence in which the priest agrees to work as a casual labourer on the construction of the railway line is paradigmatic here. As the other, indignant workers warn the protagonist that he has taken the place of several unemployed men, he makes to leave. Continuing his journey, he stops briefly twice – once after the man overseeing the workers pelts him with a stone and again to pluck a leaf from an olive tree. In his apparently contrived appreciation of nature, Nazarín is shown to be irrevocably distanced from materiality and the consequences of his actions: as he stops to admire the tree, gunshots ring out off-screen, a result of the escalating tension between the boss and the workers caused by Nazarín's hasty departure. Willis encapsulates this reading of the film: '[t]o Nazarin "nature" means "God"; but "nature", in the film's context, means "detachment"' (1978: 6).

'A nondescript landscape': the banal landscape

Given that the camerawork in *Nazarín* largely avoids showing the open vistas of the Mexican countryside, here the term landscape must be considered independently of the romantic connotations it has come to acquire.[22] Rather than thinking of landscape as simply a cluster of topographical features within the visual field of the observer, for Casey landscape provides an opportunity for the expansion of the geographical self. His argument is that '[t]he empty armature of place-cum-self needs to be fleshed out, in two opposed but complementary directions: downward into body and outward into landscape' (2001a: 689). Landscape, then, is a derivative of place, gathering and giving unity to distinct yet contiguous places, and its function within the place-world is primarily one of demarcation, a necessary component of implacement through the borders that this brings with it:

> In my embodied being I am *just at* a place as its inner boundary; a surrounding landscape, on the other hand, is *just beyond* that place as its outer boundary. Between the two boundaries – and very much as a function of their differential interplay – implacement occurs. Place is what takes place between body and landscape. Thanks to the double horizon that body and landscape provide, a place is a locale bounded on both sides, near and far. (Casey 2009: 29)

What is striking in terms of *Nazarín*, however, is that Casey's model is not seen to function as expected, and I would argue that this appears to be due to deliberate choices on Buñuel's part.

The film's shooting script is revealing of these choices. After Nazarín has left his home in the city following the fire started there by Ándara, he first approaches the band of workers constructing the railway. A reverse tracking shot reveals Nazarín, who has seemingly appeared from nowhere, as the employer of the labourers walks towards him. In the mid-distance, primitive pylons stretch away across parched earth towards rolling hills. The script tells us the setting of this scene is simply 'a broken landscape' (Buñuel 1958: 42) and the aesthetic denotations of this direction suggest on a deeper level that the protagonist's implacement here is destined to fail as the landscape itself is ruptured and broken.[23] Later, Nazarín comes across a colonel and his wife travelling along with a priest. Their horse has broken its leg and Nazarín offers to help the party. The establishing shot here is not of Nazarín framed against a backdrop of prairies and hills – though the viewer does catch a brief glimpse of this – but of the horse's head as the creature lies in the road. Indeed, given that the setting for this scene is described as 'an ordinary landscape' (Buñuel 1958: 55),[24] any aesthetic appreciation on the viewer's part should be incidental and transient. Likewise, when the trio approaches the plague-riddled village, the establishing shot is one of disease and death, showing a young victim perishing from his illness on the path leading to the village while other residents flee. Landscape is again secondary: to narrative, as the audience is encouraged to focus attention on the cause of the exodus and not on the 'ordinary road' (Buñuel 1958: 61);[25] and apparently to Nazarín himself as he is initially shown approaching the village in the same aloof manner to which the viewer has become accustomed.

This intentional invisibility of landscape through its banalisation colludes with the protagonist's neglect of his bodily realities to impede his implacement. Implacement occurs, as Casey has noted, in the arc between the body and its surrounding landscape. The border to the changing place-world is contained in landscape. The effect of Buñuel's emphasis on a prosaic *mise-en-scène* is the dissociation of Nazarín from his environment. Furthermore, that the body is always located somewhere does not necessarily signify that the body is always securely in place. Nazarín is distanced from his corporeality; his body is therefore never fully in place. Unlike in *Los olvidados*, where the emphasis on corporeality and the claustrophobic nature of the children's surroundings culminates in the representation of a dense, portending place-world, if we can indeed talk about an arc between body and landscape in

Nazarín, this is quickly undone at both ends as the priest's bodily awareness and, therefore, spatial awareness, appear of little concern.

The sick body

Nazarín subordinates of the realities of the body to his belief in the soul and this has implications for his engagement with place. As he exchanges the confines of his tenement block for the open countryside, the priest is seen to redouble his efforts to focus his attention on the metaphysical. The principle way that this is shown visually is through food.[26] Several times throughout the film, the characters are seen to eat and drink. Though their meals are modest, the act of eating is given purposeful representation. Early in the film, Nazarín is seen to eat a plate of tortillas prepared for him by señora Chanfa, the landlady of the lodge, 'with great appetite', while a little later, still in his apartment after agreeing to shelter Ándara, he is shown 'savouring the last mouthful' of another meal (Buñuel 1958: 15; 29).[27] This is last time that the spectator witnesses Nazarín eating, yet during their amblings, Ándara is seen to eat with gusto a warmed taco and to drink from a water jug in the police station after she and Nazarín have been arrested. Even before the group has abandoned the city, she and Beatriz are shown enjoying a serving of *pulque* shortly before Ándara, ensconced in the priest's apartment, nursing her stab wound, uses a bottle of tequila 'for the wounds on the inside and the outside', and is then seen to drink from the bowl of bloodied water used to bathe her wounds to slake her alcohol-induced thirst. For Nazarín, though, the act of eating becomes conspicuous through its absence during his wanderings, confirming the importance that he places on succour as opposed to sustenance. As I will show, this position appears reversed in the film's conclusion.

The need for material sustenance signals a healthy body, and Ándara and Beatriz are in tune with their corporeal needs. However, in contrast to those of the protagonists, there is a phalanx of unhealthy bodies in this film. If disabled and disfigured bodies populate the slums of *Los olvidados*, in *Nazarín* there are diseased and dying bodies. The sequence in the plague-ridden village is crucial here. The plague is a virulent strain in Buñuel's cinema, marked not only by the ailing body, but the dysfunctional one, too. Nowhere in Buñuel's cinema is this more evident than in the languid stupor and descent into madness of the Nóbiles and their dinner guests in *El ángel exterminador*. Interestingly, actress Silvia Pinal remarked of this film: 'we all came to the conclusion that it was a plague [caused by] our faults, our aggression [...] that doesn't let us move or progress'.[28] Most of the attention given to Buñuel's depiction of pestilence in *Nazarín* has focused on the dialogue as the Father Nazario attempts to administer the last rites to Lucía, the dying woman, and the ways in which her insistence on the carnal comforts of her lover, Juan, are at odds with Nazarín's vision of religious transcendence.[29] This episode, beyond the traditional physical/metaphysical binary through which it has frequently been viewed, can be read in light of the sick body to further show Nazarín's disengagement with place.

The plague sequence begins with a long shot of an 'ordinary road' that leads to the damned village as the residents flee. The trio is then confronted with a dying man on the road. Faulkner's (2004: 145) comment that Ándara and Beatriz are representative of the body rather than the spirit is pertinent here, for both women approach the village and the man with caution, conscious of their own mortality. Nazarín, however, is quick to come to the man's aid. Eamonn Rodgers believes that his manner contains a masochistic streak:

> Though in practice he has to cope with situations where he is called upon to show concern for others, engagement with what lies outside himself is seen essentially as a masochistic search for sufferings and trials which will test his self-discipline. (1995: 52)

Nazarín's perverted self-interest suggests his engagement with the sick body is essentially hollow: the ambiguity contained within the infirm and the afflicted, between life and death, enables him to focus his attention on the souls of the dying and, through a masochistic and narcissistic process, his own. Seen another way, the threat of degenerative illness to the body is re-envisaged through the priest's habitus as a generative force for the spirit. Such is the protagonist's visible sense of satisfaction during this episode that he is described in the script as 'a different man. It could be said that this is *his environment* and he takes pleasure in it' (Buñuel, 1958: 65, my emphasis).[30] That Buñuel specifies Nazarín's enjoyment here is interesting: ethically, Ándara's enjoyment of food and tequila and Beatriz's daydreams of carnal pleasure are ultimately no more shameful than Nazarín's masochistic revelling in disease. Indeed, when coupled with Faulkner's view that the two women stand for the body to Nazarín's spirit, and Willis's view that Nazarín's displays of emotion are predominately 'mechanical' (1978: 6), the two women could be said to exhibit a greater morality – certainly within the Buñuelian narrative – in that they embrace their carnal condition.

Trigg explains that, in illness, our relationship to the places that we inhabit is mediated through that illness:

Figure 11: Disorientating, disembodying illness. (Producciones Barbachano Ponce)

the whole world is mediated through the ill body, so that place and time assume a highly singular appearance that conforms to the strains of the human body. In such a case, […] the intimacy between self and world, so far assumed as a taken-for-granted given of the life-world, is experienced as a self-conscious lack. (2012: 114)

In this way, the tacit engagement between place and self is undermined by our ill body and we feel estranged from both. The estrangement brought on by infection is communicated visually in this episode. One of the most remarkable shots of the film occurs at this moment: a child is seen stumbling along a side-road, dragging behind her a bed sheet. The frame acts here not as a stable reference point, but rather as a destabilising one as the child almost wanders out of its left edge and the reverse tracking shot reveals more linen hung out to dry, momentarily obscuring the lower right-hand part of the shot (see Figure 11). This shot 'contains all the desolation of the disease; its effect, the way it empties the world, rather than its showy, baroque horrors. The sheet is all the girl has left of her home' (Wood 1993: 47). In his zeal to come to the aid of the plague victims, Nazarín aligns himself with diseased and defunct bodies. After entering the village and consulting with the mayor, the trio is shown going into a house to comfort a crying infant. The body of the child's recently deceased mother is quickly covered by the priest with a sheet, leaving only the feet visible (a shot reminiscent of Evvie's dead grandfather's feet protruding from under the blanket in *The Young One*) and it is not coincidental that Nazarín charges Ándara and Beatriz with the infant's care while he focuses his attention on the dead mother.

Following a brief scene in which Juan, the lover of the dying woman, Lucía, tells the town's mayor that government help to deal with the crisis is arriving, Buñuel cuts to a disorientating shot of Beatriz, from the shoulders down, as she washes a cloth in a bowl of water in Lucía's house. Once again, the protagonist's thoughts are of the hereafter and he advises Lucía: 'think that this life is only a road'. The exchange between the two as the dying woman refuses the last rites and calls out for the carnal comfort of her lover is well documented. Willis finds that 'carnality is *new* to Nazarín', and that the protagonist is compelled to confront 'an order – personal, sexual – unknown to him' (1978: 6). The clash of one order against another – one habitus against another – is never more jarring in Buñuel's cinema. The protagonist does not belong, either in this place or to this order: when Juan returns, Nazarín and Beatriz are thrown out of the residence. Willis perceptively remarks that 'Nazarín's neutrality in physical affairs leaves him in effect *bodiless*' (1978: 6) an assertion which renders his later sermon to the two women on the bittersweet nature of death – 'Death is like that: happy and sad. Happy because it frees us from life's chains and sad because we love our flesh' – an empty platitude. To be rendered effectively bodiless is to be rendered without place:

> If there are experiences in which my body does not figure, then these experiences will lack a here [...]. Hence herelessness inheres in certain intellectual and mystical experiences in which we rejoin a conceptual or religious 'there,' an 'on the other side' [...] that has no proper here. (Casey 2009: 51)

Crucially, Nazarín remains alone in his detachment from both body and place. Responding to Nazarín's lamentation that he has failed Lucía after her lover returns and they are thrown out of the house, Beatriz exclaims, 'I wanted that, too', referring to the corporeal comfort that Juan can give his partner, rather than a desire that Nazarín should deliver Lucía's soul to the religious 'there', as Casey would have it. Realising Beatriz's engagement with the material aspects of the body – and therefore habitation – Nazarín leaves 'doubly defeated' (Buñuel 1958: 69).[31]

A return to place?: The film's ending

The orthodox reading of the film's ending is predicated on a religious-humanist binary. Encapsulating this view, Edwards concludes that '[f]rom the ashes of spiritual disillusionment, Nazarín is finally born again into the world, the priest rejected for the man' (1982: 134). Though his reading of the film's conclusion reveals a similar ingredience of religious pride, for Rubinstein there is no binary. He concludes that Nazarín, aware now of his unjustified pride, becomes a Christian through his new-found humility (1978: 240). My reading moves beyond the two in its central focus on what has frequently been invoked as a mere by-product of the protagonist's secular/religious epiphany: place. Both Edwards and Rubinstein refer to this aspect of the film – for Edwards Nazarín is born again into the world, while for Rubinstein the landscape in the film's conclusion is that of the Gospels – and it is instrumental in the viewer's understanding of the ending.

Following his and Ándara's arrest for the tenement block fire as they are camped on the hill above the third town they have visited, Nazarín is condemned to join a gang of prisoners frogmarched through a series of villages on their way back to the capital to be jailed. Locked in a cell and beaten by a man accused of parricide, he speaks with another prisoner who says: 'you on the good side and me on the bad side. Neither of us are much good at all.' This is the protagonist's first epiphany, as the viewer witnesses a close-up shot of the priest's face, lined now with contemplative realisation. Willis writes that 'Buñuel, who took his hero out of the film a few scenes earlier, now restores him to it, with an altered perspective' (1978: 7). Although I have argued that Buñuel encourages a schism between the priest and his place-world from the first moments of the film, rather than merely a few scenes previously as Willis claims, this contemplative realisation is one of purpose and place: to be taken out of the film and then returned to it, is to begin to be re(im) placed. This process will happen again at the very end of the film. When offered a pineapple by a roadside fruit seller while he is being marched through the countryside, Nazarín at first refuses the act of charity then tearfully returns to accept it. Fuentes has commented on the way in which the film's cinematography works to communicate the idea of imprisonment in these final sequences:

> In Nazarín's walking through desolate landscapes (followed by multiple shots in many of which the camera, at ground level, focuses on the prisoners' feet) there is a circular movement: the retracing of the paths that he set out on 'to be closer to God', only to find himself biting the dust, surrounded by reprobates. (1993: 134)[32]

Besides communicating a sense of confinement, the close-up shots of the prisoners' feet as they walk are representative of the connection between the body and the earth. The protagonist's body, previously denied, now begins to come to the fore. The bandage on his head is not an emulation of Christ's crown of thorns, but a visual reminder of the priest's own flesh after being attacked in the jail cell; where food and drink were previously rejected, the pineapple he accepts is an acceptance

Figure 12: Nazarín accepts his body and its place in the world. (Producciones Barbachano Ponce)

of his corporeal urgencies (see Figure 12). Also, Nazarín is affected by this gesture of kindness, shown to be weeping as he eventually walks out of the frame as the film ends. To be affected by a gesture is to be seen as being 'here' in every sense of the word, as '[p]art of the absoluteness of the here is that I cannot detach it from my body-self and thus from the place to which this body-self now gives access' (Casey 2009: 52). Whether the ending represents Nazarín's embrace of his fellow (wo)man or his renewed sense of Christian humility is debatable. Either interpretation, however, would necessitate a reciprocal relationship between self and place: the schism between the ethereal priest and his place-world has begun to diminish. In accepting his own flesh, integral to his self, Nazarín has started to move towards a primitive habitation. Edwards sums up this shift succintly:

> By the end of the film it is not so much a case of contrasting shots reflecting the gap between the world and Nazarín's spirituality but of the gap narrowed progressively to the point where the priest is seen to be aware of his own worldliness. (1982: 136-7)

Conclusion: placing the body

My approach in this chapter is a departure from that of the previous two, representing a shift from depictions of exterior space towards the complex matrix of the body-self and place. Such an analysis necessitates an exposition of the reciprocal nature of place and body-self; a geographical-philosophical consideration of the place-world allows for this. In borrowing from the disciplines of phenomenology and geography, I have proposed film-focused readings with the aim of illuminating the representation of both self and place. The point I really wish to stress here is that my readings do not necessarily constitute a radical departure from common interpretations of these films, but are instead an inflection of their critical focuses: Evans's discussion of the uncanny within the slums depicted in *Los olvidados* has links to Tuñón's investigation of the symbiosis between the broken body and the broken city; similarly, Edwards's reading of the narrative of *Nazarín* as the hero's physical and spiritual journey into the world chimes with Willis's assertion that at the heart of the narrative is a dichotomy of passion/detachment. A common theme in the often philosophical analyses of these films, then, is place – an aspect of the films which, building on previous readings that have paid less attention to this, I have brought to the fore.

Unlike those of *Nazarín*, the places in which the characters in *Los olvidados* are positioned are frequently cramped and dingy locations, augmenting the viewer's sense of claustrophobia. The *idios* of place is writ large in this film. As I have shown, the attention that Evans draws to the Mexican national narrative of La Malinche within the film, embodied by Marta, is an expression of idiolocalism. Casey explains the power that place exerts over people as an emulsifier of entities, with the potential to determine interpersonal relationships as place comes lastingly, or fleetingly, into the self. In this way, the 'how' and 'why' are intrinsically linked to the 'where'. The idiolocal, therefore, 'is not merely idiosyncratic or individual; it is also collective in character' (Casey 2009: 23). Marta thus represents the historical-mythical figure of the consuming, rejecting, abject Malinche and her inscription in place. The street children's body techniques are generated by, and necessary to, their place-world of the slums as they interact with the discrete locations in their immediate surroundings.

Where the urchins of *Los olvidados* are shown to be immersed in their surroundings through Buñuel's foregrounding of the body in this film, Nazarín repudiates his connection to his surroundings by denying his. Throughout the narrative he is aligned with the infirm and the dead body, praying for Beatriz's sick niece and tending to the victims ravaged by plague. The dislocation of the protagonist from the needs of the body and the requirements of place is made all the more apparent by the constant presence of his female disciples, both of whom appear more in tune with their bodily needs. Beatriz's preoccupation with the carnal leads to her hysterical outburst when her mother suggests that she loves Nazarín not because he is a priest, but because he is a man, while Ándara's occupation as a prostitute is reinforced as her sweetheart Ujo proclaims: 'I don't care if you're a whore, I want you to be with me.' The women's grounding in the physical is not a comment on their gender, however, as their male counterparts Ujo and Pinto are also shown to be so. In contrast, Nazarín's love for the women is indistinguishable from his general sentiment towards the world, as when he explains that he loves them equally while gazing absently at the snail on his hand, before exiting the frame and leaving the two women to bed down alone as the trio are camped outside one of the nondescript villages. Nazarín therefore remains isolated from those around him in a position of constant existential outsideness, a position that becomes more apparent when the film script is taken into consideration. Unlike the script of *Los olvidados*, with its frequent references to specific locations such the stable belonging to Meche's family and Pedro's house, that of *Nazarín* works to preclude any such affinity between the protagonist and the places – often qualified simply as 'ordinary places' – in which he is shown. The ending of the film, however, suggests the protagonist's will to return to the world through the acknowledgement of his body.

The difference in the way that the respective films depict the characters' relationship to their immediate surroundings goes beyond questions of *mise-en-scène*. Pedro remains affected by the idiolocal, abject character of the slums even while at the farm school, and Nazarín remains aloof from himself and his contemporaries in his own squalid apartment. It is not, therefore, as straightforward a question as one of setting, of the affectivity of the urban versus that of the rural, as I signalled at the start of this chapter. Edwards understands this, writing that '*Nazarín* differs from *Los olvidados*, for there the same characters reappear throughout the film. Its focus is, therefore, limited, while the effect of *Nazarín* is much more panoramic' (1982: 135). If we take the depiction of the character-place matrix to be the unspoken subject of Edwards' observations here, his argument speaks to the one I have developed in this chapter. There are ultimately many similarities between the two films. For their thematic and stylistic differences, they are profoundly philosophical pieces of work. Their narratives both explore the connection between self and place through the use of the body, an immediate visual object for the viewer. As such, the story of both films can be read as a search for belonging, a concept that requires the collusion of self and place. This search for belonging can be explored more concretely via the various home-places that are represented in Buñuel's films of this period, and this will be my focus in the following chapter.

Notes

1   For a discussion of the broad similarities and contrasting elements between *Los olvidados* and the Italian neorealist genre, see Jones (2005: 18-31).

2   Faber also finds flaws in a naturalist reading of the film, due to its tendency to assimilate the causes of social issues into a medical discourse. I would agree, given the vitriolic reactions by Buñuel's bourgeois Mexican acquaintances to the film, suggesting the difficulty on the observer's part of retaining a clinical, impartial distance from the world on screen.

3   [Era, y continúa siendo, necesario que el cine reflejase con toda la crudeza posible la miseria de un mundo, como único y desesperado modo de conseguir que de ese mundo desaparezca la miseria, o al menos como única manera de no justificarla y bendecirla].

4   For a detailed comparison of Galdós's novel and Buñuel's film, see Sinnigen (2008: 190-245).

5   The film was not embraced by every institution influenced by Catholicism. Producer Manuel Barbáchano Ponce's application to shoot the film in Spain invited an excoriating response. The Francoist censors' verdict, in the Buñuel archive of the Filmoteca Española, reads: 'this film cannot be approved [for filming], not even in Mexico. It has a demonstrative crudeness, a narrative audacity that is negative from any point of view'. [no puede aprobarse esta película, ni aun localizándola en Méjico. Tiene una crudeza expresiva, un desenfado narrativo que resulta negativa desde todos los puntos de vista] (*Nazarín* [material de tesis]. 1958. Madrid, Filmoteca Española, Archivo Rosa Añover (AÑO/01/08).).

6   In an interview with the Mexican newspaper *Novedades* in 1950, Buñuel states that his motivation for making *Los olvidados* was a 'strand or genre that I had been developing since I made "Tierra sin pan"'. [línea o género que venía cultivando desde que hice "Tierra sin Pan"] (Peña Ardid and Lahuerta Guillén 2007: 559). Numerous Mexican and European press cuttings related to the film are meticulously collated in Peña Ardid and Lahuerta Guillén's volume. See especially pp. 466-633.

7   For Mark Polizzotti, *Los olvidados* would not have been possible without *Tierra sin pan*. In his view, '[w]hat *Land without Bread* and *Los Olvidados* share more than anything [...] is a tone, both visual and moral. It is our sense of shock they mean to provoke, rather than our sense of humour; it is our complacency they seek to undermine' (2006: 18).

8   It should be noted, however, that geographies with 'other' focuses (for example, queer or feminist), actively seek to reposition the 'othered' subject at the centre of spatial discourse. See, for example, Browne, Lim and Brown (2007). This is a strand of work within film studies, too. See, for instance, Wallace (2009) and Macleod (2014).

9   Casey's earlier work on place explains the term 'implacement'. Unlike its virtual homonym emplacement, implacement evokes the immediate placement of the subject and communicates the action of 'getting in or into, and it carries connotations of *imm*anence that are appropriate to the inhabitation of places' (2009: 367, n. 9).

10 [[la] visión ideologizada, triunfalista, del México de la revolución institucionalizada].

11 [un melodrama atípico].

12 A *chamaco* is a colloquial Central American term used to mean a 'kid'. The script is published in Peña Ardid and Lahuerta Guillén, eds. (2007: 77-300).

13 [la patria violenta que alimenta con cruel condescendencia la fortuita unión de voluntades que los adolescentes practican].

14 [cuerpo roto].

15 As a further example of the damaged body, in Mexican Spanish *cacarizo* means 'pockmarked', a reference perhaps to the scars left on the character's face by some unknown illness.

16 [la ciudad que presenta Buñuel más parece una ciudad rota, desintegrada, enferma y supurante, como los cuerpos de varios de los personajes del filme].

17 Casey uses the term 'lived body'. I suggest that the term 'self' indicates a more fairly weighted balance between the somatic and the psychological.

18 Rivera-Cordero's parallel alludes to Octavio Paz's *Labyrinth of Solitude* (1961) and his theorisation of Mexico (Marta) as a Malinche-type figure while Mexicans (Pedro) are sons and daughters of *la Chingada* – the gash created by the verb *chingar* [to fuck] being essentially abject. For more on the intertextual references between *Los olvidados* and Paz's *Labyrinth of Solitude*, see Acevedo-Muñoz (2003: 74) and Faber (2003: 237-8).

19 The original Spanish is *el gallón de la banda*. *Gallón* carries a meaning of bully. However, the etymology renders the meaning ambiguous: *gallo* actually means rooster and the suffix –ón serves to make this larger and more imposing.

20 [Estas películas [*L'Âge d'or, Los olvidados, Robinson Crusoe, Nazarín*] pueden ser gustadas, y juzgadas, como cine pero también como algo perteneciente al

universo más ancho y permanente de esas obras, preciosas entre todas, que tienen por objeto tanto revelarnos la realidad humana cuanto mostrarnos una vía para sobrepasarla].

21 [rayando en la miseria]. I use the term shooting script to refer to the version used during filming. There are other versions of this script, as Martínez Herranz (2011) details.

22 On Buñuel's fixation on the mundane in this film and Figueroa's role as director of cinematography, see Faulkner (2004: 142-3).

23 [un paisaje quebrado].

24 [un paisaje cualquiera].

25 [camino cualquiera].

26 Food is a prominent motif in the Buñuel's cinema. Bikandi-Mejias (2000: 27-8) positions the use of food within a carnivalesque trope due to the focus that this brings to the body's orifices. With specific reference to *Nazarín*, Rubinstein submits that '[i]n its perverse attentions to food, *Nazarín* stands second only to *The Discreet Charm* in the Buñuel canon' (1978: 241).

27 [con gran apetito]; [mascando el último bocado].

28 [todos llegamos a una conclusión de que era una peste [causada por] nuestras fallas, nuestras agresiones […] que no nos deja movernos ni progresar]. 'Interview with Silvia Pinal', *El ángel exterminador*, dir. Luis Buñuel (Criterion, 2008) (on DVD) disc 2.

29 On this theme, see Fuentes (1993: 134) and Willis (1978: 6). De la Colina and Pérez Turrent view the ethics of the plague sequence as metonymic of those of the entire narrative, namely that '[t]he plague stands for evil. It is impossible to stop it, but within the plague one can give hope and love' (1992: 109).

30 [un hombre distinto. Se diría que aquél es su ambiente y en él se goza].

31 [doblemente vencido].

32 [En este andar de Nazarín por desolados parajes (seguido por múltiples planos, en muchos de los cuales la cámara, a ras de tierra, enfoca los pies de los presos) hay como un movimiento circular: el desandar de los caminos por los que se lanzó «a estar más cerca de Dios», para encontrarse mordiendo el polvo y rodeado de gente baja].

Chapter 5
Questions of Belonging: The (Im)possibility of a Home-place

The notion of home is a wide-ranging concept in research within the humanities and social sciences, and is informed by disciplines from human geography and anthropology to philosophy and psychology. It is, as Jeanne Moore (2000) notes, a singularly loaded term, encompassing micro-levels of individual dwelling to macroscopic concepts such as country, nation and questions of global unity. The sheer breadth of writing on the home has given rise to surveys of the literature in an attempt to venture points of correlation and contention between the multifarious perspectives represented across disciplines. In cinema, for example, Johannes von Moltke (2005) considers how the representation of *Heimat* – a term left in the original German – in German films dealing with questions of rootedness and locality (the *Heimatfilm* genre) can encompass an entire nation and even form the basis of an imagined community for German audiences, while David T. Fortin has examined the representation of home and architecture in science-fiction film, as 'most SF narratives seemingly center on notions of homelessness, homecomings, threats to and invasions of home, and journeys from it' (2011: 11). Similarly, Tyson Lewis and Daniel Cho (2006) carry out a reading of postmodern representations of home in Hollywood cinema, especially in horror and science-fiction genres, to argue in favour of a new formulation of home beyond its bourgeois historical materialist conceptualisation. In her cross-disciplinary review, Shelley Mallett asks whether home is '(a) place(s), (a) space(s), feeling(s), practices, and/or active state of state of being [sic] in the world?' (2004: 65). Home, undoubtedly, can be all of these and the evocative medium of film has the potential to address these ideas and to propose answers to Mallett's question.

In this final chapter I draw on largely phenomenologically-inspired readings and interpretations of home – the final suggestion Mallet offers in her definitions of home above – applying these to particular films in Buñuel's Mexican corpus. In doing so, I continue to take a spatial approach to the director's Mexican work, to demonstrate how questions of belonging – often prefigured in Buñuel's narratives by the negative, as *non*-belonging – is a trope around which the characters coalesce, sewing an aesthetic and thematic thread through Buñuel's body of work from this period and, thus, a specific way of interpreting it. As I outlined in chapter one, highlighting the relevance of space in these films allows us to link the commercial and auteurist strands of Buñuel's Mexican output. This chapter continues this linkage, revisiting in turn the island heterotopias of *Robinson Crusoe* and *The Young One*, the liminal spaces of the jungle and the desert in *La Mort en ce jardin* and *Simón del desierto* and the body-self within the place-worlds of *Los olvidados* and *Nazarín* to consider the importance they give to questions of belonging and how they represent this filmically. Buñuel made a great number of films in Mexico and to each of these pairs I add a further companion film: *La Fièvre monte à El Pao*, *Abismos de pasión* and *El ángel exterminador* respectively. It will be shown that, in their respective situations (in the figurative and spatial senses of the word), the characters are often rootless in their search for belonging within Buñuel's 'frequently faceless and impersonal' Mexican canvas (Smith 1995: 26). This completes the approximate move from the outside in, from typologies of exterior space to the implacement of the body-self within the place-world, and finally to what is the kernel of the self-place matrix – the home – will be realised through a consideration of the ways in which Buñuel's cinema depicts questions of belonging. Importantly, in adding three further companion films, this will allow for a richer, more illustrated discussion whilst forging fresh stylistic, thematic and philosophical links within Buñuel's cinema and pointing towards possible areas for future research.

The phenomenology of home

Pallasmaa highlights the social and psychological dynamics at work in the creation of a home. For him, home is not simply a shell or an edifice, but is bound up with

> psychology, psychoanalysis, and sociology [...] Dwelling, or the house, is the
> container, the shell for home. The substance of home is secreted, as it were, upon

the framework of the dwelling by the dweller. Home is an expression of the dweller's personality and his [or her] unique patterns of life. (1995: 132)

Pallasmaa's focus remains largely on the home as the site of experience, meaning that home comes into being primarily through the occupant. He takes his cue from Bachelard's *Poetics of Space*, in which the philosopher explores the oneiric house, an image imprinted in the psyche of all dwellers as he claims, 'the house image would appear to have become the topography of our intimate being'. Bachelard's tenet is simple: 'that all really inhabited space bears the essence of the notion of home' (1994: xxxvi). This presumption is potentially questionable in its apparent disregard for cultural and social contexts (indeed, this is one criticism often levelled at phenomenological approaches within the discipline of geography);[1] however, Pallasmaa (1995: 133) indicates that the characteristics of the oneiric house are culturally conditioned. Bachelard's oneiric house, problematically, privileges the white, middle-class, heterosexual male dweller.[2] We are obviously far from the failed home that Buñuel presents us with in *Los olvidados* here. However, attempting to move beyond Bachelard's tacit bourgeois, patriarchal Eurocentrism, Pallasmaa argues that what is vital is the intuitive understanding of home as a 'complex condition, which integrates memories and images, desires and fears, the past and the present' (1995: 133). This presents the basis for an intersubjective conceptualisation of home, which is then shaped by the individual's interaction with his or her environment, as home becomes 'a gradual product of the dweller's adaptation to the world' (1995: 133).

This wider understanding of home beyond its purely material foundations is more relevant to Buñuel's cinema where the protagonists of films such as *Nazarín* or *Simón del desierto* lack a material shelter and, within the Buñuelian repetitious cycle, a past. Janet Donohoe questions the inside/outside binary that a more material conception of home brings with it, believing this 'leads to misunderstanding, as does the language of security and refuge when speaking of the home place' (2011: 30, n. 5). It will be clear by now that Buñuel unpicks the idea(l) of home, and the films in this book counteract this misunderstanding. Crusoe's island, for instance, is a no-place bound inextricably to the home sphere of the dominant culture that pervades it, whilst Simón – who would be free even 'in a jail cell', according to Buñuel (de la Colina and Pérez Turrent 1992: 179) – is as trapped by his liberty in the liminal vistas of the desert as he is in the poky nightclub. Equally problematic are the protagonists' houses, where these structures are actually represented. Neither Evvie's cabin nor Pedro's shack could be described in terms of security and refuge.

It is, therefore, something of a misnomer to contend that Buñuel's protagonists are homeless, even though this may frequently be the case, as this term is often perceived in its material sense. Marina Pérez de Mendiola notes that the films of this period transmit 'a sense of uprooting' (2006: 29). I would argue the term rootless is a more accurate description of many of Buñuel's characters of this period, and one that relates to the lack of a home rather than the want of a house. Attempting to extricate the idea of home from its materialistic underpinnings, Anthony Steinbock highlights that:

> The home is not something we 'possess,' but a phenomenological structure of co-existence. If we do wish to speak of 'possession,' then the home cannot be conceived along the lines of ownership; rather, the home would be that communal sphere *to which we belong.* (1994: 218–19)

This communal sphere to which we belong – or from which we are excluded or exclude ourselves – I term a home-place and I see this as a continuation of the place-world, which was the focus of the previous chapter, moving from representations of the geographical body-self as it enacts and is implaced in its surroundings to the more intimate question of belonging. Underscoring Buñuel's Mexican films discussed thus far, as well as the others I include in this chapter, there is an exploration of the *process* of dwelling, rendered by Steinbock as a process of belonging.

The island home-place: *Robinson Crusoe* and *The Young One*

Focusing on *The Young One* and *Robinson Crusoe*, in chapter two I explored Buñuel's predilection for the use of the island as setting. Martín notes Buñuel's fascination with island spaces, eliding this in turn with a more general trope of confinement which, he asserts, is especially prevalent in the films of the Mexican period, where Buñuel places his characters in 'closed places, without an apparent exit, [and] he exposes them to extreme situations that bring to the surface their contradictions and their misery, and in the end he redeems them or condemns them'. This journey Martín terms the 'road to perfection' and his semantic field clearly points to the protagonists' attempts to refine and redeem themselves (2010: 742).[3] Martín's argument is pertinent, but rather than considering this within a narrative of religious redemption, as has so often been done when it comes to Buñuel, I view this as part of the protagonists' search for a more secular, earthly belonging and, with it, a home-place. Neither the island spaces in these films, nor the unseen mainland, offer any such road to perfection.

The depiction of both Crusoe's desert island and Miller and Evvie's game-preserve is far from the idyllic setting of an island as both Edenic paradise and site of romantic adventure. The insularity of both islands actually appears to draw Evvie and Crusoe out of themselves via a series of limit-experiences, and we see a change in their behaviour and, in Evvie's case, a fundamental alteration in her interaction in that space. Her limit-experience as a result of her rape extricates her from her own being and the fade-in shot of the island's coastline following this act serves as a visual motif of her being 'drawn out' of herself. The shot is fleeting and may appear insignificant, but its role as the foremost instance of narrative rupture should not be underestimated. Crucially, it is the only high-angle establishing shot of the island's coastline in the film and it follows what is arguably the film's most controversial moment. It would not be an underestimation to say that Evvie is, out of all Buñuel's characters in the films I am writing about in this book, the most natural, organic and the most close to belonging willingly to her environment until this moment.

Michael Zimmerman says that '[i]f we conceive ourselves and treat ourselves as things, we can hardly expect to be "at home"' (1985: 250). Evvie's limit-experience that I explained in chapter two during her rape by Miller does just this: it prematurely awakens her cognisance of her corporeality and her awareness of herself as a (sexual) object, external to and at odds with her environment. The shot of the island's coastline could be seen in this way as Evvie's being torn from her environment. The spatial and the temporal *mise-en-scène* is therefore replete with symbolism: more than marking a new day, it signals the rupture in her natural attachment to her home-place and the dawn it depicts is a portent of Evvie's premature awakening and loss of security (see Figure 13). Her relationship with her home-place is irrevocably altered: she is no longer the incarnation of Artemis, as Santaolalla (2004: 102) puts it; she no longer pets the deer in the yard nor does she tend to the bees. Indeed, a scene cut from the final version of the film showed Evvie, after her second violation, savagely kicking a coyote caught in a trap alongside Traver as he attempts to flee the island (Archer 1960: x5). The effect of her bodily awareness is clear as she is seen wearing a coat over her dress on the morning following the rape despite the continuous heat, where she had previously shown little awareness of her developing body after showering in front of Traver. Also, Miller's attempts to placate her with mainland commodities are overtly sexual: lipstick and stockings. Via the Buñuelian

Figure 13: Evvie's
premature awakening.
(Producciones Olmeca)

fetish object – for instance, the close up shot of Evvie's feet in the high-heeled shoes as she waits on the pier to be taken to town with the Reverend Fleetwood – Evvie is shown to be caught between here and there, between the insularity of the island and the space beyond its borders. She expresses no wish to stay on the island, which has been her home for an unspecified amount of time. Fetishism is important not just here but in Buñuel's cinema generally: Rubinstein points out that 'Buñuel's fetishes are things […] in a world whose desperate souls share no community' (1978: 243). Although Rubinstein's statement most clearly recalls the animated postcard and the disparate group of *La Mort en ce jardin*, it is also clearly applicable to *The Young One*, whose budding community is tarnished by Miller's racism and lust.

In a similar way to Evvie's rape, Crusoe's isolation undermines his ontology. Buñuel communicates the full extent of this during the scene in which Crusoe screeches hysterically for help, running into the roaring waves to try and escape 'this tomb, this prison'. As I outlined in chapter two, Crusoe considers himself *outside* of all places, lamenting his lack of purpose and meaning, removed from the world as the island subsumes his very identity. Unlike the island in *The Young One*, which could potentially become a home for Evvie, Crusoe's is an island landing-place, and the flotsam and jetsam of the ship washed ashore with the hero in the opening sequence and subsequently plundered from the shipwreck by Crusoe are the only traces of his original cultural and territorial home-place of England. In a similar way to the fetish objects in *The Young One*, those in *Robinson Crusoe* are deliberate reminders of the dominant space and culture in the insular space. Rubinstein notes that fetishes are 'failed metaphors, or ruined metaphors, functioning for Buñuel as the natural parody of metaphor' (1978: 243). I would argue that, especially in the case of these two films, the objects are not failed metaphors

but metonyms, and the *mise-en-scène* of one scene in particular mocks Crusoe's hollow attachment to home.

The scene I am referring to is the hallucination sequence. Here, Crusoe's cave fortress, furnished with the bourgeois comforts of home, appears incongruous and ridiculous (see Figure 14). This sequence is important when we consider the hero's original home-place. It is the most overtly surrealist part of the film and it begins as Crusoe is in his hammock, ravaged by fever. Gazing off-screen, he begins to talk with an image of his father, who ignores his pleas for water and promptly sets about washing a pig. The conversation begins on a spatial note as Crusoe's father, now in shot and responding to his son's amazement at finding him on the island, says, 'Yes here. Here, here, here, here, here. Not there, but here. Where else would I be? Are you not here?'. He then admonishes his son for leaving his native country, where he 'had the best of all possible worlds'. Undoubtedly ironic, this statement is the direct inversion of Buñuel's often-cited view that, the lasting impression his cinema should leave us with is 'to repeat [...] that we do not live in the best of all possible worlds' (Edwards 2005: 90). The artificiality of dwelling, or rather, the unrealisable nature of dwelling even within Crusoe's home culture is suggested through the ridiculous, metonymic nature of the fetish items in his fortress, many of which are of little use to him, as well as the plush curtain, the upholstered chair, the candelabra and the pig, remnants of his English manor that accompany the image of his father. They are skewed fractals depicting a whole that is constantly absent as England remains unseen in the film. This accumulation of fetish items superimposes one cultural milieu onto another and indicates the vacuous nature of existence in either setting, mocking Crusoe's attempt to recreate in microcosm his home culture on the island before it has fully begun and parodying the home culture itself, from which Crusoe, in his own words, 'broke loose'.

The relevance of the island spaces as heterotopic sites, as I discussed in chapter two, is not lost when considering questions of belonging and non-belonging. Johnson contends that heterotopias 'disrupt and test our customary notions of ourselves' as '[t]hese emplacements exist out of step and meddle with our sense of interiority' (2006: 84). Evvie's and Crusoe's islands are unsettling precisely because they are not depicted, in the spirit of de la Mare's romanticism and More's perfected society, as utopic spaces. They show that home can and does fail. Heterotopias are also 'disturbing places'. We should not take this in a purely figurative sense, but rather a literal one of displacement: they 'display and inaugurate a difference and challenge the space in which we may feel at home' (Johnson 2006: 84). As the island becomes a crisis space for Evvie, she appears more conscious of her existence in her home-place and is thus disturbed as the artificiality and arbitrariness of her residence there is made clear. The layering of cultural milieus on Crusoe's island, meanwhile, works on the principle of metonymy, parodying the bourgeois comforts of a longed-for but absent and incomplete home from which the hero escaped and pointing to the ambivalent and incomplete home he has fashioned for himself. Most crucially of all, both protagonists, as well as the racial 'others' in the characters of Traver and Friday, leave their islands without a burning desire to stay, and both do so moving towards uncertain futures and, in Evvie's case, another temporary residence in the children's home.

Ojeda as failed home-place in *La Fièvre monte à El Pao*

Alongside Buñuel's two English language productions, I want to consider the island of *La Fièvre monte à El Pao* as a failed home-place. This 1959 Franco-Mexican co-production forms the third movie of Buñuel's 1950s Francophone triptych, along with *Cela s'appelle l'aurore* and *La Mort en ce jardin*. The filmmaker's own disparaging comments on this film – Buñuel admitted he did not care for the project, accepting only because he needed the money (de la Colina and Pérez Turrent 1992: 143) – place it firmly in the group of so-called studio potboilers. Unsurprisingly, critics scouring the director's films of the period for traces of Buñueliana see little of value in a narrative-driven film about totalitarian politics with an involved plot. Much like *La Mort en ce jardin* the political intrigue in this film is complex. Unlike the former film, whose narrative style bears a similarity to the Western adventure film, paradigmatically *La Fièvre monte à El Pao* is closer to melodrama. Indeed, in her review of the film Dilys Powell, highlights that the alternative English title of this – *Swamps of Lust* – is an apparent stumbling block to any semblance of artistic integrity Buñuel might have displayed in this movie, as, quite simply, 'Bunuel's [sic] best and most Bunuellish [sic] films do not have titles such as "Swamps of Lust"' (1960: n.p.). The film is set on the fictional island of Ojeda, off the coast of an unspecified Latin American country, which functions as a large-scale penitentiary for two thousand political prisoners who oppose the mainland dictatorship of Carlos Barreiro. When the despotic governor of the island, Vargas, is assassinated by a member of Ojeda's police force, his secretary, the young and ambitious Ramón Vázquez, is promoted to director of the island's penitentiary, serving under a now even more tyrannical governor, Alejandro Gual. Political manoeuvring is balanced against the film's decidedly melodramatic plot, with the depiction of desire between Vázquez and Inés, the widow of the murdered governor of Ojeda, and Gual's attempts to possess Inés and to falsely incriminate Vázquez as an accomplice to Vargas's murder. Vázquez in turn allows a rebellion to break out among the prisoners while Gual is absent, leading to Gual's execution and Vázquez's promotion to governor. I want to consider the significance of the spatial characteristics of Ojeda in illuminating the way in which the protagonists, specifically Inés and Vázquez, are portrayed in their island-residence, while considering the island as a heterotopia will show that its potential as a home-place is precluded.

The pseudo-documentary opening of the film functions as an anti-travelogue, presenting a contemporary society every bit as miserable as that which Buñuel presents us with in Las Hurdes.[4] Ojeda, the voiceover instructs, is located somewhere off the American continent, although its precise position is of little concern to those outside Barreiro's regime, as no tourist has stepped foot on the island in years. There follows a series of shots of the native islanders' dilapidated shacks and the prisoners' labour camp, part of the island's penal infrastructure. This opening montage reveals a sense of autocratic space construction by means of autochthonous place destruction: it could be Crusoe's rudimentary mutineer colony taken to sinister extremes. As Paule Sengissen (digitised press cuttings in BFI Library) points out, the pseudo-documentary – and the film as a whole – presents the viewer with an image before cutting to another image that negates the previous one; the film is in perpetual negation and is another example of the 'yes, but' dialectic Kyrou sees in Buñuel's cinema. The sweeping aerial panorama of Ojeda's verdant coastline gives way to a travelling shot of rows of dilapidated shacks in the mid-distance where the exploited natives reside; the image of the grand colonial buildings, remnants of Spanish occupation, are countered by images of prisoners labouring in the fruit fields; finally, the graveyard containing ex-prisoners becomes the luxurious mansion of Ojeda's governor.

This sprawling residence is the home of Inés, Governor Vargas's wife, and becomes the home of her lover, Vázquez, after the Governor is shot. Unlike in both *Robinson Crusoe* and *The Young One*, the mansion house here offers the comforts and trappings befitting the political elite. It appears to provide Vázquez and Inés some respite from 'sequence after brutal sequence, [...] against the bitter, cruel and often stifling background that is Mexico' (National Film Theatre programme notes: *La Fièvre monte à El Pao*, digitised press cuttings in BFI Library). One scene in particular appears to establish the house as a 'felicitous space' that 'protects the dreamer, [...] allows one to dream in peace' (Bachelard 1994: xxxv, 6). This quixotic view of the house is depicted filmically as Inés and Vázquez stroll leisurely in the mansion's gardens following her husband's assassination, framed in long shot by the trees as they stop to reminisce about their pasts. Inés admits that it has taken her years to discover freedom, having escaped from her controlling parents and violent husband, before expressing her joy that a new life lies ahead of the pair. This cocoon-like ideal of the home is undone throughout the film, contrasted with a much later scene, following the outbreak and suppression of the prisoners' revolt, where the pair is shown in the lounge, arguing over the implications of signing a falsified statement implicating them in the death of Inés's husband. Here, the establishing shot is of the lovers from behind a translucent curtain, communicating a sense of their luxurious imprisonment. Inés implores Vázquez to escape with her: 'It doesn't matter to where. [...] Spread your ideals elsewhere – the world is very big.' When contrasted with her earlier admission that it has taken her years to find her freedom, the viewer may wonder whether Ojeda has only ever provided a semblance of it. According to Bachelard:

> A house that was final, one that stood in symmetrical relation to the house we were born in, would lead to thoughts – serious, sad thoughts – and not to dreams. It is better to live in a state of impermanence than finality. (1994: 61)

Considering the film within the broad Buñuelian aesthetic dyad of confinement and liberty that is relevant to all the works I look at in this book, it becomes clear during this film that Inés's controlling husband and her privileged yet conspicuous position within Barreiro's regime suggest that the house, and by extension the whole island, is in a state of totalitarian finality. Cast adrift from the mainland, Ojeda is an exiled isle and an isle of exile, appearing to confirm Gual's significant remark in an earlier encounter with Inés as he attempts to blackmail her: 'beautiful Inés, exiled to Ojeda'. Gual's statement mirrors John MacGregor Wise's view that '[t]he space called home is not an expression of the subject. Indeed, the subject is an expression of the territory, or rather of the process of territorialization' (2000: 301). As a character *subjected* to the finality of her milieu, from which there seems to be no escape, Inés represents a disavowal of Bachelard's conception of the topophilic, dream-filled home.

In reality, the mansion is simply an extension of the island's penal institutions. Fuentes considers that the narrative develops between what he terms as two chrono-topes: the penal colony and the mansion and government buildings. The mechanisms of power and corruption are omnipresent, reinforcing his observation that there is no distinction between inside and outside power structures. Furthermore, he identifies the constant of surveillance as one of the film's principal motifs, likening the island to a panoptic watchtower (ibid.). The motif of the colour white serves to link the two chronotopes: the car in which Vázquez first arrives at the mansion to inform Inés that her presence is required at the annual celebrations to honour Barreiro is white, as is Inés's dress and the uniform of Colonel Olivares, whom Vázquez witnesses kissing Inés in this scene. The starched white uniform of Ojeda's military society is echoed in the ubiquitous white venetian blinds, a vital aspect of the film's *mise-en-scène*. The blinds in the governor's office remain closed as the post changes hands from Vargas to Gual to Vázquez, and are a visual metaphor for the social ordering of the island, based on surveillance. In the scene in which newly-appointed governor Gual gives Vázquez responsibility for the island's penitentiary, he makes a point of closing the blinds, stating that he detests the sun. Likewise, the end of the film sees Vázquez peering out from behind the blinds at Inés who is fleeing Ojeda following Vázquez's refusal to leave and their separation. The blinds symbolise the panoptic power of Ojeda's institutions and, paradoxically, the curtailing of liberty of those whom they simultaneously shield and imprison, and, crucially, they are seen not only in governmental buildings but also in the mansion's bedroom. Furthermore, in the scene where political prisoner Cárdenas is telling Vázquez about the prisoners' plan to revolt, a crude map of Ojeda can be seen on the wall onto which the light filtering through the blinds is projected, running across the island and across Cárdenas and Vázquez in a bar-like effect: the island as a whole is behind the bars of surveillance

Figure 15: Blinding blinds. A Panopticon prison. (Filmex/ Le Groupe des Quatre)

from the mainland (see Figure 15). This pervasion of authority in both the institutional and domestic realms simultaneously locates the characters within the totalitarian space of the island and places them opposite it. The island as home-place is always mediated by its relationship to Barreiro's mainland dictatorship.

Finally, whereas Crusoe's island is presented as an ou-topic no-place and the game-preserve of *The Young One* is a subverted eu-topic good place, Ojeda comes to represent a conflation of the two. In fact, the three islands are all failed utopias. In a variety of ways, the influence of the respective dominant cultures makes its presence felt, mediating the relationship between the characters and their supposed home-places in manners rendered subtly or explicitly by the films' respective *mise-en-scène*. Whether or not they escape their islands, the protagonists are all rootless. Evvie and Crusoe move towards uncertain futures, Inés is killed on her way to the airport as the driver of her car is shot for speeding through a check point as she tries to flee Ojeda and Vázquez remains alone and, in Fuentes's words, totally disorientated (2000: 133).[5] It is ultimately their (dis)location between states of rootlessness, or ou-topia, and imprisonment within the hierarchical political order, or subverted eu-topia, that prevents their adaptation to the world.

A home-place on the limen?: *La Mort en ce jardin* and *Simón del desierto*

Writing about the ending of *La Fièvre monte à El Pao*, Fuentes believes it is 'the greatest antiphrasis in all of Buñuel's cinema and the ending in which the director distances himself most from his protagonist' (2000: 133).[6] Buñuel's distancing from his protagonists is likewise evident, and arguably to a greater extent, in *La Mort en ce jardin* and *Simón del desierto*, two films that, as I showed in chapter two, can be fruitfully interpreted through the framework of the spatial liminal. The conclusions of the respective films are largely inconclusive. Chark and Maria in the jungle and Simón in the desert-disco are equally or more disorientated than Fuentes would have Vázquez, and in a manner rendered more explicit than that of *La Fièvre monte à El Pao* through the *mise-en-scène* of their endings; the nightclub and the jungle, below their surface function as arenas of narrative development, are examples of Deleuze's formless, uniform originary worlds. The protagonists of both films are caught within a vicious cycle as the former suffer corporeal degradation and disintegration in the jungle and the latter is removed from his literal desert only to be forever imprisoned in a further, figurative one. Their journeys defy Kim Hopper and Jim Baumohl's assertion that 'liminal passages are usually undertaken in well-mapped territory from which the voyager is expected to return' (1996: 4). Here there is no return, nor the chance to make a home in the interstices. In short, the creation and representation of a home-place is problematic on the limen.

I am returning to *La Mort en ce jardin* and *Simón del desierto* in order to consider what this pair can tell the viewer about the idea of home. Undoubtedly, in these two films Buñuel appears preoccupied with questions of belonging, specifically the dynamic of belonging or non-belonging within a certain community – of exiles in a foreign country, or a community built on a religious order – and both films, for their shortcomings, speak philosophically to what it is to be at home (or not) with others. Steinbock's development of Husserl's concept of a homeworld/alienworld is key in this reading. This dyadic construct forms the framework for how we experience the familiar and the foreign, and integral to the homeworld/alienworld pair is the reciprocal relationship that the two share: the former is constructed and re-constructed in connection with the latter. As Steinbock puts it simply, 'a home is formed through *appropriation* and *disappropriation*' (1995: 222). In this way:

> The *homeworld* is the taken-for-granted, tacit sphere of experiences and situations marking out the world into which each of us is born and matures as children and then adults. The homeworld is always in some mode of lived mutuality with the alienworld, which is the world of difference and otherness but is only provided awareness because of the always already givenness of the homeworld. (Seamon 2013: 160)

Steinbock is clear that we should not privilege the homeworld as that which is familiar over the alienworld simply because this is unknown, as 'neither [...] can be regarded as the "original sphere" since they are in a continual historical becoming *as* delimited from one another' (1994: 208). This concept is particularly revealing in terms of *La Mort en ce jardin* and *Simón del desierto* where the co-generative ethic of this duality of experience is frequently thwarted: the construction of a home-world after contact with the alienworld is not possible, either because the protagonists remain estranged from both the home and the alien, as is Simón, high on his pillar, or because they are thrust into a claustrophobic, unfurling alienworld with no access to the co-constitutive home, as is the group in *La Mort en ce jardin*. Finally, it is also important to acknowledge the changing nature of the homeworld, given that it requires us to participate actively in its construction and its reinforcement. What is at first unfamiliar can, through experience, become familiar. This idea of a generative bleeding of the home into the alien and *vice versa* leads Steinbock to posit the two as liminal experiences in that their borders, while porous, are fundamental to their constitution (1994: 208). Put simply, 'making ourselves at home as our world to which we belong entails more than a "sub-liminal" belonging, but an active responsibility for setting limits, for repeating, for renewing the homeworld' (Steinbock 1995: 227).

Here is where liminality finds its resonance with the construction of home. It is this limit-setting process in which the protagonists of *La Mort en ce jardin* and *Simón del desierto* fail: Castin and the group are forced out of their village in the jungle and into the boundless wilderness, while Simón's horizontal existence in the nondescript scrubland and vertical existence is inherently limitless. The punctuation of establishing panoramic shots of the vast rainforest and desert in the two films – three of the former during the final third of the film alone – does not only suggest the importance and magnitude of the setting but also a deeper connection between the exterior space and the psychology of the characters. As opposed to the community of the Francophone villagers in *La Mort en ce jardin*, Simón is an isolated figure against a backdrop about which Wood writes '[Figueroa's] images are as much about the desert as about Simón, and we can almost see the thinness of the air' (2009). Friendships, for Simón, are rather thin on the ground, too. Steinbock's focus on acts of appropriation such as repetition, ritual and communication as a means by which we make and reinforce our homeworlds makes clear that these acts are intrinsically communal and therefore often shared by homecomrades, or 'subjects qualified constitutively and intersubjectively in terms of a home; they are

"transcendental comrades," "co-bearers of our world"' (1995: 223). This is the very irony at play in *Simón del desierto*: as the spatial liminal of the boundless desert and firmament becomes the ontological liminal, Buñuel shows Simón to be incapable of such appropriation and interaction.

The scene in which a fellow monk attempts to instruct the preacher in the concept of personal property shows Simón's estrangement. Clutching the sack used by the protagonist to winch his meagre sustenance up the column, the monk makes as if to steal the bag, intending to provoke a conflict. However, Simón cannot appropriate the sack any more than he can reciprocate the discourse of the monk, stating: 'I don't understand you. We speak in different tongues.' Fuentes ventures that this interpersonal disjuncture is 'perhaps the most dramatic Buñuelian enactment of the theme of a lack of communication and dialogue among men' (1993: 156).[7] The camera closes in on the two monks during this sequence, framing them against the formless backdrop of sky (see Figure 16). Behind Simón, the rope at the edge of his pillar is visible, its arbitrary nature revealed as the few metres square area at the pinnacle of the column is not separate from the surrounding smooth space and can never demarcate a successful dwelling. This is because the unfurling smooth-liminal-originary world of the desert, like that of the discotheque after it, is *neither* home *nor* alien for the protagonist, who, despite being a fifth-century desert father, is closer to 'the first astronaut, alone on a Space Platform' (Durgnat 1977: 138). To this end, Simón's final words to the Devil are revealing: preparing to leave the disco, he tells her, 'Have fun. I'm going home'. However, he cannot go home, as his pillar is now neither-home-nor-alien to another tenant. As the Devil struts onto the dance floor, the camera cuts to a mid-close up shot of Simón's pensive expression, suggestive of his realisation that he is, and likely always has been, homeless both in a material and a spiritual sense. His use of the word home, whether meant in a purely physical sense, or used to denote spiritually or secularly what Steinbock describes as 'that communal sphere to which we belong' (1994: 218), therefore rings hollow.

In contrast to Simón's isolation, the group of Francophone diamond miners in *La Mort en ce jardin* are ostensible homecomrades, linked by a common origin familiar to them all. On the one hand, unlike Simón, the band of outlaws 'have [a] home-world as their original basis and point of departure for […] making the acquaintance of alien worlds', but on the other, they are the embodiment of 'an entire community [which stands], with respect to this home-world, in the relationship of one who has lost something' (Landgrebe 1940: 48). The question of whether they have lost their home-place or whether they have actually collectively renounced it seems pertinent here. Despite his dream of returning to France, in one of the film's most surrealist sequences Castin tears up a photograph of the Arc de Triomphe after burning another. As Wise says, a photograph

> glows with memories […] of experience, of history, of family, friends. What creates the glow is the articulation of subject (homemaker) to object (home-marker), caught up in a mutual becoming-home. But that becoming opens up onto other milieus, other markers, other spaces. (2000: 298)

Coming after the scene depicting the snake carcass being devoured by ants, Castin's act is crucial in revealing the group's idea of home – here, France – to be an illusion. As the camera fades to black on the reanimated serpent, the Champs Elysées appears in the frame. The roar of motor engines and car horns is jarring and incongruous following the jungle soundscape. The scene lasts no more than a few seconds before the sound cuts out and the soundtrack of the jungle fills its place. As Buñuel cuts to a reverse angle shot of Castin's hand holding the photograph in front of the campfire, the scene is revealed for what it really is: not an allusion to the home-place, but an illusion of it. As Castin destroys the memento in the fire and the camera's gaze lingers while it crumples into oblivion, the viewer is placed firmly among the drifters, complicit to some degree in the destruction of the illusory home (see Figure 17). The liminal jungle is an impenetrable space and the remnant of the group's home culture cannot open up into their present originary milieu. Indeed, echoing Malaguti's comments on the element of repetition inherent in

Figure 17: 'Au revoir, Paris'.
Destroying the symbol
of home. (Producciones
Tepeyac/Film Dismage)

Buñuel's cinema, Giorgio Tinazzi argues that Buñuel's films, 'in demonstrating a substantial closure of the world they represent, very often have a circular structure, […] that world does not have any exits' (1978: 119).[8] For all the critical attention that *Le Charme discret de la bourgeoisie* has received in comparison with *La Mort en ce jardin*, the latter film demonstrates more palpably the claustrophobia of perpetual repetition. Even when the circles the group trace around the jungle seem to be broken by the characters' discovery of the wreck of the aircraft and the consumerist fetish objects the cadavers of its passengers can provide – here also metonyms of an absent place and culture, as in *Robinson Crusoe* – there is no exit and the objects are equally meaningless. The jewels coveted by Djin and Maria appear ridiculous in this context and the group's immersion in the alien means that

> The elements on which the [film's] scenario is based are given as totally abstract, money for example, without any link to a possible practical use governs the events and the behaviour of the characters in places that are equally abstract. (Rebolledo, 1964: 98)[9]

With the abstraction of material objects comes the characters' isolation from one another. Steinbock contends that 'the identity of the individual […] is revealed as a homecomrade in communal and historical interaction. Who we are is *how* we are home' (1995: 223). Here, we can remember Malaguti's use of the term *azzeramento* – literally, a setting at zero – that I outlined in chapter three to refer to Buñuel's quite deliberate use of repetition to undermine any sense the viewer may have that his characters are progressing. The trek through the jungle is repetitive and every day is Groundhog Day. As a result, the generative ontology described by Steinbock is precluded in this film. The characters, although well-rounded, are liminal beings in their instable position in time as well as space, as almost the entire film appears *in medias res*, as indeed does *Simón del desierto*. The prolonged contact with what is unfamiliar within a volatile situation is rendered cinematographically as a rupture in everyday experience, and this transposes the anthropological basis of liminality onto a phenomenological level, which is especially relevant to this film. Steinbock writes that events such as the death of a child or a parent (here, Castin), the dismissal of our co-workers and, thus, our communal goals (here, the dissolution of communitas) or a war (here, the civil unrest in the mining village), 'are just some examples of the disruption of a homeworld experience that give rise to an explicit "limit-situation" [*Grenzsituation*] that calls into question [the] power to appropriate' (1995: 241). In short, as a point of contrast to Simón's location neither here (in the home) nor there (in the alien), in this film the group is forced into the alien, a state that demands 'a rupture or discontinuity of experience' (Donohoe 2011: 34) evidenced filmically by the tearing and burning of the photographs of home and the abstraction of material items.

'Don't leave me in this abyss': the abyss as home in *Abismos de pasión*

Alongside *La Mort en ce jardin* and *Simón del desierto*, Buñuel's 1954 film adaption of Emily Brontë's *Wuthering Heights* gives rise to considerations of a home-place on the limen in both its spatial and philosophical dimensions. *Abismos de pasión* represents the completion of a project Buñuel began in the 1930s when he drafted a screenplay of the novel with Pierre Unik, the cameraman on *Tierra sin pan*.[10] The sublime force of *amour fou* between Catherine and Heathcliffe – here Hispanicised as Catalina and Alejandro – attracted Buñuel, who claimed that, unlike Defoe's *Robinson Crusoe*, he had always had admiration for Brontë's novel (de la Colina and Pérez Turrent 1992: 104). Indeed, the surrealist 'spirit' of the novel, evident in parts of Buñuel's adaptation, has earned this Mexican melodrama more scholarly attention than it might otherwise have received and Buñuel himself went as far as to claim that, with a more careful casting, it could have been his best film (Evans 1982: 10).[11] Wolfram Schütte even ventures that only *Abismos de pasión*, after

Tierra sin pan, 'returns to the beginnings, lights the surrealist fire once again with an immense gust of passionate, time- and place-uprooting force' (1974: 27).[12] The film's narrative, as that of the novel, takes place between two dwellings. Between the ramshackle abode known as *la granja* [the farm], inhabited by Catalina's alcoholic brother Ricardo and which Alejandro appropriates after his ten-year-long absence from the area, and Catalina's ordered residence with husband Eduardo and sister-in-law Isabel, is the arid landscape of the Mexican state of Guerrero, to replace Brontë's Yorkshire moors. Here once again, the landscape plays the dual role which it often does in Buñuel's work, not least in *La Mort en ce jardin* and *Simón del desierto*, transcending its utilitarian function as setting and recalling Martialay's (1969: 8) observation that landscape in Buñuel's cinema often becomes a character in its own right. This is the arena in which the struggle between dwelling and non-dwelling is played out.

The exterior shots depict a charred, barren landscape from the opening of the film as the credits roll over the image of a lifeless tree. Establishing shots of the two dwellings punctuate the film, suggesting the passage of time and functioning as rudimentary spatial referents that demarcate the precipice of the abyss of the film's title. Throughout the film, the characters are often shown in long shot, appearing dwarfed by the surrounding landscape. The vast distance between Eduardo and Catalina's estate and the miserable farm on which Alejandro resides is presented as 'an irreparably closed space between the hills that seem to stretch on to infinity' (Rodríguez and Sinardet 2003: 440).[13] Apart from Alejandro, this is a space where nothing comes and nothing goes, as Rodríguez and Sinardet point out. Like those of *La Mort en ce jardin* and *Simón del desierto*, they see this as another Deleuzian originary world, 'a space *undomesticated* by man' (2003: 441, my emphasis).[14] The term 'undomesticated' is important, because the tension between the domesticated and the undomesticated, here rendered as the home and the alien through Eduardo and Alejandro respectively, comes to the fore in this film.

In the vein of liminality, we can see Alejandro as a Trickster figure and in this way he bears many similarities to the fugitives in *La Mort en ce jardin*. Tricksters are '[a]lways marginal characters: outsiders, as they cannot trust or be trusted, cannot give or share, they are incapable of living in a community' (Szakolczai 2009: 155). Alejandro's lack of (hi)story, his liminal *azzeramento* following his ten year absence, renders him rootless: there is no doubt he is one of Buñuel's orphans. Furthermore, he is clearly allied with the exterior, scorched hills, illustrated most clearly in one scene in particular. As Alejandro, Catalina and Isabel are out walking, Catalina mocks Isabel's growing feelings for Alejandro. Ashamed, Isabel flees between the sand dunes; Alejandro is shown racing along the top of the dune, sliding down it to trap her before frantically kissing and biting her neck in a paroxysm of sadomaso-chistic desire. Home and the interior are for him exclusively utilitarian, as he is shown numerous times entering and exiting *la granja* at dawn and dusk and is seen to eat and drink there. Horvath and Thomassen write:

> *not having a home,* deeply felt human relations and existential commitments, the Trickster is not interested in solving the liminal crisis either. Quite on the contrary, being really at home in liminality, *or in homelessness,* his real interest lies in its oppo-site, in perpetuating such conditions of confusion. (2008: 13–14)

Alejandro is the epitome of chaos, sowing disorder and disruption in the seem-ingly perfect world of Eduardo and Catalina's manor house. He is the antithesis of the ordered and detached Eduardo; shortly before Alejandro returns to the manor to look for Catalina, breaking and entering through a window, Eduardo is shown inserting a butterfly into his entomological display cabinet while on another occasion we see him ordering the books in his study. For Eduardo, Alejandro is a remnant of the alien that has returned to disrupt his hermetic homeworld of the manor. It is significant that Eduardo is the only character never shown outside the manor or its courtyard; the return of Alejandro disrupts his staid order and, in true Buñuelian style, reveals his bourgeois existential security to be an arbi-trary construct. Anchored solely in the familiar, it is not difficult to see Eduardo as the inverse of both Simón, who does not have a home- or an alienworld, and the characters in *La Mort en ce jardin,* whom Buñuel condemns to forever negotiate the alien, cut off from what is familiar. It would not be an exaggeration to argue that, ultimately, Eduardo's pretence of marital security and home as a refuge does nothing more than illustrate Steinbock's view that 'an idea of home as an homog-enous sphere, impervious to the alien, [...] may just be an insidious way of covering over a deeper sense of homelessness that intrudes in all our lives' (1995: 233).

The much-remarked upon ending of the film sees Alejandro fatally shot by Ricardo as he stands over Catalina's corpse after breaking into her tomb. This is patently the most surrealist sequence in the film. Alejandro seems to be an early incarnation of Don Jaime, the pseudo-necrophile of *Viridiana,* as he kisses his dead lover before his sublime hallucination of Catalina's return, her arms outstretched to welcome him to the abysmal afterlife. In reality, the hallucination is Catalina's

Figure 18: 'Into the abyss.
(Producciones Tepeyac)

brother, Ricardo, and his arms are not outstretched but are in fact aiming a shotgun at Alejandro. María Serjo Richart disavows any potential ambiguity that the film's conclusion might contain, reading the ending as Ricardo seals the lovers in their tomb as 'the saddest conclusion: there is nothing after death' (2002: 32). Certainly, unlike William Wyler's 1939 Hollywood adaptation where the ghosts of Cathy and Heathcliffe are reunited in the afterlife, Buñuel's is a more linear and logical conclusion. However, in eschewing Wyler's romantic metaphysics, Buñuel's heroes are locked in the abyss of death, a paradoxical state of infinite finitude. To this end, Philip Strick (National Film Theatre Programme Notes, digitised press cuttings in BFI Library) is right to suggest that the entire narrative is concerned with margins and thresholds torn open; none more so than that of death (see Figure 18). Despite having a clearly defined narrative, this film arguably adheres to a more radical surrealism than either *La Mort en ce jardin* or *Simón del desierto* through its treatment of *amour fou*. This paroxysmic force is the vehicle through which Catalina and Alejandro embrace their liminal immortality through repeated references to passion and death: Catalina proclaims, 'Alejandro means more to me than my soul'; Alejandro implores her spirit, 'Haunt me. Make me crazy. But don't leave me alone. Don't leave me in this abyss'. Alien to Eduardo's stale, hermetic love, the trope of *amour fou* is not shown to be negative, and here is where its relevance to questions of dwelling can be seen.

Through the foregrounding of *amour fou* and the extra-existential position of the Trickster figure the position of death as *other* is reversed, allowing Catalina and Alejandro to embrace their liminality in a way that Simón and the Francophone fugitives cannot, because we see that they embrace their sense of homelessness, being at home in their rootlessness and ultimate death. This is the film's paradox. Their romanticised deaths within the film's Gothic aesthetic contrast with the detached, etymological impetus that leads the anodyne Eduardo to capture his collection of insects in his makeshift laboratory in order to 'keep them intact'. For Catalina, death as a destructive product of *amour fou* brings with it a freedom that is lacking in Eduardo's smothering attentiveness (in her own words the vultures she shoots 'pass without feeling anything to the freedom of death', as opposed to Eduardo's insects). On the evening of Alejandro's return, Catalina tells her husband, 'your love and mine will end with death. The love I have for Alejandro is inhuman. Catalina is really a reincarnation of Lya Lys's character in *L'Âge d'or*, writhing in ecstasy at the thought of having murdered her own children, albeit her veneer of respectability does not slip as much as this earlier version of herself. Death is the key to Alejandro and Catalina's being together. Paul Harrison writes: '[t]o evoke the concept of dwelling is always to attempt to re-call, to restate or rephrase, an *ur*-concept; it is to describe an originary spacing'. By this, Harrison means that we 'will always constitute [our] distances, perspective, gaze, or narrative *from* the intimacy of dwelling' (2007: 627). Death, for the rootless Tricksters Alejandro and Catalina, is this originary spacing in reverse, in the sense that while the scorched abyss between the manor and *la granja* is an obstacle to dwelling together, in the tomb the lovers have achieved their infinite finitude. As Peter Evans and Robin Fiddian put it: 'Alejandro's «quiero morir contigo» [I want to die with you] […] is […] a complicated revelation of an individual's desire for liberation from the prison of mortality' (1988: 66). Dwelling as belonging is only possible – paradoxically – for the pair in death.

The body and the home: *Los olvidados* and *Nazarín*

In contrast to the exterior spaces of the jungle and the desert in the discussion of *La Mort en ce jardin* and *Simón del desierto*, my reading of *Los olvidados* and *Nazarín* in chapter four centred around the representation of the body-self in the place-worlds of the respective films. Casey's concept of the place-world resonates with the idea(l) of a home-place. A home can be thought of as the kernel of a more extensive territorial place-world and just as the body is instrumental in our negotiation of the place-world, so it is paramount when we construct a home. Steinbock even ventures that, when taking home as a place which structures our experiences and behaviour, 'it might not be too strained to speak of the lived-body precisely as a "home-body"' (1995: 233). Here, I reconsider the narratives of *Los olvidados* and *Nazarín* as giving rise to the protagonists' search for a place of belonging – a home – within their respective territories, and the way in which Buñuel frames questions of bodily representation is therefore vital.

To explore the absence of a home-place in *Los olvidados* I want to return to Pedro's dream sequence, when he returns home to sleep. Low-key lighting along with discordant music signal that this is an alternate reality, one that gives representation to Pedro's trauma, based on lack. The lack here is of a nurturing parent (more specifically, a mother) and of a home. Fredrik Svenaeus asks:

> What if the repressed which recurs in uncanny anxiety is something that was once the most familiar and which has now through the process of repression become the most estranged? What if it has to do with the most basic loss there is – the loss of the first object, the mother [...]? (2000: 6)

Svenaeus's use of Freudian psychoanalysis and the uncanny lends itself well to this film. In chapter four, I read Marta also as an embodiment of the abject and a cipher for the place-world on an increasing scale from neighbourhood to city to nation. Her most immediate and intimate link, however, is arguably with the home. She is the archetype of the long-suffering, downtrodden single mother fettered to her domestic duties, and is seen outside of the home only on two occasions: when visiting Pedro in the youth court following his sentencing to the farm school and at the end of the film, when out searching for her son after seemingly being struck by an attack of remorse over her treatment of him. According to Kirsten Jacobson:

> It is [...] essential to our normal daily experience of both the body and home that they are for the most part neither thematically noticeable to us nor are they for the most part actively manipulated or called upon by us. Instead, the body and home recede from our attention while we engage with our daily projects. (2009: 370)

The deliberate use of slow motion during the dream sequence is striking not only visually, but also for what it communicates to the viewer in terms of this argument. Buñuel claimed that he had always liked the use of slow-motion, 'because it gives an unexpected dimension to even the most trivial gesture; we see details that we cannot perceive at normal speed' (de la Colina and Pérez Turrent 1992: 56). Here the use of slow motion, so rare in Buñuel's cinema, jolts the viewer, who fixates on every bodily movement. Buñuel's desire is to make us conscious of the bodies in the frame and their position within the domestic setting: home and the body are purposefully not given as natural here; as portents of the Gothic mode they do not recede from our attention. As Marta advances with the gristly chunk of flesh, Freud's return of the repressed is recast as an awakening, for Pedro and the watching audience, of the abundant lack of a home-place and corporeal warmth. As the embodiment of the uncanny, Marta's body is a reminder that Pedro will forever be, as Svenaeus asserts in general terms, 'sensitive to this a priori homelessness of existence which will announce itself in the uncanny' (2000: 7). As a symbol of the formless abject, Marta denies her son's longed-for assimilation with her, and condemns him to a position as 'an exile who asks himself where' (Kristeva 1982: 8), searching for a home in the uniformly bleak slums.

Buñuel presents the slums as disturbing and threatening, a claustrophobic place that contains little prospect of a home-place. Yet one opportunity presents itself from outside: the farm school where Pedro is sent after his trial. The alternative ending that Buñuel filmed for *Los olvidados* is crucial here. This was discovered in 1996 in the archives of the Filmoteca of the Universidad Nacional de México (UNAM) [the National University of Mexico]. In interview, Francisco Gaytán, the then director of the Filmoteca of the UNAM stated that in all likelihood Buñuel shot this alternative ending to avoid possible censorship, and that it was probably a decision imposed on him by the film's producer, Óscar Dancigers (Dey 1999: 289). It shows Pedro fighting with Jaibo in Meche's stable. Their destinies are reversed: here it is Jaibo, not Pedro, who falls and is killed. Pedro then returns to the farm school having reclaimed the director's fifty pesos stolen by Jaibo earlier in the film. After reclaiming the money, Pedro briefly meets Ojitos, who lends him his poncho as they sleep under a makeshift shelter. The final shot, the briefest but the most important, has Pedro marching triumphantly away from a static camera through the open gates of the farm school, accompanied by extra-diegetic fanfare (see Figure 19). It seems that this is a potential place where he can belong. This ending, which bears none of the disturbing power of the original, is made all the more remarkable if we consider Tuñón's reading of what drives this film. She asserts that the broken city we are presented with in *Los olvidados* is '[a] fitting setting for his [Buñuel's] characters who are always searching, a setting that parallels the tortured

Figure 19: Welcome home.
(Ultramar Films)

and dismembered bodies' (2003: 87).[15] *Los olvidados* lays before the viewer a painful search: for love, for security, for acceptance. While the original ending, notably with the camera placed at the bottom of a garbage heap as it tracks the rolling motion of Pedro's tortured corpse down the hill, implicates the viewer in the action of Meche and her grandfather, this alternative ending encourages a distancing of the viewer from the uncomfortable social realities of the film through its static camera, the idea of karmic retribution for Jaibo and a salvation narrative for Pedro. The farm school is the end of this search, a place where bodies are 'rehabilitated within the collective', a collective that is uniform and *in* uniform (Dey 1999: 275). Dey reads this ending as a disavowal of the poetics of cruelty within the rest of the film and believes that Pedro's assimilation into the homogenous group is anti-ethical in its negation of individual responsibility. I agree that this saccharine ending is an inflection at odds with the rest of the film: the title relates directly to the dynamic of the film: that these 'forgotten ones' will be constantly searching. Here, Pedro has found and has been remembered. To view this ending as merely an exercise in censorship manipulation would be to reduce its relationship to the original to mere prescriptive functionality. Rather, it functions in dialogue with Pedro's earlier dream sequence, representing a realised belonging – the inversion of the uncanny home and abject place-world. The ultimate cruelty, however, is that this ending is more incredible within Buñuel's narrative than the original.

Whereas Pedro is trapped in a claustrophobic place-world with no home at its centre, Nazarín remains aloof from a sparse place-world with no centre. In chapter four I argued that Nazarín can be considered a kind of existential outsider, perhaps the most concrete example after Simón in his desert of the alienated man across Buñuel's cinema. Nazarín's disavowal of his corporeality in a film where Buñuel repeatedly highlights this is the primary stumbling block to his connection to his surroundings, a dislocation that Buñuel obviously intended to be communicated filmically as, according to the shooting script, the protagonist wanders through 'ordinary road' after 'ordinary landscape'. Yet, as opposed to the liminal Simón, Nazarín is constantly confronted by place, moving through an ever-changing set of landscapes, and by the body as this is ravaged by disease.

The default body type in *Nazarín* is the decaying, diseased or defunct body, with which the hero readily aligns himself in his attempt to sublimate flesh into spirit. The ill body is a constant reminder of Nazarín's lack of a home-place. Jacobson suggests that in

> cases of temporary disjunction with our home or body [fatigue, illness], the possi-
> bilities for acting that are usually open to us through our body or home are somehow
> hindered, and attention is thereby drawn to our body or home. (2009: 371)

This resonates with the way in which the body and the home are brought to the viewer's attention through the staging of Pedro's dream sequence in *Los olvidados*. In *Nazarín*, besides the plague episode, the earlier sequence in which the priest prays for Beatriz's sick niece is important here. Nazarín is surrounded by women – Beatriz, her sister, Ándara and several others – and begins to pray for the girl. However, the women suddenly descend into a state of collective hysteria: one flings herself on the floor while Ándara beats her chest reciting an incantation. Beat-

Figure 20: Nazarín is reminded of his body. (Producciones Barbachano Ponce)

riz's sister touches Nazarín with the flower of a sugar cane, transferring this to her daughter in what María-Dolores Boixadós (1989: 98–99) terms a synthesis of Christian-pagan ritual, and another woman grasps desperately at Nazarín's body (see Figure 20). The scene ends not in religious communion but in a communal carnal paroxysm. Nazarín appears downcast as he is reminded of his physicality. Pain and slander he can easily sublimate via religious faith, but the hero's cognisance of his body brings with it a realisation of a lack of place for this body. Fittingly, the following scene shows Nazarín once again in distance shot on the village's periphery, ready to continue his journey.

A more literal nomad than Simón, Nazarín's peripatetic existence and changing surroundings mean that a successful habitation – a holding of place – is the protagonist's main challenge. Wise writes, 'the nomad is the continual struggle between spatial forces and identity, the struggle to make a home, to create a space that opens up onto other spaces' (2000: 305). This is, in essence, the tension at the heart of *Nazarín*. The reversal of the hero from giver to receiver in the film's final sequence as he accepts the pineapple from the roadside fruit-seller, together with an increasing focus on the body via a series of close-ups on the prisoners' feet as they march and a reinterpretation of Nazarín's head bandage as a marker of his bodily vulnerability rather than a crown of thorns stigmata, is the priest's 'discovery of the reality of man' (Paz 2012: 43) through a spatial lens: his preliminary engagement with place.[16] There is irony here, however. Dey (1999: 163) bemoans the humanist rebirth/theological epiphany readings of the ending. Her desire is that the viewer see beyond the images on screen and acknowledge the ambiguity in the ending. In light of the focus on the home-place, this element of ambiguity in the film's final frames inflects ironically my conclusions in chapter four: certainly, Nazarín has moved towards a preliminary habitation, but when he is finally present-in-place and present-in-body – a form of liberation – we find that his body is following the road to physical confinement in prison. After he has accepted the pineapple, the final frames of the film show an anguished Nazarín, described in the script as dominated by 'un gran dolor' (Buñuel 1958: 104), tracking the hero in mid close-up as he moves along the road. Ultimately, the camera halts, leaving Nazarín to walk out of the frame, inviting the viewer to contemplate his fate. Just when his nomadic existence opens up to other spaces, his trajectory will be an arrested one, in a literal and metaphorical sense, and Nazarín's imprisonment will be an enforced, artificial home-place, whereby 'home can […] become a concretization of human misery: loneliness, rejection, exploitation, and violence' (Pallasmaa 1995: 134).

Housed nowhere and everywhere shut in: *El ángel exterminador*

Perhaps the film of Buñuel's Mexican period that most explicitly negates the idea of the home as a place of comfort is *El ángel exterminador*. Shot in 1962, it is a seminal contribution to Buñuel's body of work as a whole, in terms of both form and content. For some Buñuel scholars, the abject misery of the dinner guests imprisoned in the salon reprises the denigration of the middle classes in *L'Âge d'or*, creating an intertextual dialogue between the two films (Poyato 2011: 152–55). Following an evening at the opera, a group of guests return to the mansion of their hosts Edmundo and Lucía Nóbile to dine. After dinner they find themselves inexplicably trapped in an opulent room adjacent to the larger parlour to which they have retired for some after dinner entertainment, although nothing blocks their exit. The film's original title was to be *The Shipwrecked on Providence Street*; the title invokes the idea – metaphorical this time – of an island as a site of isolation from which there is no escape, and in some ways this is a continuation of *Robinson Crusoe*, except this time the characters do not manage to master their environment.[17] Again, the film's focus on the body in place raises philosophical questions of belonging and alienation that speak to my spatial readings of all the films in this book. The absent home-place is arguably never more conspicuous in the whole of Buñuel's cinema than it is in *El ángel exterminador*; as the victims of Buñuel's metaphorical shipwreck remain stranded in the salon the home figuratively and physically crumbles around them. They are the inverse of Bachelard's truism that we should be '[h]oused everywhere and nowhere shut in'. His argument is that the dweller should remain open to other possible dwellings through dreams as '[i]t is better to live in a state of impermanence than one of finality' (1994: 62; 61). Applied to *El ángel exterminador*, this idealism falters: Buñuel does not give his characters the possibility of an elsewhere as they are *housed nowhere and everywhere shut in*.

Quite obviously, space is crucial in *El ángel exterminador*. As Rebolledo signals, space is important firstly as a 'container', used not only to frame the action but also to contain the characters (1964: 142–47). Pietsie Feenstra (2003: 123–27) grounds what she sees as the film's project to demythologise the upper classes in the film's spatial dynamics, and maps this onto an inside/outside binary pair, whereby the guests are the insiders and the gathering crowd and institutional presence of the police and army outside the mansion are outsiders.[18] However, Feenstra does not consider the possibility that the guests may in fact be outsiders, yanked from the reassuring but artificial comforts of their collective place-world through a process of exteriority. This is where the filmic portrayal of the body in place comes to the fore as the twenty-one characters are subjected to corporeal disintegration.

The guests' prolonged imprisonment has obvious bodily implications. Aside from the scatological allusions in the recurring shots of the Chinese urns in the closet that the guests use to alleviate themselves, there are numerous scenes in which the characters perform perfunctory bodily tasks: Alicia is shown cutting her toenails; Silvia is chastised by Juana and her brother Francisco for combing her hair absent-mindedly; various male characters are seen shaving their legs. However, Buñuel goes beyond the merely somatic to show the psychosomatic effect of the guests' imprisonment. Buñuel's intention to focus on the body here is beyond doubt. According to the staging directions in film's shooting script: '[t]he Director will show with discretion the various "tics" that some of the guests have developed: pulling out hair, twitching of eyes, getting rid of blackheads from the nose' (Buñuel 1962: 66).[19] Blanca is shown to pull out clumps of hair, and Francisco's face repeatedly contorts with rage. Furthermore, when the fiancés Beatriz and Eduardo commit suicide in the closet in an act of *amour fou*, their blood seeps underneath the closed door. These psychosomatic discharges and bodily fluids betray an increasing exteriority of what they hope to keep hidden, rendered in criticism of the film as the bestial instincts of man.[20] When taken together with the decomposition of the salon, this degradation has crucial implications for the home.

The claustrophobic room which acts as the prison of the náufragos is, like their bodies, pockmarked by their attempts to burst the water pipe and fuel a fire to roast the three sheep, originally intended as a practical joke during the dinner party, that later wander into the salon. The state of their bodies mirrors that of the room, exposing what is hidden beneath a superficial semblance of respectability and security. For Pérez Soler, the interior becomes 'the site where all those dreaded miseries from which it [the bourgeoisie] has sought to escape actually emerge' (2003: 409). The use of the verb 'emerge' is interesting. There is palpable sense of something emerging in *El ángel exterminador*: more concretely, what surfaces from the disintegration of the mansion and the body is anxiety. According to Heidegger:

> In anxiety one feels '*uncanny*'. Here the peculiar indefiniteness of that which Dasein finds itself alongside in anxiety, comes proximally to expression: the 'nothing and nowhere'. But here 'uncanniness' also means 'not-being-at-home'. (Heidegger 1962: 233)

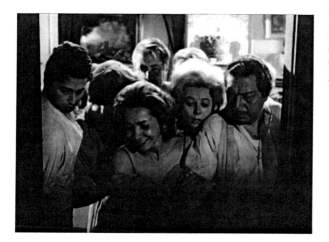

Figure 21: It came from inside the closet: the emergence of anxiety. (Producciones Gustavo Alatriste)

Anxiety's symptom is therefore an uncanny affliction. The uncanny as Heidegger explains it is a lack (a nothing and a nowhere) and a not-being-at-home: a lack of home. The fact that Buñuel chooses the house as the space in which to bring this anxiety to the surface is an acerbic comment that exposes the characters' forced domesticity as a pretence, an idea that Pallasmaa, writing more generally about the affect of architecture in cinema, identifies: '[a]nxiety and alienation, hardly hidden by surface rationalization, are often the emotional contents of today's everyday settings' (2007: 35). One sequence in particular, through its striking cinematography, vividly illustrates this. After the fiancés Beatriz and Eduardo have committed suicide in the closet and Juana has alerted the group to the puddle of blood oozing under the door, the doctor tentatively opens the closet as the rest of the guests jostle like morbid voyeurs behind him. Buñuel then cuts to a mid-distance shot from inside the closet space as the characters are seen peering in, their faces contorted in dread (see figure 21). The viewer must assume that the object of their repulsion is the pair of bloody corpses but, crucially, the object of their gaze is largely out of the frame, save for a fleeting shot of the fiancés' heads as the guests are being shepherded away. The visual ambiguity in this *mise-en-scène* as the characters look in the direction of the camera, almost breaking the fourth wall, is key. Heidegger claims that anxiety is not directed towards a particular material object, but rather towards an indefiniteness, rendering it fundamentally existential. It should be noted that for Heidegger this mode of being is not inherently negative; indeed, it is necessary to disclose 'the world as world', in the sense that it individualises a person's being-in-the-world, preventing this from getting lost in the general, impersonal 'they' and from acquiring a 'tranquillized self-assurance' (Heidegger 1962: 232, 233). In this striking shot, the guests are looking beyond the camera, into the empty space the audience cannot see because Buñuel will not show it. Buñuel's closet here is the nothing and the nowhere of Heidegger's anxiety.

Things do not improve for Buñuel's shipwrecked souls. As I have argued elsewhere (Ripley 2016), even though they eventually escape the salon, the diners do not manage to escape their collective alienation, as the final sequence of the film in the church suggests. A lateral tracking shot of the characters, clad respectably once again, shows their apathy as the service comes to an end. Attempting to leave the church, they, and the other faithful, find they are again imprisoned, this time on a larger scale. Thus, anxiety as represented in this film does not appear to give rise to a level of attunement of being-in-the-world, or 'why we are open to the world as a possibility for ourselves', as Svenaeus (2000: 8) puts it, due to the simple fact that this anxiety is repeated and expatiated. The choice that faces the diners, to acknowledge the uncanny homelessness that underpins their existence, has consequences they are not prepared to face. The only certainty, then, is one of confinement without resolution. Thus, this ending visualises more sardonically the essence of Nazarín's fate and forms a thematic intertext with the ending of *Simón del desierto*. It is the Buñuelian repetitive cycle *par excellence*, as proposed by Deleuze, and the more the characters are confined within, the more they are externalised. Imprisonment is mapped onto micro and macro territories, from home to church to world. They are housed nowhere and everywhere shut in.

The Marxist inside/outside interpretation of this film's spatial dynamics is too inflexible a distinction, then. Robert Miles believes a 'concern with border crossing and identification with insiders or outsiders is central to, indeed is the entire pretext for the development of the narrative'. Ultimately, he affirms the validity of a philosophical reading of this film. He writes that the film 'is structured by the perpetually unstable dynamics of belonging as it performs them' (2006: 180). I would argue this film does not perform the dynamics of belonging, but shows us the extreme consequences of unbelonging, underscoring in various ways all of the films I have looked at in this book. The increasing externalisation of the characters' bodies and psyches through the emergence of carnal fluids and compulsions hollows out the meaning of the home. This space shifts from Bachelard's apotheosised image to an uncanny receptor for the accumulating toll of decay and death, and the unsettling events on screen are also transposed onto the viewer. Gutiérrez-Albilla claims that Buñuel's own existential anxieties in this film 'express the idea that human beings have become aware of the absurdity of the world' (2008: 93). As the mask of tranquillised self-assurance slips, anxiety that the viewer sees on screen induces discomfort in the audience off screen, for 'what surfaces in anxiety is human existence as such: every "thing" in the world – every project – reveals itself as empty against the backdrop of a basic meaningless – a homelessness of life' (Svenaeus 2000: 8). To posit a rigid inside/outside binary here is to dull the film's impact, forcing us to adopt a faux working-class-hero position and identify automatically with the home help rather than the bourgeoisie. The disturbing potential – I use the term with both its emotional and spatial meanings – of the film is brought out by a more flexible reading that acknowledges the film as a comment on the façade of rational human existence. Ultimately, this interpretation is more faithful to Buñuel's directive to the viewer settling down to watch the film: '[i]f the film that you are about to see seems to you enigmatic or incongruous, that is how life is also. […] Perhaps the best explanation for *The Exterminating Angel* is that, rationally, there is none' (Miles 2006: 179, n. 15). Buñuel's non-explanation of this film leads us to believe that celluloid reality has the potential to expose the celluloid, or artificial, aspect of our reality; a case of reel life exposing real life, as Aitken and Zonn put it (1994: 5). Perhaps with this film, more than any of his others, Buñuel understood the affective potential of film, as '[c]inema and architecture, as all art, function as alluring projection screens for our emotions' (Pallasmaa 2007: 32).

Conclusions: an impossible home?

In all the films I have discussed in this book, the characters' interaction with and action in their environments is frequently founded on negation and doubt. Read as philosophical texts, the films seem to espouse Novalis's thought that philosophy 'is really homesickness, an urge to be at home everywhere' (O'Donoghue 2011: 21, n. 2). It is this impulse to be at home that appears precluded in Buñuel's Mexican cinema. As the images of home, or a possible home, are undermined filmically, the various ideas of home are systematically undone in the films I have included here, creating mutual points of convergence.

Bachelard writes that 'our house is our corner of the world. As has often been said, it is our first universe, a real cosmos in every sense of the word' (1994: 4). The home as primordial location from which to set out into the world is negated in *Simón del desierto*, as Simón remains stranded in the desert, just as it is in *La Mort en ce jardin*, because the diamond miners of the anonymous Latin American republic are cut off from their origins. My focus on liminal space in chapter three highlights the protagonists' positions between spatial referents. Bringing this into dialogue with considerations of home and belonging, it becomes apparent that the characters' respective surroundings – the desert and the jungle – are unequivocally closed worlds, surroundings which do not open onto other, different spaces and which undermine Wise's assertion that '[h]ome [...] is a collection of milieus, and as such is the organization of markers (objects) and the formation of space' (2000: 299). The protagonists' liminal *azzeramento* – a setting at zero, temporally without past or future and spatially without a here or there – renders them unable to distinguish a homeworld from an alienworld. Furthermore, the ill-fated lovers in *Abismos de pasión* are the embodiment of the Trickster, an extra-existential figure at home in a liminal homelessness, rendered as the abyss of the film's title. The parched landscape of this film does unfold onto another milieu: the infinite finitude of death. Ironically, only in death can the lovers be said to have achieved a belonging, inverting the depiction of the home-place as origin.

Similarly, home as something to be constructed is not possible in the above films. Wise writes that 'home is a becoming within an always already territorialized space (the home, the house, the domestic)' (2000: 301). The implication here is obviously that the result of such action, the process of becoming, is intrinsically salutary. However, for the dinner guests in *El ángel exterminador*, the mansion becomes nothing more than a container, de-territorialised and fragmented to its inhabitants, while the guests themselves become primitive figures. Indeed, Pérez Soler points out that 'the domestic interior becomes the bourgeois' tomb. In this way, Buñuel takes the idea of dwelling as casing to a macabre – but cogent – ending' (2003: 411). For all his efforts, Crusoe's island is also a casing of sorts, making his escape impossible. However, unlike the closed desert and jungle, it is penetrated by other milieus that themselves remain incomplete, fragments of another life as the world beyond its shores is emptied of all meaning. This lack of meaning undermines his prospective home. A refugee of sorts, Crusoe's attempt to recreate his previous 'middle station' of life – admired now in retrospect – is only partially successful and is readily abandoned in favour of a return to the previous world from which Crusoe felt the need to escape. For his part, Nazarín's realisation of himself as an autonomous being implies that he has become aware of his body and the place that it occupies. According to Trigg, '[h]ome is thought of as a thing to be salvaged from the wreckage of memory, there to be reinserted into the living self, as though it had accidentally fallen by the wayside but now demanded recollection' (2012:

195). The pineapple that the priest tearfully accepts salvages a sense of being aware of his physicality and his place. However, as Nazarín exits the frame in the final shot, returned to the world, he is ironically moving towards nothing more than 'the sterility of a new and definitive isolation' (Fuentes 1970: 141).[21]

The connotation of home most difficult to disavow – the home as a protective shelter – is systematically subverted in *Los olvidados*. Bachelard's initial metaphor for the house is a cradle, where 'life begins well, […] enclosed, protected, all warm in the house' (1994: 7). Pedro's shack is pervaded by the cruelty of the surrounding place-world while the *idios* of this place-world is expressed through his mother's body in the dream sequence. The structure provides little protection or maternal warmth, and given the elision of the caring, wholesome mother with the home and the homeland, the vitriolic public reaction to the images of maternal neglect could easily be interpreted as an outcry against the representation in Buñuel's film of a failed home as much as a perverted motherhood. For Evvie, the game-preserve is a site of coercion, leading to her forced sexual initiation. Buñuel counters the association of the island with an idyllic retreat from the opening sequence of *The Young One*, as Traver is faced with the hostile sign to would-be trespassers. Miller's abortive utopia, like Crusoe's, is caught in the skein of cultural influence and the intrusion of the mainland society, against which the island comes to be constituted as a heterotopic space of crisis (for Evvie) and deviation (for Miller), is omnipresent. Furthermore, for Evvie at least, this crisis heterotopia will merely be replaced by another: the children's home – for children with no home. In this way, Evvie echoes Nazarín: as both characters become aware of their bodies, both move on to uncertain, and presumably institutionalised, futures. Finally, the opulent mansion and plush bureaucratic interiors of Ojeda inhabited by Inés and Vázquez in *La Fièvre monte à El Pao* are not impervious to the ubiquitous gaze of totalitarian power. As a satellite state, Ojeda is in a condition of authoritarian finality. Heidegger's often-cited definition of dwelling is that it is a 'staying with things' (1971: 151); that is, 'cultivating a relationship to the broader environment, allowing the indeterminacy of place to grow within us as we adapt to a world of new horizons' (Trigg 2012: 195). The *mise-en-scène* of this film suggests that the protagonists are staying *under* and *behind* things, oppressed by the heat, the starched white uniforms and the constant surveillance behind closed doors and blinds. Vázquez's political idealism leads not to change, but indirectly causes Inés's death and his own certain death: Ojeda offers no indeterminacy, imposing only a state of finality.

Notes

1   For an overview of this approach see Seamon and Sowers's summary of existential geography (2009: 666–71).

2   Feminist scholars have challenged Bachelard's implicitly classed and gendered writing, whereby the home is a haven. Joshua M. Price (2002), for example, considers the home as the site of concealment for violence against women, while Beatriz Muñoz González (2005) investigates the contradictory emotions experienced by Spanish housewives in their domestic labour.

3   [lugares cerrados, sin salida aparente, los expone a situaciones extremas que sacan a la luz sus contradicciones y miserias, y al final los redime o los condena]; [camino a la perfección].

4   Javier Herrera (2006: 145–57) uses the term *anti-viaje* [anti-voyage] to describe Buñuel's movement in Las Hurdes, contrasting Buñuel's journey in the region to that of Alfonso XIII in 1922. Herrera claims that the King's visit was an exercise in propaganda, intended to counter the claims of backwardness and neglect associated with the region.

5   [totalmente desorientado].

6   [la mayor antífrasis de todo el cine de Buñuel y el final en que el director más se separa de su protagonista].

7   [quizá la más dramática escenificación buñueliana del tema de la falta de comunicación y de diálogo entre los hombres].

8   [a dimostrazione di una chiusura sostanziale del mondo rappresentato, hanno assai spesso una struttura circolare, [...] quel mondo non ha uscite].

9   [Les éléments de base du scénario sont donnés comme totalement abstraits, l'argent par exemple, sans aucun rapport avec une utilisation pratique possible régit les événements et le comportement des personnages dans des lieux tout aussi abstraits].

10   Julie Jones (1997: 162, n. 1) believes *Tierra sin pan* foreshadows the latter in its use of a primitive and barren landscape as setting.

11   In addition to Jones's article cited above, Sam Ishii-Gonzalès (2003) and Michael Popkin (1987) are analyses framed by surrealism.

12   [kehrt zu den Anfängen zurück, entfacht das surrealistische Feuer noch einmal mit einem gewaltigen Windstoß leidenschaftlicher, zeit- und ortaufhebender Gewalt].

13 [un espace irrémédiablement clos entre des collines qui semblent s'étendre à l'infini].

14 [non domestiqué par l'homme].

15 [[un] escenario preciso para sus personajes que siempre buscan, escenario paralelo a los cuerpos torturados y desmembrados].

16 [descubrimiento de la realidad del hombre].

17 See Dey (1999: 86–129) for more on the link between the two films.

18 See also Marsha Kinder (2009), who reads this along class lines, writing that 'the film also spatializes the sharp class division between insiders and outsiders'.

19 [[e]l Director irá mostrando con discreción los distintos "tics" que han ido adquiriendo algunos invitados: arrancarse pelos de las cejas, guiño de ojos, sacarse capinillas [sic] de la nariz]. The word *capinilla* is not in the dictionary of the *Real Academia Española de la Lengua* and appears to be Buñuel's own invention. It is close to *espinilla*, the word for blackhead. There is a scene where Silvia Pinal's character is shown squeezing spots on her nose in front of the mirror.

20 Michel Estève (1978: 248) believes that the bourgeois guests become wolf-like in this film.

21 [la esterilidad de un nuevo y definitivo aislamiento].

Conclusion

umming up the characters in Buñuel's films, Humberto Ávila Dueñas says simply that they are 'on a constant search to reach something that is impossible for them to achieve' (1994: 289).[1] He is writing specifically about Buñuel's Mexican period and his words inform my reading of the films in this book. This search is palpable in Buñuel's cinema and often forms the subtext of different focuses in criticism: the surrealist impulse towards libertarianism in *L'Âge d'or*, for example, or thwarted sexual desire in any number of the filmmaker's movies, none more so than *Cet obscur objet du désir*. Clearly, Ávila Dueñas's observation is also a recasting of Carlos Fuentes's metaphorical 'search for the authentic self' of Buñuel's characters, Michel's ideal of de-alienation and Chaspoul's belief that Buñuel's characters never come to successfully inhabit the places in which they find themselves, as I outlined in chapter one. Paradoxically, then, the originality of my reading of the Mexican films works to a large extent from within traditional Buñuel scholarship, expanding both the potential meaning and relevance of critical literature on Buñuel and possible readings of the film texts themselves.

As I have explained, the spatial dynamics of these films have been frequently intimated by researchers and critics, yet ultimately left largely undeveloped. The interdisciplinary critical approach to this body of work that I have employed in this book supports an alternative reading of these films, simultaneously freeing up the commercial strand of the Mexican cinema from genre-based analysis and elaborating an alternative interpretation of the more auteurist films beyond tried-and-tested paradigms in Buñuel studies. This has enabled a complementary reading of films traditionally considered more auteurist and the so-called studio potboilers independently of frameworks previously used to situate the two together, such as those informed by psychoanalysis and sexual theory. My intention is that this book should serve as a springboard for further research, particularly on Buñuel's Mexican films, as the number of extended studies of the works of this period remains relatively low, even if writing on the period has advanced over the course of the past few decades.

The research in this book also has implications for approaches in film studies. As what García Riera terms 'an authentic "Author"' (1960: 55), Buñuel's work has traditionally been viewed from an auteur perspective, in turn supported by established theoretical paradigms in film analysis. Indeed, Linda Williams identifies four main branches of Buñuel criticism: the surrealist Buñuel, the realist Buñuel, the auteurist Buñuel and the formalist Buñuel, and the proponents of each branch (1996: 199–206). In terms of spatial analysis, an auteur-biographical approach has coloured analyses of transnationalism and exile in Buñuel's cinema, often seeking to *place* his films in claiming them for Mexican, Spanish or French national cinemas. Ironically, though, if we foreground the importance of a spatial reading informed by philosophical themes of freedom and alienation that are already fundamental to various branches of Buñuel criticism, the underlying *placelessness* of these largely realist films is highlighted, and we do not have to read Buñuel's films through Buñuel-the-man to see this. Although Williams ultimately locates Buñuel's films in the surrealist tradition, she acknowledges that the director's movies constantly resist categorisation, that they 'wiggle out of this tenuous grasp and force us, once again, to question our critical methods' (1996: 205). My own intention in developing readings of the Mexican films informed by human geography, anthropology and philosophy has been to wiggle out of and question tried-and-tested analytical frameworks with regards to Buñuel, and show how previous scholarship on the filmmaker can open up fresh avenues for exploration, not only in Buñuel studies but more broadly within film studies.

In reading the film text spatially, this book takes inspiration from the spatial turn in analysis in the humanities and social sciences. As an inherently visual medium, cinema can utilise space and setting to add another layer of meaning to the narrative. Melbye terms this deeper meaning 'cinematic allegory'. By this he means a particular mode of narrative that moves beyond the literal towards the symbolic. As such, these 'narratives invite a second interpretation beyond the immediately visible world that is otherwise sufficient in more conventional films to entertain an audience' (2010: 3). Buñuel's Mexican cinema works on both levels. The films over which he was able to exercise a greater level of authorial control still function as traditional narrative cinema, even if they are tricky to place when it comes to genre. The more commercial movies, as I have read them alongside their more auterist counterparts, retain the same potential to disturb us as viewers through their symbolism. My analysis approximates Melbye's definition of cinematic allegory applied to both of these strands, using them as a foundation from which to consider the representation of belonging in film. As such, aside from its thematic focus on space, this book roughly fits in to the growing appraisal of film as a possible philosophical text, a promising discipline that Daniel Shaw (2008: 4) argues is in its infancy, and is finding useful outlets in journals such as *Film-Philosophy* or groups such as the Society for the Philosophic Study of the Contemporary Visual Arts. I do not claim that this is the sole method of interpreting the texts, nor am I proposing any intentional fallacy, and my reticence stems in part from the large number of auteurist approaches to Buñuel that focus on well-known themes in his work. However, it is worth recalling that Buñuel read philosophy during his time in Madrid at the *Residencia de Estudiantes* and avoided dictating monolithic meaning in his films: 'there is an element of mystery, of doubt, of ambiguity. I'm always ambiguous. Ambiguity is part of my nature because it breaks with immutable preconceived ideas' (de la Colina and Pérez Turrent 1992: 182–3). In glimpsing another possible reading beyond the level of narrative, one that questions the concept of a stable dwelling place, I am conscious of Buñuel's commitment to breaking fixed idea(l)s.

The question remains, then, in what way the argument put forward in this book inflects Buñuel's cinema. Should we take these films in a wholly pessimistic spirit? I am convinced that such a judgement would be contrary to Buñuel's adherence to ambiguity. The question is a complex one with no easy answer. We can look to Wood's essay on Buñuel's Mexican films in this respect, however:

> Luis Buñuel said more than once that his films were designed to show us that we do not live in the best of worlds. They certainly do that, but the formulation scarcely seems strong enough, or flexible enough. […] Buñuel's films display a world which *must* be changed, which is intolerable. But they offer no indication of how this world can be changed; indeed, they usually intimate that it cannot. (1993: 41)

Buñuel's cinema provides no exit from the disturbing and upsetting (used here in a spatial, as well as literal, sense) worlds that it portrays. The narrative linearity of his commercial and auteurist Mexican movies, as opposed to the formal complexity of the later French films, veils a marked exploration of the fundamental human need to find a place in a world that continually prevents this. Wood is quite right that this underlying reading has, perhaps, gone largely unnoticed by viewers and enthusiasts of the director's Mexican films. As such, the questioning of what it means to be securely in place, depicted in the films included in this book, is not necessarily as pessimistic as it might seem. Read philosophically, I argue these films inflect Wood's hypothesis that we do not live in the best of worlds, because they really suggest that such a utopian vision does not exist and is itself deceptive. Indeed, the pursuit of a utopian ideal – be it Miller's perverted counter social structure, Nazarín and Simón's relentless sublimation or the misplaced belief in the stability of the bourgeois position in *El ángel exterminador* – is the cause of many of the characters' states of dissatisfaction, instability and uncertainty.

Hugo Santander proposes that Buñuel is ultimately an existential director. Santander's summation of what he considers Buñuel's ethic is important here:

> Throughout his films, Buñuel debated ethics in a negative way – for, as Dante, he is interested in the tortures of the doomed. His cinema invites viewers to recognize their animality – to listen to *instinct* before logic, in order to conciliate life and death, heaven and earth, the universe and the particular, men and society. (2002)

Just as François Truffaut argues that Buñuel's cinema is based upon a principle of negation, as he 'never makes films for, always against' (1982: 261–62), the films of the Mexican period define their characters by what they are not and what they do not have – contentment and belonging – exploring in a negative way human interaction with the world. The binary pairs Santander lists, typical of Buñuel's cinema, are palpable in the Mexican films, and the play between the two is rendered spatially: Alejandro and Catalina's struggle to achieve death over life in a barren landscape; Nazarín's ambivalence towards his self and society as an existential outsider; Simón's liminal positioning between heaven and earth, and the desert and nightclub that extend this position horizontally. Santander suggests that the key to liberation for Buñuel's protagonists, and the spectators, lies in their recognition of their earthly, imperfect nature. Wood, though, questions the viability of this liberation. He believes Buñuel's cinema suggests that

> Perhaps we do see things as they are; their nudity is what is intolerable, and we hasten to cover it with words and explanations, theories, nationalities, contexts.

There is no way out of this procedure, it seems; we cannot bear much reality. (1993: 51)

If we take the nudity to which Wood refers to be the realisation of our precarious position – as much in a literal, spatial sense as in a figurative, contextual one – in the world, the films' humanity lies precisely in the way that they reveal, viscerally, our own nudity to us. This is the value of Buñuel's cinema as art. From its inception in the eye-slitting sequence in *Un Chien andalou* to its completion, as the seamstress sews up the hole in the bloodied garment at the end of *Cet obscur objet du désir*, Buñuel's is an instinctive cinema that disturbs and upsets us. Space, as cinematic allegory, is the ideal canvas on which to expose, aesthetically and philosophically, our pursuit of liberty as a phantom at the same time as Buñuel depicts a profound humanity, and even sometimes a biting comedy, in our relentless search.

Note

1 [en una búsqueda constante para conseguir algo que les es imposible lograr].

References

Filmography

The Adventures of Robinson Crusoe, dir. by Luis Buñuel (Orbit Media, 2007).

El ángel exterminador, dir. by Luis Buñuel (Criterion, 2008).

Death in the Garden [*La Mort en ce jardin*], dir. by Luis Buñuel (Translux Films, 2009).

Das Fieber steigt in El Pao [*La Fièvre monte à El Pao*], dir. by Luis Buñuel (Kinowelt, 2010).

Les Hauts de Hurlevent [Abismos de pasión], dir. by Luis Buñuel (Films sans Frontières, 2006).

Nazarín, dir. by Luis Buñuel (Yume Pictures, 2006).

Los olvidados, dir. by Luis Buñuel (Films sans Frontières, 2001).

Simon of the Desert [*Simón del desierto*], dir. by Luis Buñuel (Criterion, 2008).

The Young One, dir. by Luis Buñuel (Optimum, 2006).

Bibliography

Acevedo-Muñoz, Ernesto R. (2003) *Buñuel and Mexico: The Crisis of National Cinema*. Berkeley, CA: University of California Press.

____ (2013) 'Transitional Triptych: The Traps of International Cinemas in Buñuel's *Cela s'appelle l'aurore*, *La Mort en ce jardin*, and *La Fièvre monte à El Pao*', in Rob Stone and Julián Daniel Gutiérrez-Albilla (eds) *A Companion to Luis Buñuel*. Oxford: Wiley-Blackwell, 340–61.

Aitken, Stuart C. and Leo E. Zonn (1994) '*Re*-Presenting the Place Pastiche', in Stuart C. Aitken and Leo E. Zonn (eds) *Place, Power, Situation, and Spectacle: A Geography of Film*. Lanham: Rowman & Littlefield, 3–25.

Anon. (1974) 'Die mexikanische Kreidekreis', *Der Spiegel*, 21 January, 112–14.

Aranda, Francisco (1976) *Luis Buñuel: A Critical Biography*, ed. and trans. David Robinson. New York: Da Capo Press.

Archer, Eugene (1960) 'Buñuel's "Dixie" down Mexico Way', *New York Times*, 29 May, x5.

Arias, Santa (2010) 'Rethinking Space: An Outsider's View of the Spatial Turn', *GeoJournal*, 75, 29–41.

Ávila Dueñas and Iván Humberto (1994) *El cine mexicano de Luis Buñuel: estudio analítico de los argumentos y personajes*. Mexico City: Instituto Mexicano de Cinematografía.

Bachelard, Gaston (1994) *The Poetics of Space*, trans. Maria Jolas. Boston, MA: Beacon.

Barbáchano, Carlos (2000) *Luis Buñuel*. Madrid: Alianza.

Barro Hernández, Mario (2016) 'Ese oscuro objeto de análisis: estudios sobre Luis Buñuel (con una indicación sobre su etapa mexicana)', *Bulletin of Spanish Studies*, 93 (4), 623–38.

Bateson, Gregory (1935) 'Culture Contact and Schismogenesis', *Man*, 35, 178–83.

Baudrillard, Jean (1994) *Simulacra and Simulation*, trans. Sheila Faria Glaser. Ann Arbor, MI: University of Michigan Press.

Baxter, John (1994) *Buñuel*. London: Fourth Estate.

Bazin, André (1978) '*Los Olvidados*', trans. Sallie Iannotti, in Joan Mellen (ed.) *The World of Luis Buñuel: Essays in Criticism*. New York, NY: Oxford University Press, 194–200.

Bermúdez, Xavier (2000) *Buñuel: espejo y sueño*. Valencia: Ediciones de la Mirada.

Bernardi, Auro (1999) 'Introducción', trans. María E. Schettino Valencia, in Auro Bernardi (ed.) *Buñuel: cittadino messicano – ciudadano mexicano*. Genoa: Le Mani, 8–11.

Bernardi, Sandro (2002) *Il paesaggio nel cinema italiano*. Venice: Marsilio Editori.

Bikandi-Mejias, Aitor (2000) *El carnaval de Luis Buñuel: estudios sobre una tradición cultural*. Madrid: Akal.

Blum, Ryan H. (2010) 'Anxious Latitudes: Heterotopias, Subduction Zones, and the Historico-Spatial Configurations within *Dead Man*', *Critical Studies in Media Communication*, 27 (1), 55–66.

Bogue, Ronald (2003) *Deleuze on Cinema*. London: Routledge.

Boixadós, María-Dolores (1989) 'Nazarín el anarquista: literatura y cine, Galdós y Buñuel', *La Torre: Revista de la Universidad de Puerto Rico*, 3 (9), 91–103.

Boscaljon, Daniel (ed.) 2013 *Resisting the Place of Belonging: Uncanny Homecomings in Religion, Narrative and the Arts.* Farnham: Ashgate.

Bourdieu, Pierre (1977) *Outline of a Theory of Practice*, trans. Richard Nice. Cambridge: Cambridge University Press.

Brosseder, Claudia (2000) 'Der zitternde Fuß. Buñuels Obsessionen', *Frankfurter Allgemeine Zeitung*, 26 July, 52.

Browne, Kath, Jason Lim and Gavin Brown (eds) (2007) *Geographies of Sexualities: Theory, Practices and Politics.* Aldershot: Ashgate.

Buache, Freddy (1973) *Luis Buñuel*, trans. Peter Graham. London: Tantivy.

Buñuel, Juan Luis (1978) 'A Letter on *The Exterminating Angel*', in Joan Mellen (ed.) *The World of Luis Buñuel: Essays in Criticism.* New York, NY: Oxford University Press, 254–56.

Buñuel, Juan Luis and Rafael Buñuel (2000) 'Afterword', in *An Unspeakable Betrayal: Selected Writings of Luis Buñuel.* Berkeley, CA: University of California Press, 265.

Buñuel, Luis (1958) *Nazarín/Luis Buñuel* [typewritten script with handwritten emendations]. Madrid, Filmoteca Española, Archivo Buñuel (AB 541).

_____ (1962) *El ángel exterminador/Luis Buñuel* [typewritten script with handwritten emendations]. Madrid, Filmoteca Española, Archivo Buñuel (AB 527) .

_____ (2001) [1982] *Mi último suspiro*, 2nd edn, trans. Ana María de la Fuente. Barcelona: Plaza & Janés.

_____ (2003) *My Last Sigh*, trans. Abigail Israel. Minneapolis, MN: University of Minnesota Press.

Buñuel, Luis and H. B. Addis (1960) *'The Young One': A Screenplay* [typewritten script with handwritten emendations]. Madrid, Filmoteca Española, Archivo Buñuel (AB 524).

Buñuel, Luis and Julio Alejandro (1964) *Guión de Simón del desierto.* [typewritten script with handwritten emendations]. Madrid, Filmoteca Española, Archivo Buñuel (AB 1479).

Casey, Edward S. (2001a) 'Between Geography and Philosophy: What Does It Mean to Be in the Place-World?', *Annals of the Association of American Geographers*, 91 (4), 683–93.

_____ (2001b) 'Body, Self and Landscape: A Geophilosophical Inquiry into the Place-World', in Paul C. Adams, Steven D. Hoelscher and Karen E. Till (eds) *Textures of Place: Exploring Humanist Geographies.* Minneapolis, MN: University of Minnesota Press, 403–25.

____ (2009) [1993] *Getting Back into Place: Toward a Renewed Understanding of the Place-World*, 2nd edn. Bloomington, IN: Indiana University Press.

Cevera, Elena (ed.) (2008a) *México fotografiado por Luis Buñuel*. Madrid: Ministerio de Cultura, Filmoteca Española, CBC.

____ (2008b) 'La exposición', in Elena Cevera (ed.) *México fotografiado por Luis Buñuel*. Madrid: Ministerio de Cultura, Filmoteca Española, CBC, 13–20.

Chaspoul, Charles (1997) 'Luis Buñuel: cinéma exilé, cinéma exilant', *Positif*, 435, 113–18.

Clarke, David (1997) *The Cinematic City*. London: Routledge.

Coates, Paul (1985) *The Story of the Lost Reflection: The Alienation of the Image in Western and Polish Culture*. London: Verso.

Conley, Tom (2008) '*Viridiana* Coca-Cola', in Joan Ramon Resina and Andrés Lema-Hincapié (eds) *Burning Darkness: A Half Century of Spanish Cinema*. Albany, NY: SUNY Press, 43–60.

Connor, James A (1993) 'Strategies for Hyperreal Travelers', *Science Fiction Studies*, 20 (1), 69–79.

Conrad, Randall (1978) 'A Magnificent and Dangerous Weapon: The Politics of Luis Buñuel's Later Films', in Joan Mellen (ed.) *The World of Luis Buñuel: Essays in Criticism*. New York, NY: Oxford University Press, 332–51.

____ (1994) 'No Blacks or Whites: The Making of Luis Buñuel's *The Young One*', *Cinéaste*, 20 (3), 28–31.

Corbucci, Gianfranco (1974) 'L'approccio brechtiano nel periodo dei film messicani' *Cinema Nuovo*, 227, 41–43.

Corby, Louise (1961) '*The Young One*', *Films in Review*, 12, 111–12.

De la Colina, José and Tomás Pérez Turrent (1992) *Objects of Desire: Conversations with Luis Buñuel*, ed. and trans. Paul Lenti. New York, NY: Marsilio.

____ (1993) *Buñuel por Buñuel*. Madrid: PLOT.

De la Mare, Walter (1932) [1930]. *Desert Islands and Robinson Crusoe*, 2nd edn. London: Faber and Faber.

Deleuze, Gilles (1992) *Cinema 1: The Movement-Image*, trans. Hugh Tomlinson and Barbara Habberjam. London: Athlone.

Deleuze, Gilles and Félix Guattari (2004) *A Thousand Plateaus: Capitalism and Schizophrenia*, trans. Brian Massumi. London: Continuum.

Delmas, Jean (1978) 'Buñuel, Citizen of Mexico', trans. Sallie Iannotti, in Joan Mellen (ed.) *The World of Luis Buñuel: Essays in Criticism*. New York, NY: Oxford University Press, 186–93.

Dey, Catherine E. (1999) 'Buñuel's 'Other' Films: Responding to Work from the Mexican Period'. PhD thesis. University of Birmingham.

D'Lugo, Marvin (2003) 'Subversive Travel: The Transnational Buñuel in Mexico', in Isabel Santaolalla, Patricia d'Allemand, Jorge Díaz Cintas, Peter William Evans, Consuelo Sanmateu, Alistair Whyte and Michael Witt (eds) *Buñuel, siglo XXI*. Zaragoza: Prensas Universitarias de Zaragoza, 89–100.

____ (2004) 'Hybrid Culture and Acoustic Imagination: The Case of *Robinson Crusoe*', in Peter Evans and Isabel Santaolalla (eds) *Luis Buñuel: New Readings*. London: British Film Institute, 80–96.

Donohoe, Janet (2011) 'The Place of Home', *Environmental Philosophy*, 8 (1), 25–40.

Durgnat, Raymond (1977) [1967] *Luis Buñuel*. rev. edn. Berkeley, CA: University of California Press.

Eco, Umberto (1987) *Travels in Hyperreality*, trans. William Weaver. London: Picador.

Edwards, Gwynne (1982) *The Discreet Art of Luis Buñuel*. London: Marion Boyars.

____ (2004) 'A Spanish Triptych', in Robert Havard (ed.) *A Companion to Spanish Surrealism*. Woodbridge: Tamesis, 79–96.

____ (2005) *A Companion to Luis Buñuel*. Woodbridge: Tamesis.

Elizondo, Salvador (1961) 'Luis Buñuel, un visionario', *Nuevo Cine*, 4–5, 2–7.

Elliott, Bridget and Anthony Purdy (2006) 'A Walk through Heterotopia: Peter Greenaway's Landscapes by Numbers', in Martin Lefebvre (ed.) *Landscape and Film*. Abingdon: Routledge, 267–90.

Endsjø, Dag Øistein (2000) 'To Lock up Eleusis: A Question of Liminal Space', *Numen*, 47 (4), 351–86.

Espada, Javier (2008) 'Fotografías para una exposición', in Elena Cevera (ed.) *México fotografiado por Luis Buñuel*. Madrid: Ministerio de Cultura, Filmoteca Española, CBC, 21–30.

Estève, Michel (1978) '*The Exterminating Angel*: No Escape from the Human Condition', trans. Sallie Iannotti, in Joan Mellen (ed.) *The World of Luis Buñuel: Essays in Criticism*. New York, NY: Oxford University Press, 244–54.

Evans, Peter William (1982) 'The Discreet Charm of the Revolutionary', *Guardian*, 5 June, 10.

____ (1995) *The Films of Luis Buñuel: Subjectivity and Desire*. Oxford: Oxford University Press.

_____ (2004) 'The Indiscreet Charms of the Bourgeoises and Other Women', in Peter William Evans and Isabel Santaolalla (eds) *Luis Buñuel: New Readings*. London: British Film Institute, 143–56.

Evans, Peter William and Isabel Santaolalla (eds) 2004. *Luis Buñuel: New Readings* London: British Film Institute.

Everett, Wendy and Axel Goodbody (2005) 'Introduction', in Wendy Everett and Axel Goodbody (eds) *Revisiting Space: Space and Place in European Cinema*. Bern: Peter Lang, 9–22.

Faber, Sebastiaan (2003) 'Between Cernuda's Paradise and Buñuel's Hell: Mexico Through Spanish Exiles' Eyes', *Bulletin of Spanish Studies*, 80 (2), 219–39.

Faulkner, Sally (2004) *Literary Adaptations in Spanish Cinema*. Woodbridge: Tamesis.

Feenstra, Pietsie (2003) 'Buñuel during the Mexican Period: Space and the Construction of Myths', in Isabel Santaolalla, Patricia d'Allemand, Jorge Díaz Cintas, Peter William Evans, Consuelo Sanmateu, Alistair Whyte and Michael Witt (eds) *Buñuel, siglo XXI*. Zaragoza: Prensas Universitarias de Zaragoza, 123–7.

Fiddian, Robin W. and Peter William Evans (1988) *Challenges to Authority: Fiction and Film in Contemporary Spain*. London: Tamesis.

Fieschi, Jean-André (1966) 'L'Ange et la bête: croquis mexicains de Luis Buñuel', *Cahiers du cinéma*, 176, 33–41.

Fisher, Jaimey and Barbara Mennel (eds) (2010a) *Spatial Turns: Space, Place and Mobility in German Literary and Visual Culture*. Amsterdam: Rodopi.

Fisher, Jaimey and Barbara Mennel (2010b) 'Introduction', in Jaimey Fisher and Barbara Mennel (eds) *Spatial Turns: Space, Place and Mobility in German Literary and Visual Culture*. Amsterdam: Rodopi, 9–23.

Fortin, David T. (2011) *Architecture and Science-Fiction Film: Philip K. Dick and the Spectacle of Home*. Farnham: Ashgate.

Foucault, Michel (1979) *Discipline and Punish: The Birth of the Prison*, trans. Alan Sheridan. London: Penguin.

_____ (1986) 'Of Other Spaces', trans. Jay Miskowiec. *Diacritics*, 16 (1), 22–7.

_____ (1991) *Remarks on Marx: Conversations with Duccio Trombadori*, trans. R. James Goldstein and James Cascaito. New York, NY: Senuotext.

_____ (2000) 'A Preface to Transgression', in James D. Faubion (ed.) *Aesthetics, Method and Epistemology: Essential Works of Michel Foucault 1954–1984*. 3 vols, II. London: Penguin, 69–87.

Fuentes, Carlos (1970) *Casa con dos puertas*. Mexico City: Joaquín Moritz.

Fuentes, Víctor (1991) 'Lo hispano-mexicano en el cine de Buñuel', in Charo Portela Yáñez (ed.) *Cincuenta años del exilio español en Puerto Rico y el Caribe 1939–1989*. Sada: Ediciós do Castro, 273–83.

____ (1993) *Buñuel en México: iluminaciones sobre una pantalla pobre*. Teruel: Instituto de Estudios Turolenses.

____ (2000) *Los mundos de Buñuel*. Madrid: Akal.

____ (2003) 'Luis Buñuel: un cine del exilio redimido', in Isabel Santaolalla, Patricia d'Allemand, Jorge Díaz Cintas, Peter William Evans, Consuelo Sanmateu, Alistair Whyte and Michael Witt (eds) *Buñuel, siglo XXI*. Zaragoza: Prensas Universitarias de Zaragoza, 137–43.

____ (2005) *La mirada de Buñuel: cine, literatura y vida*. Madrid: Tabla Rasa.

Gandy, Matthew (2006) 'The Cinematic Void: Desert Iconographies in Michelangelo Antonioni's *Zabriskie Point*', in Martin Lefebvre (ed.) *Landscape and Film*. Abingdon: Routledge, 315–32.

García-Abrines, Luis (1956) 'Rebirth of Buñuel, trans. Daniel de Guzmán', in Kenneth Douglas (ed.) *The Art of the Cinema*. New Haven, CT: Yale University Press, 54–66.

García Riera, Emilio (1960) 'The Eternal Rebellion of Luis Buñuel', *Film Culture*, 21, 42–60.

____ (1998) *Breve historia del cine mexicano: primer siglo, 1897–1997*. Mexico City: Ediciones Mapa.

Gardies, André (1993) *L'Espace au cinema*. Paris: Méridiens-Klincksieck.

Goldmann, Annie (1969) 'Les Déserts de la foi'. *Révue de l'Institut de Sociologie*, 3, 463–73.

Gómez, Libia Stella (2003) *La mosca atrapada en una telaraña: Buñuel y 'Los Olvidados' en el contexto latinoamericano*. Bogotá: Universidad Nacional de Colombia.

González Dueñas, Daniel (2000) Buñuel en México: la mirada imparcial. *Guaraguao: Revista de Cultura Latinoamericana*, 10, 191–202.

Grange, Joseph (1985) 'Place, Body and Situation', in David Seamon and Robert Mugerauer (eds) *Dwelling, Place and Environment: Towards a Phenomenology of Person and World*. Dordrecht: Martinus Nijhoff, 71–84.

Gregor, Ulrich (1965) '*Simón del desierto*', *Filmkritik*, 10, 591–2.

Gutiérrez-Albilla and Julián Daniel (2008) *Queering Buñuel*. London: IB Tauris.

Haddu, Miriam (2007) *Contemporary Mexican Cinema 1989–1999: History, Space, and Identity*. Ceredigion: Edwin Mellen Press.

Harcourt, Peter (1967) 'Luis Buñuel: Spaniard and Surrealist', *Film Quarterly*, 20 (3), 2–19.

Harper, Graeme and Jonathan Rayner (2010) 'Introduction', in Graeme Harper and Jonathan Rayner (eds) *Cinema and Landscape: Film, Nation and Cultural Geography*. Bristol: Intellect, 15–28.

Harrison, Paul (2007) 'The Space between Us: Opening Remarks on the Concept of Dwelling', *Environment and Planning D: Society and Space*, 25, 625–47.

Hayward, Susan (2004) *Simone Signoret: The Star as Cultural Sign*. New York, NY: Continuum.

Heidegger, Martin (1962) *Being and Time*, trans. John Macquarrie and Edward Robinson. Oxford: Blackwell.

_____ (1971) *Poetry, Language, Thought*, trans. Albert Hofstadter. New York, NY: Harper and Row.

Herrera Navarro, Javier (2006) *Estudios sobre "Las Hurdes" de Buñuel: evidencia fílmica, estética y recepción*. Seville: Renacimiento.

Hetherington, Kevin (1997) *The Badlands of Modernity: Heterotopia and Social Ordering*. London: Routledge.

Higginbotham, Virginia (1979) *Luis Buñuel*. New York, NY: Twayne.

Hillier, Jean and Emma Rooksby (2005 [2002]) 'Introduction to First Edition', in Jean Hillier and Emma Rooksby (eds) *Habitus: A Sense of Place*, 2nd edn. Aldershot: Ashgate, 19–42.

Hogue, Peter (1976) 'The "Commercial" Life of Luis Buñuel', *Movietone News*, 51, 1–10.

Hook, Derek and Michele Vrdoljak (2002) 'Gated Communities, Heterotopia and a "Rights" of Privilege: A "Heterotopology" of the South African Security-Park', *Geoforum*, 33, 195–219.

Hopper, Kim and Jim Baumohl (1996) 'Redefining the Cursed Word: A Historical Interpretation of American Homelessness', in Jim Baumohl (ed.) *Homelessness in America*. Phoenix, AZ: Oryx Press, 3–14.

Horvath, Agnes and Bjørn Thomassen (2008) 'Mimetic Errors in Liminal Schismogenesis: On the Political Anthropology of the Trickster', *International Political Anthropology*, 1 (1), 3–24.

Hubbard, Phil, Brendan Bartley, Duncan Fuller and Rob Kitchin (eds) (1998) *Thinking Geographically: Space, Theory and Contemporary Human Geography*. London: Continuum.

Interview with Silvia Pinal. *El ángel exterminador*, dir. Luis Buñuel (Criterion, 2008) [DVD, disc 2].

Ishii-Gonzalès, Sam (2003) *Wuthering Heights*: Buñuel, Bataille, Brontë', in Isabel Santaolalla, Patricia d'Allemand, Jorge Díaz Cintas, Peter William Evans, Consuelo Sanmateu, Alistair Whyte and Michael Witt (eds) *Buñuel, siglo XX*. Zaragoza: Prensas Universitarias de Zaragoza, 239–46.

Jacobs, Steven (2010) 'Panoptic Paranoia and Phantasmagoria: Fritz Lang's Nocturnal City', in Jaimey Fisher and Barbara Mennel (eds) *Spatial Turns: Space, Place and Mobility in German Literary and Visual Culture*. Amsterdam: Rodopi, 381–95.

Jacobson, Kirsten (2009) 'A Developed Nature: A Phenomenological Account of the Experience of Home', *Continental Philosophy Review*, 42 (3), 355–73.

Jay, Martin (1995) 'The Limits of Limit-Experience: Bataille and Foucault', *Constellations*, 2 (2), 155–74.

Jobst, Marko (2008) 'Cinema – Filming in Outer Spaces', *Architects' Journal*, 6 February 2008. Available online at https://www.architectsjournal.co.uk/cinema-filming-in-outer-spaces/586539.article [accessed 24 June 2017].

Johnson, Peter (2006) 'Unravelling Foucault's "different spaces"', *History of the Human Sciences*, 19 (4), 75–90.

Jones, Elizabeth (2007) *Spaces of Belonging: Home, Culture and Identity in 20th-Century French Autobiography*. Amsterdam: Rodopi.

Jones, Julie (1997) 'Fatal Attraction: Buñuel's Romance with *Wuthering Heights*', *Anales de la Literatura Española*, 22 (1–2), 149–63.

_____ (2005) 'Interpreting Reality: *Los olvidados* and the Documentary Mode', *Journal of Film and Video*, 57 (4), 18–31.

_____ (2013) 'Luis Buñuel and the Politics of Self-Preservation', in Rob Stone and Julián Daniel Gutiérrez-Albilla (eds) *A Companion to Luis Buñuel*. Oxford: Wiley-Blackwell, 79–97.

Jormakka, Kari (1998) 'Post Mortem Eclecticism', in Roland Ritter and Bernd Knaller-Vlay (eds) *Other Spaces: The Affair of the Heterotopia*. Graz: Haus der Architektur, 124–53.

Kael, Pauline (1978) 'Saintliness', in Joan Mellen (ed.) *The World of Luis Buñuel: Essays in Criticism*. Oxford: Oxford University Press, 270–7.

Keating, Patrick (2010) 'The Volcano and the Barren Hill: Gabriel Figueroa and the Space of Art Cinema', in Rosalind Galt and Karl Schoonover (eds) *Global Art Cinema: New Theories and Histories*. Oxford: Oxford University Press, 201–17.

Kinder, Marsha (1993) *Blood Cinema: The Reconstruction of National Identity in Spain.* Berkeley, CA: University of California Press.

____ (2009) '*The Exterminating Angel*: Exterminating Civilization', *Criterion Current*, 9 February. Available online at http://www.criterion.com/current/posts/1012-the-exterminating-angel-exterminating-civilization [accessed 24 June 2017].

Kristeva, Julia (1982) *The Powers of Horror: An Essay on Abjection*, trans. Leon S. Roudiez. New York, NY: Columbia University Press.

Kyrou, Ado (1956) 'La Mort en ce jardin', *Positif*, 19, 25–9.

Landgrebe, Ludwig (1940) 'The World as a Phenomenological Problem', *Philosophy and Phenomenological Research*, 1 (1), 38–58.

Larrea, Juan and Luis Buñuel (2007) *Ilegible, hijo de flauta*, ed. Gabriele Morelli. Seville: Renacimiento.

Leahy, Sarah (2013) 'Stars in the Wilderness: *La Mort en ce jardin*', in Rob Stone and Julián Daniel Gutiérrez-Albilla (eds) *A Companion to Luis Buñuel.* Oxford: Wiley-Blackwell, 324–39.

Leen, Catherine (2010) 'How Not to Make a Mexican Musical: Luis Buñuel and The Perils of *Mexicanidad*', in Wolfgang Berg and Aoileann Ní Éigeartaigh (eds) *Exploring Transculturalism: A Biographical Approach.* Wiesbaden: Verlag für Sozialwissenschaften, 97–112.

Lefebvre, Martin (2006) 'Between Setting and Landscape in the Cinema', in Martin Lefebvre (ed.) *Landscape and Film.* Abingdon: Routledge, 19–59.

Lewis, Tyson and Daniel Cho (2006) 'Home Is Where the Neurosis Is: A Topography of the Spatial Unconscious', *Cultural Critique*, 64, 69–91.

Lillo, Gastón (1994. *Género y transgresión: el cine mexicano de Luis Buñuel.* Montpellier: Centre d'Études et de Recherches Sociologiques.

____ (ed.) (2003a) *Buñuel: el imaginario transcultural/L'imaginaire transculturel/The Transcultural Imaginary.* Ottawa: LEGAS.

____ (2003b) 'Presentación', in Gastón Lillo (ed.) *Buñuel: el imaginario transcultural/L'imaginaire transculturel/The Transcultural Imaginary.* Ottawa: LEGAS, 7–9.

Löhndorf, Marion (2008) '…und wenn sie nicht gestorben sind…', in Gabriele Jatho (ed.) *Luis Buñuel: Essays, Daten, Dokumente.* Berlin: Deutsche Kinemathek and Bertz & Fischer, 65–84.

Lyon, Elizabeth H (1973) 'Luis Buñuel: The Process of Dissociation in Three Films', *Cinema Journal*, 13 (1), 45–48.

M. K. S (1962) 'Island of Shame', *Monthly Film Bulletin*, 29, 18–19.

Macleod, Allison (2014) 'Compartmentalized Cosmopolitans: Constructions of Urban Space in Queer Irish Cinema', in Conn Holohan and Tony Tracy (eds) *Masculinity and Irish Popular Culture: Tiger's Tales*. London: Palgrave Macmillan, 42–57.

Malaguti, Cristiana (1993) 'Buñuel messicano: la lente rovesciata dell'entomologo', *Cineforum*, 33 (5), 24–7.

Mallett, Shelley (2004) 'Understanding Home: A Critical Review of the Literature', *The Sociological Review*, 52 (1), 62–89.

Marks, Laura U. (2006) 'Asphalt Nomadism: The New Desert in Arab Independent Cinema', in Martin Lefebvre (ed.) *Landscape and Film*. Abingdon: Routledge, 125–47.

Martialay, Felix (1969) '*Simón del desierto* de Luis Buñuel', *Film Ideal*, 211, 6–11.

Martín, Fernando Gabriel (2010) *El ermitaño errante: Buñuel en Estados Unidos*. Murcia: Tres Fronteras Ediciones.

Martínez Herranz, Amparo (2013) 'The Creative Process of *Robinson Crusoe*: Exile, Loneliness and Humanism', in Rob Stone and Julián Daniel Gutiérrez-Albilla (eds) *A Companion to Luis Buñuel*. Oxford: Wiley-Blackwell, 279–301.

Martínez Herranz, Amparo (2011) '*Nazarín*: Guiones y genealogías', in Patricia Cavielles García and Gerhard Poppenberg (eds) *Luis Buñuel: dos miradas. Una aportación hispano-alemana a un cine antitético*. Berlin: Edition Tranvía, 51–80.

Mathieu, José Agustín (1980) El período mexicano de Luis Buñuel. *Cuadernos Hispanoamericanos*, 358, 156–72.

Matthiessen, Peter (1990) *On the River Styx and Other Stories*. London: Collins Harvill.

Mauss, Marcel (1979) *Sociology and Psychology*, trans. Ben Brewster. London: Routledge and Kegan Paul.

McGregor, Eduardo (2000) 'Transterrados en el desierto', *Cuadernos Hispano-americanos*, 603, 36–41.

Melbye, David (2010) *Landscape Allegory in Cinema*. New York: Palgrave Macmillan.

Michel, Manuel (1961) 'L'homme sans chaînes', *Cinéma 61*, 52, 21–30.

Midding, Gerhard (2008) 'Die Realität des Imaginären: Motive im Werk von Luis Buñuel', in Gabriele Jatho (ed.) *Luis Buñuel: Essays, Daten, Dokumente*. Berlin: Deutsche Kinemathek and Bertz & Fischer, 17–42.

Miles, Robert J. (2006) 'Virgin on the Edge: Luis Buñuel's Transnational Trope in Mexico', *Studies in Hispanic Cinemas*, 2 (1), 169–88.

Milne, Tom (1965–66) 'The Mexican Buñuel', *Sight and Sound*, 35 (1), 36–9.

Moore, Jeanne (2000) 'Placing *Home* in Context', *Journal of Environmental Psychology*, 20, 207–17.

Mora, Carl J. (2005) [1982] *Mexican Cinema: Reflections of a Society, 1896–2004*, 3rd edn. Jefferson, NC: McFarland.

Mulvey, Laura (1975) 'Visual Pleasure and Narrative Cinema', *Screen*, 16 (3), 6–18.

Muñoz González, Beatriz (2005) 'Topophilia and Topophobia: The Home as an Evocative Place of Contradictory Emotions', *Space and Culture*, 8, 193–213.

Naficy, Hamid (2001) *An Accented Cinema: Exilic and Diasporic Filmmaking*. Princeton, NJ: Princeton University Press.

National Film Theatre Programme Notes: *La Fièvre monte à El Pao* [digitised press cuttings in British Film Institute Library collection].

Nazarín [material de tesis] (1958) Madrid, Filmoteca Española, Archivo Rosa Añover (AÑO/01/08).

Noble, Andrea (2005) *Mexican National Cinema*. Abingdon: Routledge.

O'Donoghue, Brendan (2011) *A Poetics of Homecoming: Heidegger, Homelessness and the Homecoming Venture*. Newcastle-upon-Tyne: Cambridge Scholars Publishing.

Pallasmaa, Juhani (1995) 'Identity, Intimacy and Domicile – Notes on the Phenomenology of Home', in David N. Benjamin and David Stea (eds) *The Home: Words, Interpretations, Meanings, and Environments*. Aldershot: Ashgate, 131–47.

_____ (2007) *The Architecture of Image: Existential Space in Cinema*. Helsinki: Rakennustieto.

Paz, Octavio (1961) *The Labyrinth of Solitude: Life and Thought in Mexico*, trans. Lysander Kemp. New York, NY: Grove Press.

_____ (2012) *Luis Buñuel: el doble arco de la belleza y de la rebeldía*. Mexico City: FCE.

Peña Ardid, Carmen and Víctor M. Lahuerta Guillén (eds) (2007) *Los olvidados: guión y documentos*. Teruel and Zaragoza: Instituto de Estudios Turolenses, Gobierno de Aragón, Caja Rural de Teruel.

Pérez de Mendiola, Marina (2006) 'Buñuel's Mexico, Saura's Tango: An Act of Reterritorialization', *Chasqui*, 35 (3), 26–45.

Pérez Soler, Bernardo (2003) '*Heimlichkeit* Destroyed: Freud's "The Uncanny" and *The Exterminating Angel*', in Isabel Santaolalla, Patricia d'Allemand, Jorge Díaz Cintas, Peter William Evans, Consuelo Sanmateu, Alistair Whyte and Michael Witt (eds) *Buñuel, siglo XXI*. Zaragoza: Prensas Universitarias de Zaragoza, 405–11.

Pérez Turrent, Tomás (1997) '¿Existe un cine mexicano de Luis Buñuel?', *Cinémas d'Amerique Latine*, 5, 135–44.

Polizzotti, Mark (2006) *Los Olvidados*. London: British Film Institute.

Popkin, Michael (1987) *Wuthering Heights* and Its "Spirit"', *Literature/Film Quarterly*, 15 (2), 116–22.

Powell, Dilys (1960) 'Swamps of Lust', *Sunday Times*, 19 June, n.p.

Poyato, Pedro (2011) *El sistema estético de Luis Buñuel*. Bilbao: Servicio Editorial, Universidad del País Vasco.

Press cuttings on the film *Jardin* (*La Mort en ce jardin*) by Luis Buñuel, 1955–1962 (n.d.). Madrid, Filmoteca Española, Archivo Buñuel (ABR-1981), items 53, 68.

Press cuttings on the film *La joven* by Luis Buñuel, 1960–62 (n.d.). Madrid, Filmoteca Española, Archivo Buñuel (ABR-2030), item 140.

Price, Joshua M. (2002) 'The Apotheosis of Home and the Maintenance of Spaces of Violence', *Hypatia*, 17 (4), 39–70.

Rapp, Claudia (2006) 'Desert, City and Countryside in the Early Christian Imagination', in Jitse Dijkstra and Mathilde van Dijk (eds) *The Encroaching Desert: Egyptian Hagiography and the Medieval West*. Leiden: Brill, 93–112.

Rebolledo, Carlos (1964) *Buñuel*. Paris: Editions Universitaires.

Relph, Edward (1976) *Place and Placelessness*. London: Pion.

Richardson, Tony (1978) 'The Films of Luis Buñuel', in Joan Mellen (ed.) *The World of Luis Buñuel: Essays in Criticism*. New York: Oxford University Press, 125–38.

Ripley, Marc (2015) 'Panic at the Disco? The Liminal Position in Luis Buñuel's *Simón del desierto*', *Hispanic Research Journal*, 16 (1), 15–30.

_____ (2016) 'Housed Nowhere and Everywhere Shut in: Uncanny Dwelling in Luis Buñuel's *El ángel exterminador*', *Bulletin of Spanish Studies*, 93 (4), 679–95.

Rivera-Cordero, Victoria (2006) 'Transatlantic Visions: Imagining Mexico in Juan Rejano's *La esfinge mestiza* and Luis Buñuel's *Los olvidados*', *Romance Notes*, 46 (3), 309–17.

Rodaway, Paul (2011) [2004] 'Yi-Fu Tuan', in Phil Hubbard and Rob Kitchin (eds) *Key Thinkers on Space and Place*, 2nd edn. London: SAGE, 426–31.

Rodgers, Eamonn (1995) *Apurando la lección*: Luis Buñuel and Galdós's *Nazarín*. *Romance Studies*, 26, 51–9.

Rodríguez, Marie-Soledad and Emmanuelle Sinardet (2003) 'Les mondes originaires dans *Abismos de pasión* et *La joven*: de la pulsión au salut', in Isabel Santaolalla, Patricia d'Allemand, Jorge Díaz Cintas, Peter William Evans,

Consuelo Sanmateu, Alistair Whyte and Michael Witt (eds) *Buñuel, siglo XXI*. Zaragoza: Prensas Universitarias de Zaragoza, 439–51.

Rosenbaum, Jonathan (2004) *Essential Cinema: On the Necessity of Film Canons*. Baltimore, MD: Johns Hopkins University Press.

Rubinstein, Elliot (1977) 'Buñuel in Mexico', *Latin American Literature and Art Review*, 20, 31–7.

____ (1978) 'Buñuel's World, or the World and Buñuel', *Philosophy and Literature*, 2 (2), 237–48.

Sandro, Paul (2003) 'Putting the Squeeze on Thought: Buñuel's Naturalism and the Threshold of the Imagination', in Gastón Lillo (ed.) *Buñuel: el imaginario transcultural/L'imaginaire transculturel/The Transcultural Imaginary*. Ottawa: LEGAS, 33–46.

Santander, Hugo N. (2002) 'Luis Buñuel, Existential Filmmaker', *Espéculo. Revista de Estudios Literarios*, 20. Available online at http://pendientedemigracion. ucm.es/info/especulo/numero20/bunuel2.html [accessed 24 June 2017].

Santaolalla, Isabel (2004) 'Domination and Appropriation in *The Young One*', in Peter William Evans and Isabel Santaolalla (eds) *Luis Buñuel: New Readings*. London: British Film Institute, 97–113.

Santaolalla, Isabel, Patricia d'Allemand, Jorge Díaz Cintas, Peter William Evans, Consuelo Sanmateu, Alistair Whyte and Michael Witt (eds) (2003) *Buñuel, siglo XXI*. Zarazoga: Prensas Universitarias de Zaragoza.

Schütte, Wolfram (1974) 'Luis Buñuels "kleine" Filme', *Neue Zürcher Zeitung*, 26 January, 27.

Seamon, David (2013) 'Phenomenology and Uncanny Homecomings: Homeworld, Alienworld, and Being-at-Home in Alan Ball's HBO Television Series, *Six Feet Under*', in Daniel Boscaljon (ed.) *Resisting the Place of Belonging: Uncanny Homecomings in Religion, Narrative and the Arts*. Farnham: Ashgate, 155–70.

Seamon, David and Jacob Sowers (2009) 'Existentialism/Existential Geography', in Rob Kitchin and Nigel Thrift (eds) *The International Encyclopedia of Human Geography* (12 vols, III). Oxford: Elsevier, 666–71.

Sengissen, Paule (n.d.) *La Fièvre monte à El Pao* [digitised press cuttings in British Film Institute Library collection].

Serjo Richart, María (2002) 'Buñuel's Heights: *Abismos de pasión*', *Brontë Studies*, 27, 27–33.

Shakespeare, William (2011) [1611]. *The Tempest*, ed. Virginia M. Vaughan and Alden T. Vaughan. London: Arden Shakespeare.

Shane, David Grahame (2008) 'Heterotopias of Illusion: From Beaubourg to Bilbao and Beyond', in Michiel Dehaene and Lieven de Cauter (eds) *Heterotopia and the City: Public Space in a Postcivil Society*. London: Routledge, 259–71.

Shaw, Daniel (2008) *Film and Philosophy: Taking Movies Seriously*. London: Wallflower Press.

Shiel, Mark and Tony Fitzmaurice (eds) (2001) *Cinema and the City: Film and Urban Societies in a Global Context*. Oxford: Blackwell.

Sibley, David (1995) *Geographies of Exclusion*. London: Routledge.

Sinnigen, John H. (2008) *Benito Pérez Galdós en el cine mexicano: cine y literatura*. Mexico City: UNAM.

Smith, Murray and Thomas E. Wartenberg (2006) 'Introduction', in Murray Smith and Thomas E. Wartenberg (eds) *Thinking through Cinema: Film as Philosophy*. Oxford: Blackwell, 1–9.

Smith, Paul Julian (1995) 'Shocks and Prejudices', *Sight and Sound*, 5 (8), 24–6.

Soja, Edward W. (1996) *Thirdspace: Journeys to Los Angeles and Other Real-and-Imagined Places*. Oxford: Blackwell.

Steinbock, Anthony J. (1994) 'Homelessness and the Homeless Movement: A Clue to the Problem of Intersubjectivity', *Human Studies*, 17 (2), 203–23.

____ (1995) *Home and Beyond: Generative Phenomenology after Husserl*. Evanston, IL: Northwestern University Press.

Stone, Rob and Julián Daniel Gutiérrez-Albilla (eds) (2013a) *A Companion to Luis Buñuel*. Oxford: Wiley-Blackwell.

____ (2013b) 'Introduction: The 'Criminal' Life of Luis Buñuel', in Rob Stone and Julián Daniel Gutiérrez-Albilla (eds) *A Companion to Luis Buñuel*. Oxford: Wiley-Blackwell, 1–58.

Storment, Ryan Lee (2008) *Other Spaces, Other Voices: Heterotopic Spaces in Island Narratives*. Saarbrücken: VDM.

Strick, Philip (n.d.) National Film Theatre Programme Notes: *Abismos de pasión* [digitised press cuttings in British Film Institute Library collection].

Svenaeus, Fredrik (2000) 'Das Unheimliche – Towards a Phenomenology of Illness', *Medicine, Health Care and Philosophy*, 3, 3–16.

Szakolczai, Arpad (2000) *Reflexive Historical Sociology*. London: Routledge.

____ (2009) 'Liminality and Experience: Structuring Transitory Situations and Transformative Events', *International Political Anthropology*, 2 (1), 141–72.

Thacker, Andrew (2003) *Moving through Modernity: Space and Geography in Modernism*. Manchester: Manchester University Press.

Thomassen, Bjørn (2009) 'The Uses and Meanings of Liminality', *International Political Anthropology*, 2 (1), 5–27.

Tinazzi, Giorgio (1978) 'Il cammino di Buñuel', in Adelio Ferrero (ed.) *Storia del cinema: autori e tendenze negli anni cinquanta e sessanta*. Venice: Marsilio Editori, 115–23.

Trigg, Dylan (2012) *The Memory of Place: A Phenomenology of the Uncanny*. Athens, OH: Ohio University Press.

Truby, John (2007) *The Anatomy of Story: 22 Steps to Becoming a Master Storyteller*. New York, NY: Faber and Faber.

Truffaut, François (1982) *The Films in My Life*, trans. Leonard Mayhew. Harmondsworth: Penguin.

Tuan, Yi-Fu (1990) [1974] *Topophilia: A Study of Environmental Perceptions, Attitudes, and Values*. New York, NY: Columbia University Press.

Tuñón, Julia (2003) Cuerpo humano y cuerpo urbano en *Los Olvidados*', in Gastón Lillo (ed.) *Buñuel: el imaginario transcultural/L'imaginaire transculturel/The Transcultural Imaginary*. Ottawa: LEGAS, 69–89.

Turner, Victor (1967) *The Forest of Symbols: Aspects of Ndembu Ritual*. Ithaca, NY: Cornell University Press.

_____ (1978) *Image and Pilgrimage in Christian Culture*. Oxford: Basil Blackwell.

_____ (1982) *From Ritual to Theatre: The Human Seriousness of Play*. New York, NY: Performing Arts Journal Publications.

_____ (1995) *The Ritual Process: Structure and Anti-Structure*. Hawthorne: Aldine de Gruyer.

Van Gennep, Arnold (1960) *Rites of Passage*, trans. Monika B. Vizedom and Gabrielle L. Caffee. London: Routledge and Kegan Paul.

Vargas, Javier (2003) '*Los olvidados*, de Luis Buñuel: espacio y personajes de una misma poética', in Gastón Lillo (ed.) *Buñuel: el imaginario transcultural/ L'imaginaire transculturel/The Transcultural Imaginary*. Ottawa: LEGAS, 91–8.

Verástique, Bernardino (2000) *Michoacán and Eden: Vasco de Quiroga and the Evangelization of Western Mexico*. Austin, TX: University of Texas Press.

Von Moltke, Johannes (2005) *No Place Like Home: Locations of Heimat in German Cinema*. Berkeley, CA: University of California Press.

Wallace, Lee (2009) *Lesbianism, Cinema, Space: The Sexual Life of Apartments*. Abingdon: Routledge.

Warf, Barney and Santa Arias (2008) 'Introduction: The Reinsertion of Space into the Social Sciences and Humanities', in Barney Warf and Santa Arias (eds) *The Spatial Turn: Interdisciplinary Perspectives*. Abingdon: Routledge, 1–10.

Whittaker, Tom (2013) 'Out of Place, Out of Synch: Errant Movement and Rhythm in Buñuel's Mexican Comedies', in Rob Stone and Julián Daniel Gutiérrez-Albilla (eds) *A Companion to Luis Buñuel*. Oxford: Wiley-Blackwell, 226–39.

Williams, Linda (1996) 'The Critical Grasp: Buñuelian Cinema and Its Critics', in Rudolf E. Kuenzli (ed.) *Dada and Surrealist Film*. Cambridge, MA: MIT Press, 199–206.

Williams, Linda (1989) *Hard Core: Power, Pleasure, and the 'Frenzy of the Visible'*. Berkeley, CA: University of California Press.

Willis, Don (1978) 'Nazarin: Buñuel's Comic Hero Revisited'. *Sight and Sound*, 48, 5–7.

Wise, John Macgregor (2000) 'Home: Territory and Identity', *Cultural Studies*, 14 (2), 295–310.

Wood, Michael (1993) 'Buñuel in Mexico', in John King, Ana M. López and Manuel Alvarado (eds) *Mediating Two Worlds: Cinematic Encounters in the Americas*. London: British Film Institute, 40–51.

____ (2009) 'Damned if you do…', *Criterion Current*, 3 February. Available online at http://www.criterion.com/current/posts/1013-simon-of-the-desert-damned-if-you-do [accessed 24 June 2017].

Zavala, Silvio (1947) 'The American Utopia of the Sixteenth Century', *Huntingdon Library Quarterly*, 10 (4), 337–47.

Zimmerman, Kara M. (2010) 'Hermeneutics and Heterotopias in Shakespeare's "The Tempest" and the Cult TV Series "Lost"'. Honours thesis, Emory University. Available online at https://etd.library.emory.edu/view/record/pid/emory:7tm8v [accessed 24 June 2017].

Zimmerman, Michael E. (1985) 'The Role of Spiritual Discipline in Learning to Dwell on Earth', in David Seamon and Robert Mugerauer (eds) *Dwelling, Place and Environment*. Drdrecht: Martinus Nijhoff, 247–56.

Index

CPSIA information can be obtained
at www.ICGtesting.com
Printed in the USA
LVOW11s2325241117
557309LV00007B/22/P

9 780231 182355